पुरातत्त्व
पुरातत्त्व
PURĀTATTVA

Bulletin of the Indian Archaeological Society

No. 28 1997-98

Editors

K. N. Dikshit & K.S. Ramachandran

D.K. Printworld (P) Ltd.
New Delhi

Cataloging in Publication Data — DK
[Courtesy : D.K. Agencies (P) Ltd. <docinfo@dkagencies.com>]

Purātattva : bulletin of the Indian Archaeological Society, no. 28, 1997-98 / editor, K.N. Dikshit & K.S. Ramachandran.
p. cm.
Includes bibliographical references.
ISBN 8124603030

1. Archaeology — India — Periodicals. 2. India — Antiquities — Periodicals. 3. India — Civilization — Periodicals. I. Dikshit, K.N. II. Ramachandran, K.S. (Kattalai Sivasubramanium), 1939- III. Indian Archaeological Society.

First Published in 1998
First Reprinted in 2005
ISBN 81-246-0303-0
Price for volume 28 (1997-98): Rs. 800 US $ 40

Reprint authorised by
Indian Archaeological Society
New Delhi - 110 016

The Editors are not responsible for the opinions expressed by the Contributors.

Purātattva is published annually.

Manuscripts (whether in the form of articles or notes or book reviews) offered for publication should be sent to the Editor, Purātattva, Indian Archaeological Society, B-17, Qutab Institutional Area, New Delhi - 110 016.

Published and printed by:
D.K. Printworld (P) Ltd.
'Srikunj,' F-52, Bali Nagar
New Delhi – 110015
Phone : (011) 2545 3975, 2546 6019 Fax : (011) 2546 5926
E-mail : dkprintworld@vsnl.net
www. dkprintworld.com

PURĀTATTVA

CONTENTS

NOTES AND NEWS

BOOK REVIEWS

ANNUAL REPORT

Obituaris

Shri Shri-Govind Tiwari
(1910-1997)

Shri Shri Govind Tiwari who passed away on 11th Jan. 1998 at the ripe age of over 87 years will be long remembered for his distinguished services not only as an efficient photographer, but for his great humane qualities. His technical skill, artistic excellence and indefatigable industry was matched by his administrative skill as head of the photo section of the Archaeological Survey of India. He very imaginatively transformed the technical section into a Photo Library. All those who were trained by Dr. R.E.M. Wheeler, the then Director General of Archaeology in field archaeology at Taxila, Harappa and Arikamedu and were initiated by Shri Tiwari in the technical skills and niceties of archaeological photography will never forget the ever cheerful and lively personality of Tiwariji (as he was addressed by all).

Born in October 1910, on *Shard Purnima* day, Tiwarij radiated serene pleasant glow of the full moon all his life. Like many youths of his generation, he was actively associated with the freedom movement launched by Mahatma Gandhi. After obtaining his BSc. degree, he started his career as a School teacher, but learnt photography in the studio-cum lab of his friend, Shri Vishnu Dutt who later also joined the Archaeological Survey of India as photographer. After mastering all aspects of photography, Shri Tiwari joined the Archaeological Department of Jaipur State in 1940 and later shifted in 1942 to Archaeological Survey of India, New Delhi and in due course rose to be the Head of the Photo Section.

Shri Tiwari took deep interest in archaeological photography and endeared himself to one and all by dint of his excellent work, diligence and pleasant manners. He accompanied the then Prime Minister Pt. Jawaharlal Nehru and his party to Indonesia which also included Dr. N.P. Chakravarti, the then Jt. Director General of Archaeology. He also visited Afghanistan as a member of the Archaeological exploration team headed by late Shri T.N. Ramachandran, Jt. D.G. and built a rare collection of photographs of monuments, sites, museum objects which ushered, in due course, co-operation with Afghanistan in the field of conservation of the world famous monumental caves of Bamyan. Shri Tiwari was associated with Shri A. Ghosh's work of Exploration of Rajasthan. The exhibition held on the occasion of Centenary Celebration of the Archaeological Survey India in 1961 was a roaring success and the contribution of Shri Tiwari in preparing excellent enlargements was hailed by one and all as a major factor in this successful venture.

Tiwariji, was always a warm hearted host and his Laxmi Bai Nagar residence was a favourite place for visiting friends and colleagues whenever they came to Delhi on tour. I remember the warm hospitality of Shri Tiwari and his culinary skills both at Delhi as his guest or on tour in out of the way places. Over the years, I came to regard him like an elder brother. After retirement, Tiwari took lot of interest in spiritual matters, so much so that when he passed away, his mind & eyes were glued on the photograph of Govindji, the deity he worshipped constantly.

M.N. Deshpande.

Prof. G.N. Pant
(07-07-1940 — 08-04-1998)

Prof. (Dr.) G.N.Pant, Pro-Vice Chancellor, National Museum Institute, New Delhi had a distinguished career. Born on the 7th July, 1940 at a small village Singhai in distt. Lakhimpur Kheri (U.P), he passed his M.A., B.ED., Proficiency in Sanskrit examination from the University of Lucknow; got his Ph. D. from the Sagaur University and his D.Litt. from the Magadh University.

Prof. Pant's first booklet 'Indian Weapons' was published by the Indian Council of Educational Research and Training, New Delhi in 1966 and then second 'Studies in the Defence History', a bibliography by the U.S.I., Ministry of Defence. The gigantic work *Studies in Indian weapons and warfare* (1970) fetched him the President of India's Acclamation. His Bhartiya Ashtra Shastra now out of print, proved the landmark and his Indian Archery (reprinted, 1993) is acknowledged as the last word on the discipline. Some other major publications authored by Prof. Pant are *'Weapons in the Babur Nama', Catalogue of the weapon in the Junagad' Museum, Gujarat, Catalogue of edged wreapons in the Salarjung Museum, Hyderabad', 'Catalogue of the weapons in the Bharat Kala Bhawan, Varanasi', 'Catalogue of Indian arms in the Museum for Folkerkunde, Hamburg,* Germany and so on. Prof. Pant had seventeen books and more than three hundred research papers to his credit. In addition he had edited dozens of professional journals.

Prof.Pant was the president of Museums Association of India and member, ICOM; Author's Guild of India; Art and Culture Society of India; Association of Art Historians; Arms and Armour Society, London and a host of other professional/technical organizations. He was affiliated with several universities in India and has produced fifteen Ph. D. scholars. Prof.Pant finds mention in various *'who is who'* published in India and abroad.

Prof.Pant was nominated Fellow of Royal Asiatic Society (FRAS) London and a Fellow of Society of Future educators USA. as an erudite scholar. He travelled extensively and examined the art collections in the museums of Europe, USA, Russia, Africa and Southeast Asia. He presided over an international conference organized by the University of New York, USA in 1985.

Prof.Pant was felicitated by several societies and associations and won prestigious awards. apart from 'Acharya Narendra Dev Award', the 'Indian Priyadarshini award' (New Delhi, 1994), and the 'Twentieth Century Achievement Award' (USA, 1995), have been conferred upon htm. The American Biographical Institute, USA had selected Prof. Pant as the 'Man of the year, 1995'.

PURĀTATTVA

Number 28 **1997-98**

Editorial

We are happy to appraise our members of the society that the construction of our building is almost complete and we are confident that we would be able to move into it some time in early 1999.

The basement will house the administrative and other offices of the society. The other floors will be apportioned for library, laboratory, photography, graphics, etc. There were will be suites also in the second floor for visiting scholars. All modern facilities and best construction materials have been used here with marble and Kota Stone flooring and aluminium replacing iron; maintenence is expected to be minimum.

* * *

This issue is particularly devoted to the archaeology of North East India: a few articles about that region appear here.

* * *

We have decided to hold our 1999 annual conference in Delhi, so that all our members share the joy of participating in the first conference to be held in the society's own building.

An international conference highlighting the contribution of Indian archaeology to the World archaeology is being contemplated along with the annual conference.

* * *

The present issue of *Puratattva* contains a brief write up on the archaeological excavations conducted during (1997-98) in the Indus-Sarasvati site of Rakhigarhi located on the Drishdvati in Haryana; a site of utmost importance awaiting the spade of archaeologists to unravel the mysteries it entombs.

* * *

The Indian Archaeological Society deeply mourns the untimely death of Prof. G.N. Pant, Pro-Vice Chancellor/Director of National Museum Institute of History of Art, Conservation & Museology (Deemed to be University).

The Society also condoles the sad demise of Shri S.G.Tewari of the Archaeological Survey of India.

In spite of our best efforts we were not able to gather much information about Shri S. Ganesh Rao, who helped the Society in various capacities for the last 30 years and who passed away a couple of years ago. We offer our heartful condolences to the breaved family.

*   *   *

Finally, the Society, wishes to place on record its indebtedness to all those who graciously donated money and labour for constructing the building.

The Editors are beholden to Dr. S.P. Gupta, Chairman of the Board of Management of the society for his unstinted cooperation and untiring labour in generating funds for the construction work.

We are also thankful to all the contributors who had responded to our request for papers.

A special thanks is due to Sri Praveen Mehta for his ungrudging cooperation in bringing out the issue on time.

Editors

Archaeology in India : Relevance of Social Science Approach

S.C. MALIK*

Introduction

The title of this paper may sound like a rhetoric today. But many years ago when my teacher, Prof. Gordon Childe viewed archaeology as a social science in most of his works, he was ignored during his life time. During the last 25 years or more archaeology has been studied as anthropology, mostly in America, and a little less in Europe. In India not many are pursuing this approach systematically, i.e. integration of archaeology with social sciences. This hesitation, perhaps, arises because the Indian scene is dominated by the view of studying archaeology as a humanities discipline, alongwith the concomitant traditional historiographical or art methodologies. The latter continue to encourage ideographic enquiries which emphasize descriptive accounts, techniques and quantitative analysis.

Actually, there is no opposition between the two approaches, which in fact compliment each other. It is only a social science-orientation which today has allowed archaeology to widen its horizons. This is both in terms of theoretical formulations and the discoveries made thereafter. In this sense both history and archaeology, in a way, have also become more 'scientific', i.e., in terms of formulating and testing various generalizations, processes and explanations about man, society and its interaction with nature. It is erroneous to believe that the mere use of scientific techniques, as many continue to reiterate in India, makes archaeology a scientific discipline. It is crucial to formulate explicit frameworks, if archaeology is to contribute towards general explanations and processes about human cultures. Unfortunately, this interaction between generalizations both before and after fieldwork is seldom followed in India i.e., about how we know about what we know or state. Inculcating the potential for explicit research enquiry hardly exists at post-graduate levels in India.

The last hundred years or more of archaeological work in India has produced very little interpretative work along the lines mentioned above, in terms of cultural processes of any explanatory hypotheses, compared to the vast number of descriptive excavation and exploration reports. In order to move beyond merely being a fact finding discipline, beyond the mere utilization of a multitude of scientific techniques which have not brought us close to any solutions to many of the old problems, we have to create a synthesis between its scientific means and humanistic aims. This is where social science theoretical formulations become very helpful. For this purpose archaeology as a discipline needs to develop a meaningful philosophy. This is what will enable its results to be related to the present and the future. To achieve such an aim archaeology has to contribute more than just a simple time perspective about human cultures and a general

*Retd. UGC Professor of Anthropology, New Delhi.

awareness of human history. The philosophical elements need to be formulated in cooperation with the social and behavioural sciences.

The multidisciplinary approach becomes even more imperative because archaeology relies on the scarce, fragmentary durable remains for reconstructing past cultures. As a result, the evidence and the interpretation of the past so reconstructed is inferential, relying on many other disciplines, but especially on ethnographic material; and, consequently, dependent upon other socio-anthropological information which itself arises out of various theoretical assumptions with which many archaeologists are seldom familiar with. Implicitly, therefore, archaeology has been seeking support, in drawing parallels, from social science literature. However, as a discipline in its own right, it has to evolve its own theoretical models or atleast explicitly state its concepts relying on its own evidence even if these are, already at another level, available in the social sciences. It has to be kept in mind that all statements in those disciplines are themselves governed by certain other assumptions, hypothesis which need to be carefully looked into if a true integration is to take place between archaeology, anthropology and other social sciences.

We are all well aware how archaeological knowledge, is frequently being used in everyday social and political problems even if often not only erroneously but deliberately distorted for selfish motivations. This use of archaeology, for current socio-political issues, gives a tremendous responsibility for the practitioners of the discipline to make very accurate and cautious statements about the findings which reflect on the socio-cultural aspects of any part or level of this civilization, i.e., especially about practical and testable explanations about 'nonarchaeological' areas which relate to contemporary issues, when a recourse to the past is made very often in public life. This is why it is necessary to bring in strictly worked out standards of theoretical rigour in order to give careful explanatory evaluations about evolution of man, and his social and cultural behaviour.

In the above context, it may be useful to give a brief background of archaeological studies in India, to elaborate the issue of the social science relevance of archaeology in India.

Archaeology: Historical Background

Archaeology as a discipline of great value has been well known in India from the 19th century. But if one takes into account its history, it has developed from diverse interests on the part of those engaged in the work; i.e., influenced by history, geology, art and architecture along with their respective concepts. In this development excellent techniques of excavations, new typologies, distribution maps and so on along with preoccupation with unilateral evolution, diffusion, hyper-diffusion, etc. were, and continue, to be followed. These delineated historical sequences of so-called archaeological 'material culture' were classified in terms of regional complexes in the context of the vast subcontinent. In short, the collected material evidence was then seen in terms of missing links which historical hypotheses were earlier stating. For instance, not only in prehistory was this approach true, it was also a part of building a sequential examination of Harappan sites– their origin and disintegration, the problem of the second urban revolution, and so on. Most scholars, following European footsteps, were scholars of Sanskrit, and historians, who were seeking material remains to supplement the textual evidence. Even prehistoric studies, in most cases, continue even today to be a part of Ancient History, Culture and Archaeology departments. Ethno-archaeology and archaeology as a social science has as yet to take roots as a separate discipline.

However, the goals continue to be determined by 19th century models of filling in evolutionary gaps in the succession of events in a linear fashion, dominated by techno-economic frameworks. The use of elaborate techniques of scientific developments does not distract us from the fact of using outmoded ideas, in our attempt to understand man in the past in order to know ourselves in the present. For example, the concept of the "Three Age" system developed by C.J. Thomsen is based on the technological framework, followed by the techno-economic models. Without going into the historical records of archaeological studies, it is clear that modernistic– the idea of 'progress' and techno-economic models– world views dominated a study of the past-including socio-cultural stages. The evidence was thus looked into from these view-points. Later on, there is the ecological-cultural approach of normative archaeology; followed by new archaeology, symbolic and semiotic approaches to the study of the past.

At any rate, these normative, analytical, processual, post-processual, structuralist, ideographic and what not, researches are all related to the same basic paradigm of the modern or post-modern era, i.e., linked to the fragmentary approach of studying the past in order to project the future–such as to the rewriting of history for political purposes which is taking place all over the world. The important point is that the basic paradigm of anthropocentrism, competition- 'success in trade'- continues to govern research goals. The holistic paradigm has as yet to have any impact on historical and social sciences since one continues to believe that the Newtonian-Cartesian approach has served us very well. But as stated above the consequences have been disastrous at the local, regional, national and international levels.

It other words, Indian archaeology continues to be in a pre-paradigm stage, if we bear in mind the four stages of Kuhn's evolutionary progression of scientific disciplines. There are some indications that we may be moving beyond the first stage, into stating explicit paradigms, albeit little compared to what is happening elsewhere. At the first stage, conceptual ideas are not clear because each researcher thinks of building the foundation of the discipline from a personal level. The second stage is reached when either a single theory or a set of new theories are evolved to reorganise data as well as provide a set of grounded theories. The third and fourth stages are periods of normal sciences where basic grounded theories or paradigms are logically explored or tested and discarded until new paradigms are logically explored or tested and discarded until new paradigms are discovered.

A paradigm is a model of what the record of the past is like, what we can expect from it and its significance. This goal may hold true for the traditional researcher as well. But a social scientific research implies promoting the formulation of explicit models, to understand how and why we think and the manner in which we make statements, the way we do so under the umbrella of certain axioms and assumptions. We must know not only know what we are looking for but why we are looking for whatever the kind of past we are trying to understand. Since each one of us already has an image of the past, it is this that in fact is crucial in our reconstructions and interpretations. It is this changing perspective which has lead to more and more discoveries, i.e., moving beyond the empiricist traditional approach whereby all that is basically necessary is to collect facts and arrange them according to some inherent order implicit in them. There is nothing inherent or implicit in the evidence, since even in applying new analytical techniques a fundamental difference arises in the manner whereby data is viewed. The chief difference between 'old' and 'new' approaches is at all levels of research. In the social science approach, concepts and models are always to be borne in mind. For example, there are two important points which are basic for analytical procedures : (1) investigations are problem-oriented since this is what governs the analysis of data; and (2) explicit definition of each concept is essential, for the problem to be visualised needs to be sorted out on the basis of well-formulated questions which are specific for this purpose.

From unidimensional to multidimensional analysis

Until recently archaeologists have used 'culture' in a restricted sense, defining it as an assemblage of associated material traits that recur repeatedly. These material traits not only reflect a fraction of the culture but are infact only symbols of socio-cultural aspects, i.e., the total picture is richer and more comprehensive than the type fossils that often an archaeologist is occupied with.The shift has to be from a microdynamic to a macrodynamic framework, in order to bring life into lifeless assemblages of 'accidental' types, and see the interrelatedness of elements in a functioning whole. For instance, today, no longer is a single attribute-dimension-of artifact types used, and multidimensional analysis is being utilized. The rationale and justification of the research problem has changed because a change has taken place in the conceptual models. In short, since typology is a means for analysis that brings order to our observations, this ordering of phenomenon is being carried out consciously and explicitly so that functional variability is expressed beyond morphological types. Thus, it is today clear that the task of the researcher is to discover meanings in terms of three things behind the artifact, for instance; ideas, customs or mental templates and the functional and historico-evolutionary meanings.

To illustrate, the variability of the Lower Palaeolithic artifacts is governed by the interaction of : 1. physical properties; 2. intention or design which is related to functional requirements; and 3. the transmission of tradition which has to be viewed within the set of technical and morphological patterns that are functionally adequate, aesthetic and socially acceptable.

Similarly, functional variability may be seen in terms of : 1. vegetable foods, 2. the importance of hunting-fishing activities, 3. environmental variations and seasonal migration of animals on which palaeolithic groups depended; 4. the intended function of artifacts and probable use of perishable material; and 5. establishing relative chronology on the basis of these industries.

Needless to say, microscopic examinations of tools, use of statistical and other mathematical and computer techniques, etc. are being used in this multivariate analysis.

Obviously, in this attempt to understand Early Man and his culture, moving beyond techno-economic stages, within the social science approach, today we are looking into ; 1. group activities; 2. settlement patterns and mobility during seasons or any other changes to find out the territorial range and its extent; 3. economic patterns and subsistence (diet); and 4. micro-and-macro cultural patterning of available material for clarification of typology-taxonomy of cultural groups in terms of intergroup differentiation, diffusion, cultural contact, evolution and so on. Here again the geomorphological setting-glacial or fluvial-palaeobotanical-zoological, etc. data is ofcourse necessary. In short, there is a combination of the palaeontologial, geological, ecological data with the general anthropological, ethnographic, historical and archaeological disciplines.

Thus, it is clear from recent researches that archaeological studies need not be restricted by any one approach, nor strictly by 'durable' remains of 'material' culture. If there is now an increase of information about the past, it is due to the awareness of the ever-widening horizons in the realm of 'non-material' aspects which archaeologists in India often claim cannot be 'dug' up. The observer's view-point is inextricably linked with what is being observed at all levels; planning, sampling, digging, analysing, interpreting and even statistical-methodological techniques are governed by various socio-cultural and personal orientations. That is why archaeological remains represent a continuity of socio-cultural ideas of any human group, i.e., what we observed directly represents a structure of ideas and evaluations of social norms not only of past behavioural patterns but also of the present.

Some of the other existing social science orientation of archaeological material is briefly given below.

Structuralism and archaeology

Structuralism as a concept has been an important landmark in the development of modern anthropology, first emerging in the study of linguistics. Briefly, its basic premise is that just as structural units and rules govern the many forms of a language, similarly these also govern the behavioural forms of material objects. Both these cases are symbolic of socio-cultural structures that represent men-material interactions within a given community, i.e., words and artifacts are different expressions of the same system because both are products of human motor activity which results in the one case words because of the interacting nerve impulses with the 'material' air, and in the other the action of muscles under mental control (which in turn is governed by corresponding social and cultural patterning) results in artifacts that are learnt in the larger framework by technological skills.

Thus, in structural terms when assemblages are put together into various types according to their relationships to each other because of certain similarities, then, what we are trying to do is to build a pattern of structural behaviour of standard artifacts, i.e., each such groups represents wider behavioural patterns of human ideas and actions. It is impossible that it is the archaeologist who places artifacts according to what he thinks may represent similar group-patterns of a society. This is one of the problems to be faced. Nevertheless, notwithstanding difficulties, structuralism has helped archaeologists to reflect upon various rules that govern different combinations of traits and trait-complexes, and to understand rules of cultural artifacts. In a nutshell, the basic argument of structuralism as applied in archaeology is this : if there were no structural rules of society, there could be no consistence patterning and it would not be possible to integrate assemblages. It is this basic assumption that allows a comparison of artifacts and their attributes, i.e., not by mere physical comparisons but by understanding the underlying socio-cultural patterning of structures.

Beyond this, the approach of structuralism is helpful

for other problems in archaeological interpretations, such as in the areas of migration, trade, diffusion of ideas and traits, and so on; for example, ordered rules allow us to see diffusion (both primary and secondary) in a different manner. This is because the rates of diffusion of different artifacts are patterned in a variety of ways, due to attribute sharing. For instance, if people migrate, the social relationships within a group may or may not change, depending upon whether innovation or invention of 'new' artifacts is compatible in the new ecological setting, according to the local needs and demands. It is a combination of local and outside cultural patterns which is often clearly reflected in the emergence of 'newer' artifacts. Of course, at times, 'newer' artifacts are exchanged by themselves, without major socio-cultural changes, i.e., they are often reproduced superficially in a technical sense, such as 'neolithic' celts of eastern India that are copies of metal types and, therefore, do not represent a 'metal-oriented' society, rather it suggests a continuation of the older socio-economic patterns. It is in this way that the complexities of archaeological evidence in the culture-setting may be understood, rather than by means of detailed descriptive accounts.

Systems Theory and Archaeology

Today, part of the advancement in archaeology, far away from the direct application of personal experience and intelligence, is the use of mathematical and other scientific techniques for interpretative purposes. There developments are not mere refinements of quantitative analyses, because these procedures help us to gain further information about intangible aspects with greater probability, provided our orientations are social scientific. That is why the application of systems theory, or that of cybernetics (systems of communication and control, information theory, games theory, etc. which are all highly mathematical in content) has allowed the use of complex mathematical methods and computers.

General systems theory is of great significance. It is the concept of wholeness whereby total structures are comprehended. A system is any large assemblage of intercommunicating elements which may reasonably be regarded as a unit in itself. Systems range from organic to inorganic and even machine-like entities, making it possible to evolve formulations that lead to laws and generalizations. These are then equally applicable to diverse systems of a wide range, so that comparative generalizations become possible. That is why the advantage of general systems theory is that it holds good for several disciplines. It is because of these conceptual developments that the use of computers has been useful, rather than seeking in the system a mechanical mathematical model. The application of cluster analysis is well known for archaeology, anthropology and sociology because within the framework of systems theory, it allows us to perform the task of compression of classifications, to build basic foundations of types and indices of traits that indicate significant patterns of human behaviour. It is in this manner that typological refinements have become crucial in the organization of archaeological material; searching for structures within multivariate archaeological data.

Ethnography and Prehistory

It is clear today that ethnographic and anthropological data has a crucial bearing in the interpretation of archaeological material. For instance, investigations have revealed that the broad subsistence patterns of hunting, gathering and collecting— that of early vegetarian diet and a carnivorous diet– are not in any evolutionary exclusive linear sequence. Moreover, adaptive systems of human societies, as lithic industries reflect, in order to survive indicate acceleration of mental, linguistic and social growth with a division of male hunters and female gatherers. But here again there is no uniformity, it includes a great variety and levels of subsistence patterns and social organization even amongst non-agricultural 'band' societies. This may be reflected in terms of the predominance of hunting for meat, for vegetable food, fishing, gathering seeds and collecting other plants, nuts, berries and roots. It is in this context that ethnographic material becomes crucial for seeking insights into our understanding of theoretical concepts about ethnographic material becomes crucial for seeking insights into our understanding of theoretical concepts about culture-history and the evolution of Man with the proviso that such contemporary societies have not remained static and many may in fact represent a regression because of pressure of more advanced societies that left them without the optimum conditions for their development.

We may call the above approaches as systemic ones for the study of human culture, reminding ourselves that each age and generation tries to interpret and relate available knowledge in terms of its own understanding. This is why different models have to be adopted to understand reality. But models are not fictional structures, they have their own objective reality albeit it changes as we try to examine the material. Consequently, what was proved long ago or what was the truth long ago does not hold true any more, not because it was false before but because newer perspectives have altered it. The relations between the observer and the observed is constantly changing. Today, within the contemporary framework, the social science framework, the holistic vision is extremely crucial within the context of understanding a persistent longstanding civilization like the Indian one, as follows.

Civilizational Approach

There is then the civilization approach to archaeological evidence, which seems closer to the social science objective. Let us recapitulate some of these frameworks of enquiries which may provide insights into various issues, especially related to the study of civilizations, particularly the Indian.

The Study of Civilizations

Civilizations have been studied for many generations and answers to such questions have been given in many ways. For instance, under the immediate impact of Darwinism, human societies were classified in terms of the biological principle of natural selection. This resulted in a quest for locating and studying such non-European societies as would exemplify various 'natural' stages in the history of societies, it also led to the investigation of Greek, Egyptian and Chinese civilizations. For instance, approaches as that of Gibbon, Spengler and Toynbee, presumed that civilizations have a definite life course and death similar to that of an individual organism. In fact, this idea has its roots in the 13th century, and even earlier universal histories. In short, the history of such studies is a long one, and we need not go into their details here. Some of the relevant conceptual assumptions of such studies may be summarised as follows :

EVOLUTIONIST AND PROGRESS ASSUMPTIONS :

These stress predominantly the technological criteria of material progress, as formulated by Lewis H. Morgan in 1877, Engels in 1884, and following in their footsteps Childe, who from archaeological and other evidences of ethnography, characterised civilization by the presence of cities, large monuments, agricultural surpluses, writing, etc.

ORGANIC VIEW POINTS :

These consider civilizations in terms of life cycle, of youth, manhood, old age, and death—especially as enunciated by Gibbon, Spengler, Toynbee, and others.

NON-EVOLUTIONISTS DEFINITIONS :

These include such viewpoints as the consideration of truth, beauty, adventure, art and peace as chief characterises –qualities– of a civilized society. We may here also include views which characterise India by its spirituality, or other moral judgments.

LEVELS OF INTEGRATION :

(a) Sorokin and Cowell, have viewed various cultural systems at high levels of integration in such fields as science, philosophy and art. Sorokin divided cultural systems into sensate, ideational, and idealistic, depending upon the respective view points of ultimate reality. But he does not consider a total civilization as integrated since for him subsystems, even clashing ones, along may be integrated; (b) Redfield considers civilization in terms of the integration of folk and urban cultures, and the interaction of high and low traditions, (c) Kroeber views civilizations as a 'superstyle' or a 'way of life'. For example, in considering the climax or culmination of a civilization in terms of art and intellectual activities, he indicates two such periods for India; from the Upanishadic period to the development of Buddhist and other heretical religions around 500 B.C., and the Gupta period (traditional golden period) from A.D. 400-600. The delimitation of culture and civilization corresponds closely to periodization, and for him history is an end product of learning and of judgment by conscious choice, whereby we organise endless continuum of culture and past happenings.

LITERATE CIVILIZATIONAL STUDIES :

In studying societies and cultures as a whole, either in terms of social and cultural integration, or in some other form of abstraction, it was thought that in literate civilizations, as contrasted with non-literate societies, there is a possibility of greater abstraction because of the presence of historical or philosophical sources. Literate civilizations are those which accumulate a wealth of written documents of all sorts, having a rich intellectual tradition –religious, historical, legal, scientific and the like. The word civilization has been chosen because in contrast to society and culture, it implies an extra increment of scope and elaborations.

Indian Civilization :Structure and Dynamics

The complexities involved in studying a civilization such as the Indian are self-evident; not only because of the diversity of ecological zones but also the multitude of topics that cover the enormous timespan of many hundreds of years. No single dominant theme or lifestyle unitary label would suffice or be accurate. The perennial question has been, how do we describe that almost infinite cultural variety, and yet communicate the essential features or common interrelated elements which would make these typical of that civilization ? We may sum up four basic directions towards which researchers have approached its examination :

i. Cataloguing, ii. Cultural Essence, iii. Cultural Communication and iv. Indian Civilization as type based on world wide structural, and cultural processes that illustrate culture-historical or sociological principles.

The first two approaches are simple to understand; the former deals with description while the latter with contents. The third seeks out basic systems of communication and structural integration. The fourth states that alongside distinct values, lifestyles and aspects of social structuring that are unique. These have to be put within the framework of some organising conceptual principle if a coherent picture is to emerge with regard to continuity and change. Perhaps, one may see it in terms of a hierarchy of different evaluations and levels of integration rather than any unitarily integrated network. Again, lifestyles may be defined within the framework of general systems theory, in order to seek recurrent patterns within the dynamic interaction of ecological, cultural, political, economic, social, religious and other subsystems.

Our very attempt to seek cross-cultural patterns is the result of a self-consciousness, a reflection of changing concepts in general knowledge and specifically in the social sciences, especially about national identity. However, the dynamics of hisorical knowledge is also linked, this interwoven tapestry of the past, present and the future, within an existential framework. Thus whatever the Indian heritage be, it cannot be taken for granted. It is best that one clearly states this new consciousness time and again within systematically worked out conceptual frameworks, so that enduring traditions are discovered in historic depth. For instance, the growth of this civilization is interlinked now with contemporary objectives of social transformations. This implies that radical changes are taking place in traditional structures, even if chaotically. But if we are to avoid aping 'modernisms', and not consider the mere use of science and technology as indicators of modernisation, it becomes imperative to clearly state this new consciousness, bearing in mind native categories of thought and world-views, which shall be eluded to later on.

In the process of model building, seeking regularities, often a uniformity is sought overlooking inconvenient aspects. But which tradition to keep and which to discard may only be decided if the dynamic nature is kept in mind. While there are ideas, symbols and images in each socio-cultural system that contribute to the maintenance of its self-identity and self-image, imbalances and disharmonies are also created from time to time along with corrective mechanisms that are set in motion. no society can claim to be static and not changing, for it would be hard to provide empirical evidence for such a mere tradition-directed society. Even normative premises are unevenly distributed in terms of understanding and interpretation of beliefs in different segments of the population. This dynamic nature holds true equally for the rural, tribal segments with which Indian civilization is so closely tied in its rich heritage, not only culturally but also politically.

However, social sciences are not very clear always as to how to assess all these mechanisms, e.g., often some techno-economic subsystems may persist apparently while their symbolic meanings change; and, on the other hand, while social systems persist in parts, the system of meaning implicit in them undergoes perceptible changes. Then, there is the rational orientation of man, and at the ideational level when 'non-conformist' individuals change society through art and creativity, areas where a certain logic does not work as these may be autonomous of the other systems, including the environment; it is well-known that socio-economic changes have not brought about the required political changes as envisaged, and so on.

To illustrate, in summary, questions which may be asked for Indian civilization could be, by and large, as follows :

A i. If a civilization is viewed as a system, in terms of levels of integration, is not a basic assumption of conflict equally valid for our analysis ?

ii. What are the fundamental aspects of discontinuity and change in a system, and the most fruitful ones of analysing them ?

iii. What criteria do we use to identify and define cultural stages, phases, periods, beyond mere chronology ? How do we work out a time-scale to judge the rates of socio-cultural and techno-economic changes ?

B i. Can one speak meaningfully of a finite number of pre-requisites for a civilization, and in their absence, of its decline and death?

ii. Are certain crucial socio-cultural institutions more necessary for the maintenance of a system than others, and if so, what ?

C i. What are the units of our study, both for contemporary and historic times ? The units maybe ethnographic, historical *(janapadas)*, ecological, cultural or even a sampling of statistical units.

ii. How do different/similar environments lead to similar/different technological and cultural levels ? Has a detailed correlation of techno-economic levels to socio-cultural levels been worked out ?

iii. Do social and cultural spheres and values produce economic needs ? Or, do needs, physiological or ideological, create the potential for socio-cultural and technological changes ? If, however, there are multiple interacting variables involved, how is this multivariate process to be identified and analysed ?

iv. What multivariate models will explain the inter-relationships of technology and economics to culture, or even the role of technology and economics in social systems ? What models, and evidence, do we have for seeing land use, trade pattern, population density, social relations, property rights, etc. ?

v. Is pre-industrial- traditional – society inherently conservative, especially the village one? If so, what is the context and empirical evidence for it? If supposing it is not, will we not need to look at historical evidence afresh ? Do some variable have more proneness for change than others; technology, arts and crafts, economics social life, or ideology ?

D i. Under what conditions and who in a socio-cultural group migrates ? Does migration always lead to replacement and no acculturation ?

ii. When do ideas alone spread, or do ideas and trait-complexes diffuse together with techno-economics and subsistence levels ?

iii. What is the role of convergent and parallel evolution in processes of diffusion and migration ?

iv. When do cultures borrow, replace or adopt alien technology, culture, economic systems, ideology and so forth ?

v. How do we see inner differentiation and change within a given cultural unit (boundary system), instead of invoking external cultural factors as a cause for change, i.e., do we not have to take certain inner compulsions indigenous (local and regional) needs of a society ?

Conclusion

Thus, our very attempt to seek cross-cultural patterns, whether in the past or the present, is the result of a self-consciousness, a reflection of changing concepts in general knowledge and specifically in the social sciences, especially about national identity. Contemporary ideas are directly linked, therefore, to the dynamics of historical knowledge. In this way, there is an interwoven tapestry of the past, present and the future, within an existential framework. Therefore, whatever the Indian heritage be, it cannot be taken for granted. It is best that one clearly states this new consciousness time and again within systematically worked out conceptual frameworks, so that enduring traditions are discovered in historic depth. For instance, the growth of this civilization is interlinked now with contemporary objectives of social transformations. This implies that radical changes are taking place in traditional structures, even if chaotically. But if we are to avoid aping 'modernisms', and not consider the mere use of science and technology as indicators of modernisation, it becomes imperative to clearly state this new consciousness, bearing in mind native categories of thought and world-views.

In the process of model building, seeking regularities, often a uniformity is sought overlooking inconvenient aspects. But which tradition to keep and which to discard may only be decided if the dynamic nature is kept in mind. While there are ideas, symbols and images in each socio-cultural system that contribute to the maintenance of its self-identity and self-image, imbalances and disharmonies are also created from time to time along with corrective mechanisms that are set in motion. No society can claim to be static and not changing, for it would be hard to provide empirical evidence for such a mere tradition-directed society. Even normative premises are unevenly distributed in terms of understanding and interpretation of beliefs in different segments of the population. This dynamic nature holds true equally for the rural, tribal segments with which Indian civilization is so closely tied in its rich heritage, not only culturally but also politically.

However, historical and social sciences are not very clear always as to how to assess all these mechnisms, e.g., often some techno-economic subsystems may persist apparently while their symbolic meanings change; and, on the other hand, while social systems persist in parts, the system of meaning implicit in them undergoes perceptible changes. Then, there is the rational orientation of man, and at the ideational level when 'non-conformist' individuals change society through art and creativity, areas where a certain logic does not work as these may be autonomous of the other systems, including the environment; it is well-known that socio-economic changes have not brought about the required political changes as envisaged, and so on.

In the ultimate analysis, models are ideal type referents against which individual cases may be compared.

Any model, in fact, represents a structured set of systems of concepts and ideas. This does not necessarily mean that human social systems may be compared with and expected to behave as natural systems of inorganic or organic matter. Nevertheless, concepts and models are not merely heuristic devices which help to put into order our complex data and observations, these also have a self-fulfilling prophetic value, through the building up of various images to possibly realise the vision of a new society.

BIBLIOGRAPHY

Baden-Powell, H. Baden. 1892. *Land System of British India.* London.

_________ 1953 (reprint), *Indian Village Community.* New Haven.

Binford, L.R. 1962. "Archaeology as Anthropology", *American Antiquity,* 28 (2), pp. 217-25.

_________ 1965, "Archaeological Systematics and the study of culture process." American Antiquity, 31 (2), 203-210.

_________ Sally (ed.) 1968. *New Perspective in Archaeology.* Chicago.

_________ 1972. An Archaeological Perspective, New York.

Bouissac, Paul 1990. "Semiotics and the Gaia Hypothesis: Towards the Restructuring of Western Thought" in *Philosophy and the Future of Humanity,* Vol. 1, 2. pp. 168-184

de Chardin, Teilhard, P. 1959. *The Phenomenon of Man.* New York..

Childe, V. Gordon, 1946. "Archaeology and Anthropology". *South Western Journal of Anthropology,* 2(3), 243-51.

_________ 1947. "Archaeology as a Social Science", *Third Annual Report* (1946). Institute of Archeology, London, pp 49-60.

_________ 1951. *Social Evolution,* penguin.

_________ 1950. "The Urban Revolution". *Town Planning Review,* 21. pp. 3-17, London.

_________ 1954. *New Light on the Most Ancient East,* London.

_________ 1954. *What Happened in History,* London.

_________ 1956. *Piecing Together the·Past,* London.

_________ 1956. *Society and Knowledge,* London.

_________ 1957. *Man Makes Himself,* London.

_________ 1958. "Retrospect". *Antiquity,* 32. 69-74.

_________ 1958. "Valediction". *Bulletin of the Institute of Archaeology.* I. 1-8.

Cowell. F.R. 1952. *History. Civilization and Culture* (An Introduction to the Historical and Social Philosophy of Pitrim A. Sorokin). London.

Gandhi. K. (ed.) 1990. *The Odyssey of Science. Culture and Consciousness.* New Delhi.

Harris. Errol E. 1991. *Cosmos and Anthropos –A philosophical interpretation of the anthropic cosmological principle.* New Jersey. London.

Heisenberg. Werner. 1959. *Physics and Philosophy* –Glifford Lectures. George Allen and Unwin. London.

Hsu. Francis L.K. 1969. *The Study of Literate Civilizations.* New York.

Kroeber. Alfred. 1963. a. *Style and Civilizations.* Berkley.

_________ *An Anthropologist looks at History.* Berkley.

Kuhn. Thomas. 1970. *The Structure of Scientific Revolution.* Chicago.

Malik. S.C. 1968. Indian Civilization; the Formative Period– *A study of archaeology as anthropology.* Shimla. (reprinted. 1987).

_________ 1968. "Archaeology as a Source in Writing Socio-cultural and Socio-economic History". *Eastern Anthropologist.* Lucknow.

_________ 1969. "Culture Areas. Ecology and Regionalism". *Language Culture and Society.* Shimla.

_________ (ed.). 1971. *Indian Civilization: The First Phase-problems of a Source book.* Shimla.

_________ 1972. "Human Evolution; Some Reflections on its Philosophy". *Eastern Anthropologist.* Lucknow.

_________ 1973. "Models and Social Relevance of Indian Archaeology". in D.P. Agrawal (ed). *Radio-carbon and Indian Archaeology.* Bombay.

_________ 1975. *Understanding Indian Civilization– A Framework of Enquiry.* Shimla.

_________ 1975. "Prehistory as a Social Science". *Man in India.* Lucknow.

_________ (ed.). 1977. *Dissent. Protest and Reform in Indian Civilization.* Indian Institute of Advanced Studies. (IIAS) Shimla.

_________ (ed.) 1978. *Indian Movements : Some Aspects of Dissent. Protest and Reform.* I.I.A.S. Shimla.

_________ 1979. "Changing Perspectives of Archaeology and Interpreting Harappan Society" in Agrawal and Chakrabarti (eds.). *Essays in Indian Protohistory.* New Delhi.

_________ (ed.). 1986. *Determinants of Social Status in India.* I.I.A.S. Shimla.

_________. 1987. "Dual Nature of Thought". *Vishwabharati Quarterly.* Santiniketan.

_________ 1989a. *Modern Civilization-A crisis of Fragmentation.* New Delhi. (Abhinav).

_________ 1989b. "Intellectuals. Traditions and Ethnographic Studies–some basic questions. " *Man in India.* Ranchi.

_________. 1990c. "In search of Quality of Life in Anthropology : Beyond Fragmentation". *Quality of Life* I.I.A.S. Shimla.

_________ 1990d. "Holism and Life Style Studies- the Civilization Context". *Eastern Anthropologist.* Lucknow.

_________ 1992. "Matter and Consciousness". *The nature of Matter.* IGNCA. New Delhi.

_________ 1993a. "Holistic Science and Consciousness". *Nature and Man-An Integral Vision.* Indra Gandhi National Centre for Arts (IGNCA). New Delhi.

_________ 1993b. "A Question of Consciousness". Future of the Mind– Mind of the Future. IGNCA. New Delhi

_________ Saraswati. B.N. and Khanna. Madhu.(Ed.,) 1994 and *Art : The Integral Vision.* D.K. Print world. New Delhi.

_________. 1995. *Reconceptualising the Sciences and the Humanities : An Integral Approach.* Manohar. New Delhi.

Marriot. Mckim (ed.). 1963. *Village India : Studies in the Little Community.* Chicago.

_________ and Inden. R. 1974. "Towards an Ethnosociology of South Asian Caste System". Mimeographed. Chicago (IXth *International Congress of Anthropology–Ethonology).*

_________ 1974. "Caste System". *Encyclopaedia Brittanica.* London.

Mathur. K.S. and Varma. S.C. (eds.). 1975. *Man and Society,*. Lucknow.

Misra. Vidya Niwas. 1971. "Indian Concept of Civilization" in *Malik. op. cit.*

Murty. M.L.K. and Sontheimer. G.D., 1980 "Prehistoric Background to Pastoralism in the Southern Deccan in the Light of Oral Traditions and Cults of some Pastoral Communities". *Anthropos,* Germany.

Redfield. Robert. 1956. *Peasant Society and Culture.* Chicago.

__________ 1961. *The Little Community and Peasant Society and Cultures,* Chicago.

Saraswati B.N. 1973. *Contributions to the Study of Indian Civilization,* Dharwar.

__________ 1977. "Notes on Kabir: A non-literate Intellectual" in Malik. op. cit.

Schroedinger. E. 1948. *What is Life.* Cambridge. U.P.

Sheldrake R. 1980. *A New Science of Life.* London.

Singer, Milton (ed.). 1959. *Traditional India; Structure and Change,* Philadelphia.

__________ (ed.). 1968. *Structure and Change in Indian Society,* Chicago.

Sorokin. Pitrim A. 1962. *Social and Cultural Dynamics* (Four volumes), New Jersey.

Toynbee. Arnold J. 1947. *A Study of History* (Six volumes), London.

The Palaeolithic Evidences From Pathalgarwa In Bihar†

D.K. Bhattacharya and Manoj Kumar Singh*

Introduction

During 1994-95, Shri Rathindra Nath Tagore and Surendra Nath Kar both of Shantiniketan discovered a single Acheulian handaxe from Bhimbandh region (25°3'50"N and 86°23'55"E) of Munghyr district in Bihar. Subsequently R.C.P. Singh[1] and N.K. Bose[2] also explored the same area and recorded fresh antiquities. These initial interests in the region, however, did not culminate in any further systematic investigation till as late as 1972 (published in 1978), P.C. Pant and Vidula Jayswal took up a systematic excavation at a site called Paisra, which is about 18 km north-east of Bhimbandh. The excavation confirmed that a late Lower Palaelolithic occupation in the Kharagapur hills is extremely advanced and probably widely spread. Two things became clear as a result of the Paisra excavation. Firstly, unlike Tagore and Kar's finds from boulder deposits, these were both open air as also factory sites. Secondly, here we might be dealing with a really very late Lower Palaeolithic culture. In this regard the stratigraphic occurrence of microliths immediately overlaying the Acheulian layer is also a very significant point. A radiocarbon date for this microlithic layer measured 7420± 110 B.P. (5470±110 BC).

The present work[3] reports another large and rich site from the Kharagpur ranges which lies within the same physiographic region. Locally the site is called Pathalgarwa and is located near the village Jamuniya (25°5'N 86°20'E) in Jamui district. The nearest railway station is Jamui (Malepur) and the site is about 35 km south-west from here. During 1996 the present authors undertook a survey of the Kharagpur hills and discovered a large number of Palaeolithic, Mesolithic and Neolithic sites from these hills spread over the districts of Nawada, Giridih, Munghyr and Jamui. Pathalgarwa was discovered during this field work in December 1996 (Fig. 1).

The Site

The Kharagpur ranges constitute a number of low hills of irregular formation. The hills are also the watershed region for the higher ranges that surround them. Vegetal cover in these lower benches is much thicker and this has caused the formation of a layer of soil cover on the bare rocks. On a horizontal surface such soil cover is from 10 to 30 cm. thick, but in areas which are depressed or wide crevices in the rock such soil deposits can be as much as 1.50 to 4.0 m thick. Pathalgarwa is situated on one of

* The first author is a professor in the Deptt. of Anthropology University of Delhi while the second is a Research Scholar in the same Deptt. and University.

† This paper is dedicated to the memory of Prof. A.K Ghosh of the Deptt. of Anthropology, Calcutta University. Calcutta.

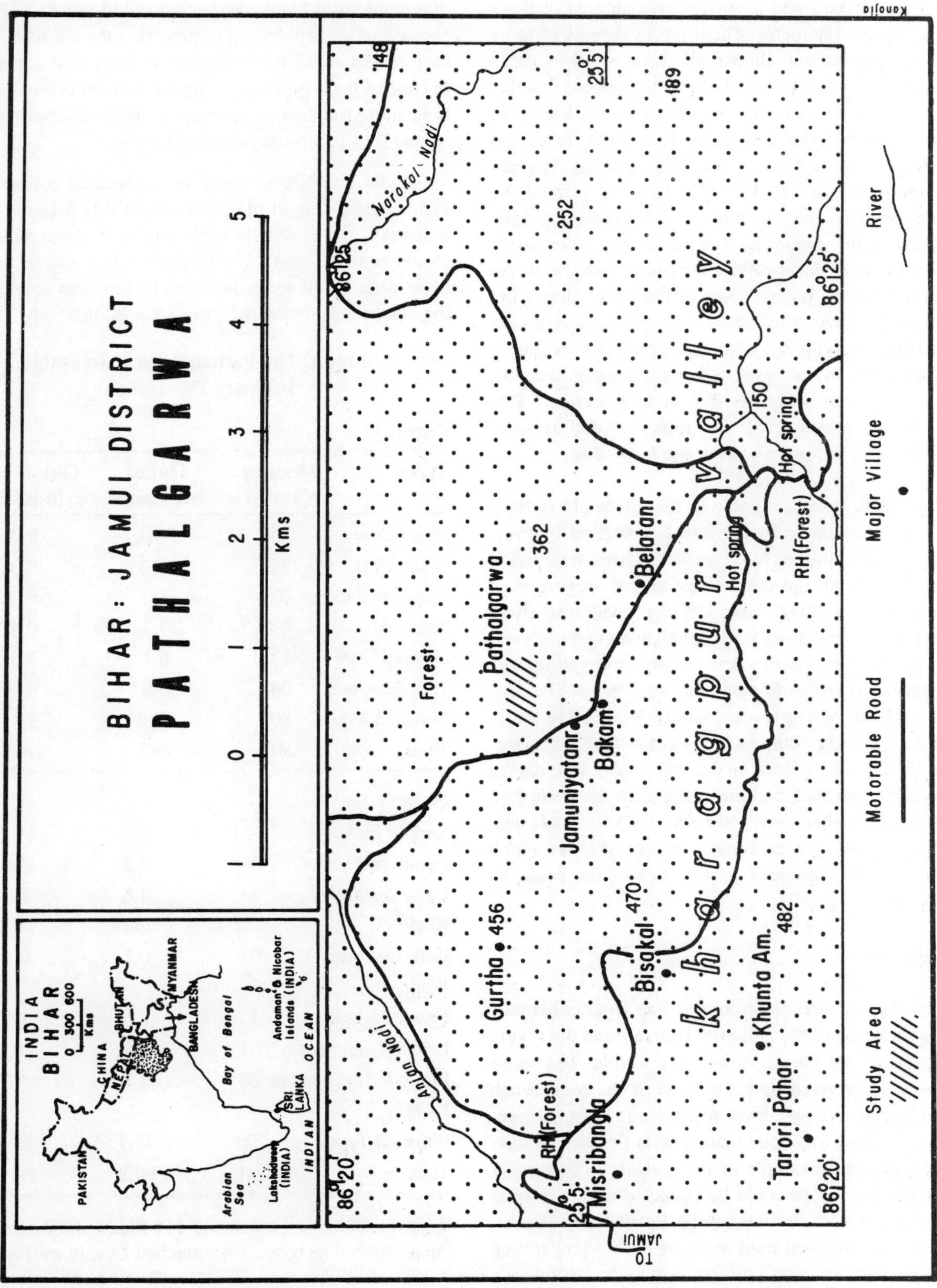
BIHAR : JAMUI DISTRICT
PATHALGARWA
Kms
0 1 2 3 4 5
INDIA
BIHAR
0 300 600
Kms
PAKISTAN
CHINA
NEPAL
BHUTAN
MYANMAR
BANGLADESH
Bay of Bengal
Arabian Sea
Lakshadweep (INDIA)
SRI LANKA
Andaman & Nicobar Islands (INDIA)
INDIAN OCEAN
Kanojia
Narokol Nadi
Anjan Nadi
Forest
Pathalgarwa
Gurtha 456
Jamuniyatanr
Bakam
Belatanr
362
252
189
150
Hot spring
RH (Forest)
Misribangla
Bisakal 470
Khunta Am. 482
Tarori Pahar
Khargapur Valley
86°20'
86°25'
25°5'
148
TO JAMUI
Study Area
Motorable Road
Major Village
River

these rocky benches and is spread over an area of more than one square kilometre. There are evidences of large flake beds present on almost all those suitable rocks which are jutting out. It would, therefore, appear that this was not only a factory site but also a major source of quarrying raw material. Numerous such large flakes and cores almost cover the entire area. The area largely comprises pre-Cambrian rocks. The base is formed by quartzite, phyllite, slate, sericite, schist, intrusive granite and quartz veins. Near the site an entire exposure of quartzite is visible wherever laterites have been cut through modern activities. Most of the lower slopes laterite forms the upper crust along with alluvium. Artefacts occur in clusters with this alluvium which is very thin in the higher parts. In the lower and sloping region the alluvium is almost as much as 2-4 m in thickness. This alludes to the presence of the implementiferous layer being right after the period of laterite formation.

The soil deposits available in the ditches have been dug out at many places by the forest authorities to cover temporary roads constructed. Theses roads are required to bring trucks within the deep forest where logging is in progress. These diggings have left readymade and sharp angular profiles of deposits. In Pathalgarwa one such soil profile was present and this was closely observed for any colluviational effect of implementiferous band. The profile available at Pathalgarwa is nearly 3 metres in thickness and is entirely composed of compact and homogeneous red soil. The colour of the soil tends to be darker towards the upper half, and these represent the watershed activity of the higher slopes bringing kankary loads during rains. No tool or even angular chunks of rocks which are otherwise so numerous on the rock bench could be found in this soil profile.

The Industry

A method of random collection was roughly planned for the picking up of the antiquity from around the region where most of the jutting rocks were visible. The entire area has been covered upto the limit of the rock bench where it begins to slope down towards the seasonal rainfed channel. This was done mainly with the idea of having a representative sample of the main activity area. A total of 844 specimens could be collected in this manner to be transported to the laboratory. Large flake chunks, which might have been used as cores for the preparation of suitable tool blanks and types could not be collected because of the problem of transporting the load. Naturally such pieces are also not counted in the statistical tablets. In spite of these precautions undertaken there would seem to be more finished types in our collection which got lifted and thus incorporated in the sample.

Table 1 shows the break up of the total collection of Pathalgarwa. One of the most remarkable features of the industry is the extremely fresh condition of the tools. The fractures are so sharp and fresh that they appear to have been made on the same day. This feature was not noted in the specimens collected from the boulders by earlier workers. In all 130 cores and 411 flakes and blades have been finished as types. Unretouched Levalloise flakes are

Table 1. The Pathalgarwa Palaeolithic Industry Percentage

Cores

Types	Absolute Number	Out of total cores	Out of total Industry
Flake Core	76	36.1	9.0
Blade Core	28	13.3	3.3
Retouched Core	02	1.0	0.2
Nncleate	07	3.3	0.8
Discoid Core	13	6.1	1.5
Tortoise Core	04	2.0	0.4
Finished Types	80	38.0	9.4
Total	210	99.8	24.6

Flakes

Simple Flake	144	22.7	17.0
Retouched Flake	56	8.8	6.6
Levallois Flake	31	4.8	3.6
Blade	158	25.0	18.7
Core trimming Blade	01	0.1	0.1
Crested Blade	13	2.0	1.5
Levalloisian Point	02	0.3	0.2
Psedudo levalloisian Point	06	1.0	0.7
Finished Types	223	35.1	26.5
Total	210	99.8	24.6

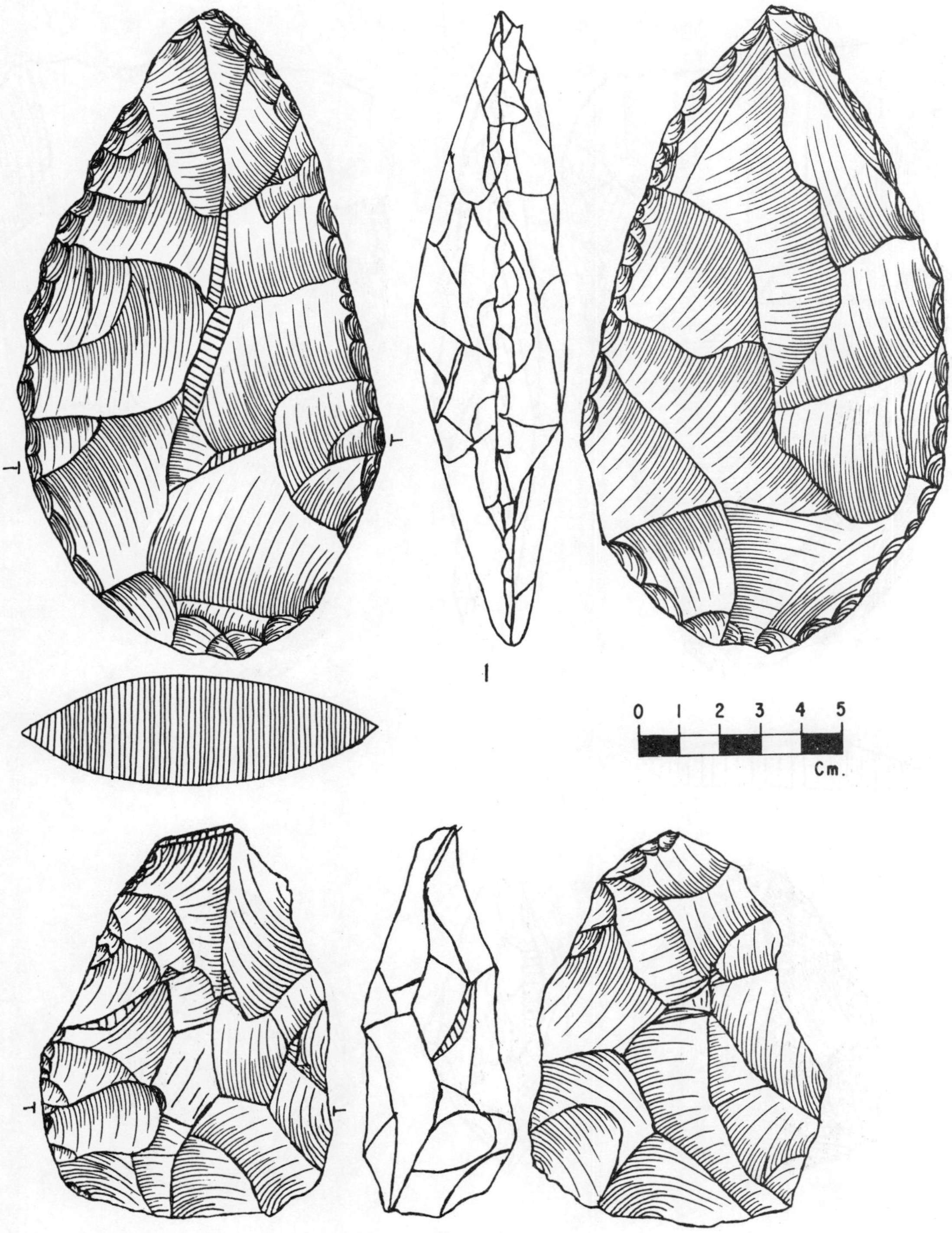

Fig. 2 A

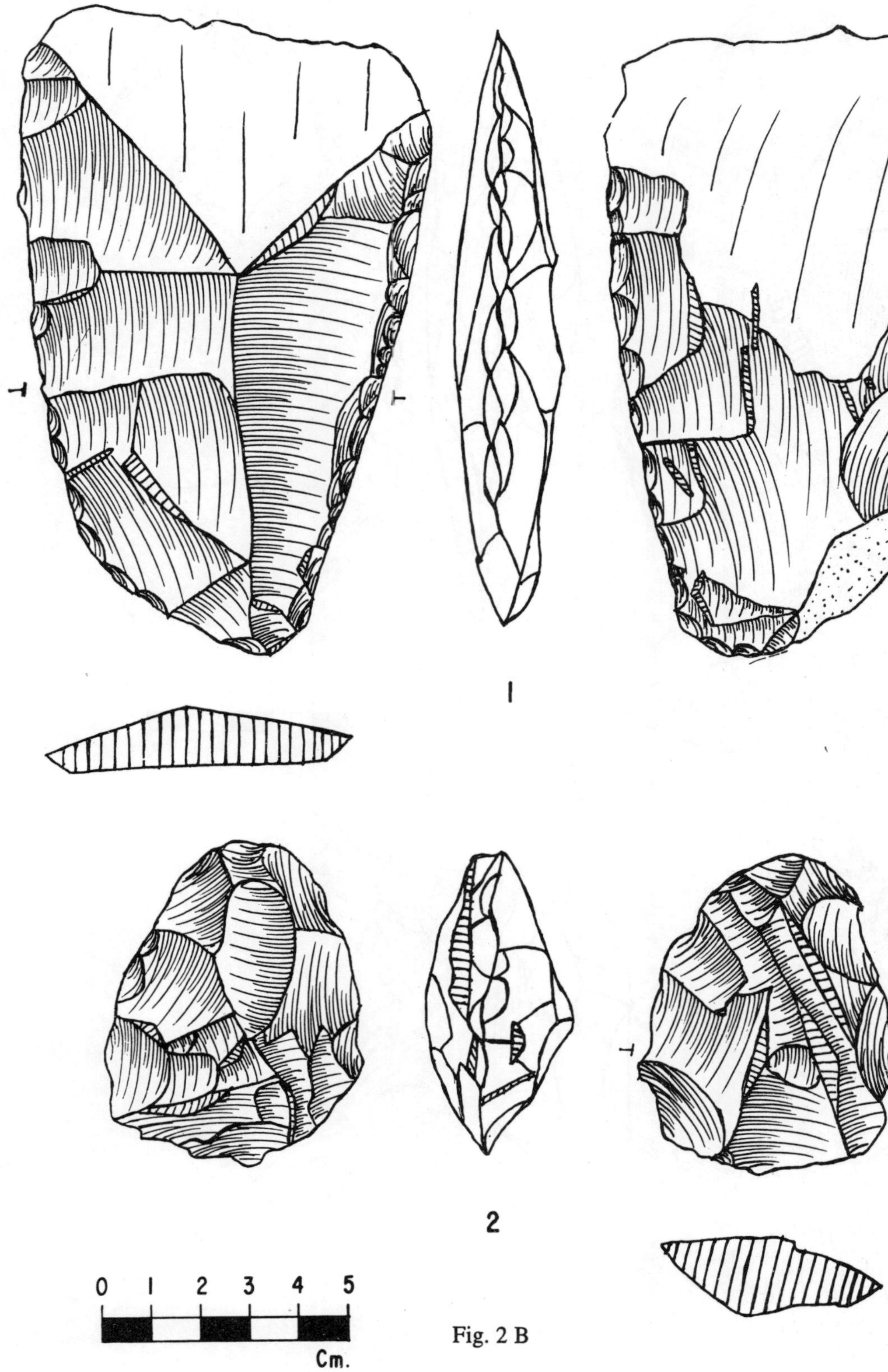

Fig. 2 B

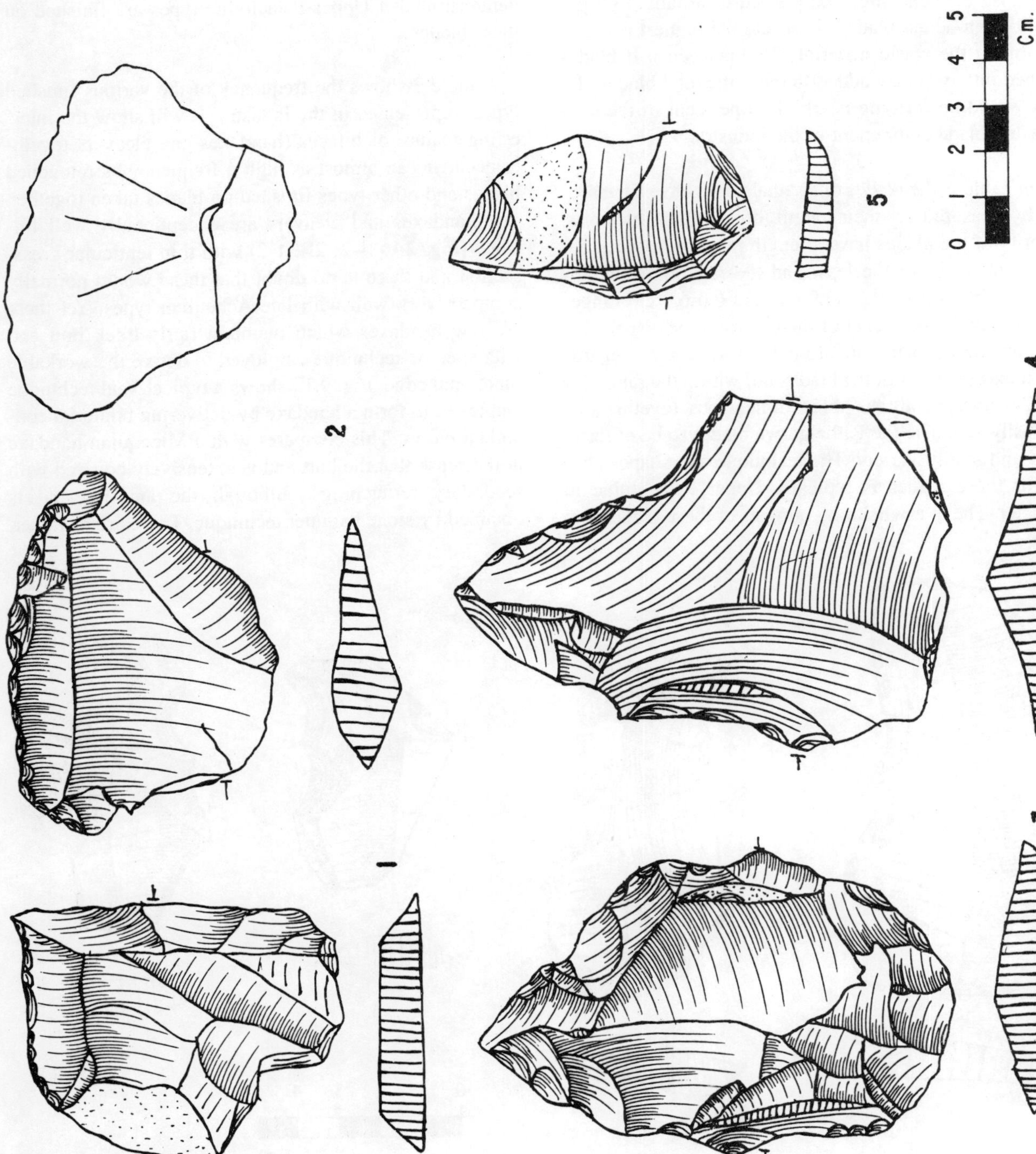

Fig. 3

31 in number (4.8 per cent) but besides these there are some others which have been retouched into types and if these are taken into account the total percentage of Levalloise element might be pushed to around 13.6 per cent. Untretouched blades constitute the highest percentage among the waste material (25.0 per cent). If blades finished into types are added to these the total blades element would be forming nearly 45.0 per cent of the total flake and blade component of the industry.

In Table 2, the blades of Phathalgarwa have been separately measured for their length, breadth and thickness. Majority of the blades have a length ranging between 5.0 to 7.9 cm although the least and the maximum lengths recorded fall between 2.0-2.9 cm and 6.0-6.9 cm ranges respectively. In the aspect of their breadth the dispersal is much less and concentrate around 2.0-4.9 cm. As regards their thickness most of the blades fall within the range 1.9 cm. Considering all the three dimensions together one can easily visualise the Pathalgarwa blades to be of fairly broad and sturdy variety. The technique and shapes chosen for these blades is typically Upper Palaeolithic in character. The overwhelming number of these blades and the identical manner of their detachment leaves no doubt that blade manufacture formed a cultural imperative among the people of Pathalgarwa. This can be further demonstrated if Upper Palaelothic types are finished on these blades.

Table 3 shows the frequency of the various finished types represented in the industry. It will show the interesting feature of bifaces (handaxes and cleavers together)occurring in almost as high a frequency as retouched blades and other types finished on blades taken together. The handaxes and cleavers are exceptionally well finished (Fig. 2A. 1--2; 2B. 1-2) with thin lenticular crosssection and there is no doubt that these would normally compare very well with late Acheulian types. Yet there are few handaxes which maintain fairly thick butt end with specific technique employed to derive the workable functional edge. Fig. 9.1., shows a typical Vaal technique employed to form a handaxe by delivering bilaterial concoildal blows. This compares with a Micoquian handaxe in the sense that the butt end is extensively covered with secondary retouchings, although the anterior end is obtained by stone hammer technique. There are however,

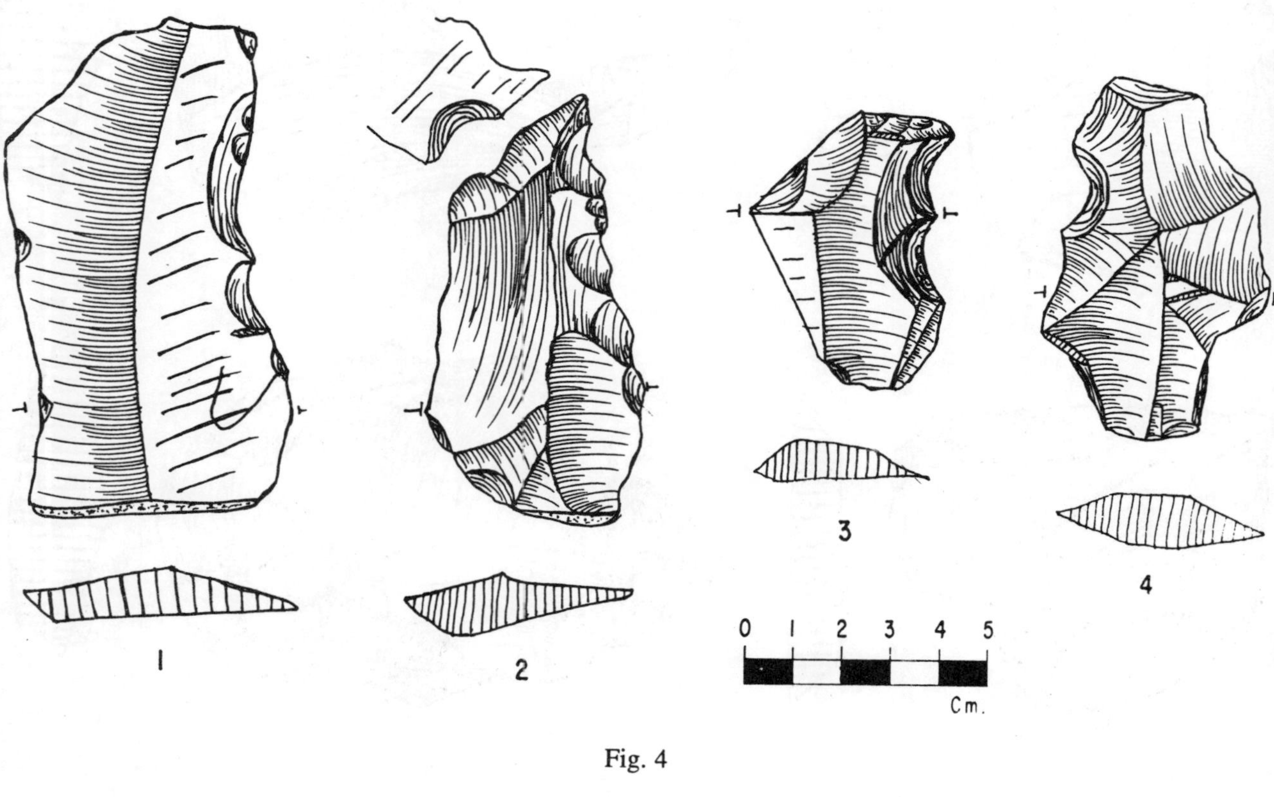

Fig. 4

some which appear to be diminutive in shape and look more like having been shaped out of exhausted cores

Table 2: Measurement of the Blades of the Pathalgarwa Industry

Range	Length	Breadth	Thickness
0.0-0.9			33
1.1-1.9		3	95
2.0-2.9	1	29	18
3.0-3.9	4	58	10
4.0-4.9	13	43	2
5.0-5.9	33	16	
6.0-6.9	38	2	
7.0-7.9	26	6	
8.1-8.9	13	1	
9.0-9.9	13		
10.0-10.9	4		
11.0-11.9	8		
12.1-12.9	3		
13.2-13.9			
14.3-14.9	1		
15.4-15.9			
16.5-16.9			
17.6-17.9	1		
Total No. of Blades	158	158	158

(Fig. 2B.2.). The cleavers are prepared on thin like flakes with a narrowed down butt end (Fig. 2B.1.). But unlike a typically Acheulian flake cleaver these hardly represent the parallelogram cross-section. These are thin flakes whichhave been minimally trimmed along the two lateral borders and seldom at the butt end. The transverse edge is formed by planning the intersection of two flat scars sloping towards the anterior end.

Continuing with Table 3, we find that the largest number of finished types represented in this industry is that of varieties of side scrapers (total = 31.6 per cent)[4]. Many of these are prepared on Levalloise flakes. Tortoise cores found are not very many (only four in number). The intersecting point about these cores is that these are medium sized (Fig. 8. 1-2) and are almost exhausted cores. So many flakes have been taken out of them that they look almost flat in some instances. Retouchings are bold and contiguous and compare very well with the manner of retouchings done on blades (Fig. 3.2-4). Notches and denticulates are fairly high in frequency and in some cases these are also prepared on blades (Fig. 4.1-4) . In fact one of the specimens (Fig.6.6) is finished perfectly into a Tayac point. Besides these, point as a type seem to be not much favoured (Fig. 3.1). There are some massive flakes which are specially thinned out by taking out large scars anterio-posteriorly. The lateral borders are then given extensive retouchings to emphasize the pointed region (Fig. 10.1). These specimens are counted as 'hand points' in the manner of Bosinski's[5] analysis of Bockstein material. End-scrapers and burins occur in almost same frequency but these are not finished in the typical Upper Palaeolithic manner known from south-west France[6]. In fact there are some burins which are prepared on flakes and are actually vec-alterene[7] in type (Fig.6.3). There are others which are prepared on notches (Fig. 6.1). There are 4 backed blades of moderate length which distinctly demonstrates the ultimate expertise of blade tool technology (Fig. 5.1). A number of these blades have pronounced crest running along their length on the dorsal surface(Fig. 7.1). Obviously, these indicate attempts to shape cores suitable for further removal of blades. In other words, the blades at Pathalgarwa cannot be taken as mere random and chance production. Instead this can be taken to indicate a regular expertised blade production, which can be an additional proof of the industry being of Upper Palaeolithic culture. In the same way a denticulate prepared on the lateral border of a blade recalls the French Upper Perigordian in type (Fig. 4.2). If end-scrapers (Fig.6.4), retouched blades (Fig. 5.3,4) and burins (Fig.6.2) are taken as typical Upper Palaelothic types then Pathalgarwa represents more than 21.3 per cent of these total tools. In contrast to that handaxes and cleavers total 26.2 per cent while side scrapers represents 31.6 per cent. End-scrapers at the site are not only prepared on suitable blades by there are two finely finished carinated end–scrapers also found in this collection (Fig. 7.2 and 3). These are finished exactly in the manner of the specimen of Aurignacian tradition. Naturally these can be taken as another significant factor in deciding Pathalgarwa as an Upper Palaeolithic in character.

Table 3. The Pathalgarwa Tool Types Percentage

Types	Absolute Number	Out of total types	Out of total Industry
Handaxe	43	14.1	5.0
Vaal Handaxe	02	0.6	0.2
Flake Handaxe	03	1.0	0.3
Unfinished Handaxe	10	3.3	1.1
Cleaver	18	6.0	2.1
Fragmented Cleaver	02	0.6	0.2
Unfinished Cleaver	02	0.6	0.2
Single Slide Scraper	77	25.4	9.1
Double Side Scraper	03	1.0	0.3
Convergent Side Scraper	10	3.3	1.1
Transverse Side Scraper	05	1.6	0.6
Alternate Side Scraper	01	0.3	0.1
Carinated End Scraper	02	0.6	0.2
Notch	12	4.0	1.4
Denticulate	12	4.0	1.4
Notched Blade	08	2.6	1.0
Hand point	01	0.3	0.1
Borer	04	11.3	0.4
Burin	10	3.3	1.1
Axial Burin	01	0.3	0.1
Bec alterne Burin	06	2.0	0.7
Retouched Blade	29	9.5	3.4
Retouched Blade alternate	02	0.6	0.2
Disc	04	1.3	0.4
End Scraper	19	6.2	2.2
Truncated Blade	02	0.6	0.2
Burin on notch	02	0.6	0.2
Tayac Point	01	0.3	0.1
Cutaux a dos	02	0.6	0.2
Backed Blade	04	1.3	0.4
Point	06	2.0	0.7
Total	303	99.2	25.6

Discussion

The nature of the Pathalgarwa industry raises many theoritical issues in archaeology. Semantically as well there would be a difficulty to name such an industry with any of the chrono-cultural terms used in archaeological methodology. That is, both typo - technologically as well as chronologically this industry does not fit in any of the available sub-divisions of Palaeolithic, if Lubbock[8] or Lyell's[9] methods are adopted. It is difficult to prove any marked change in our approach from this one hundred-and-thirty-five years old method even today. One of the paradoxes of our subject is that although it is undergoing change in a totally unprecedented speed and depth its basic analytical frame hardly shows any appreciable change. We seem to be more and more depending on rules which are least negotiable. Probably this is because our thinking for the last few centuries has been having an

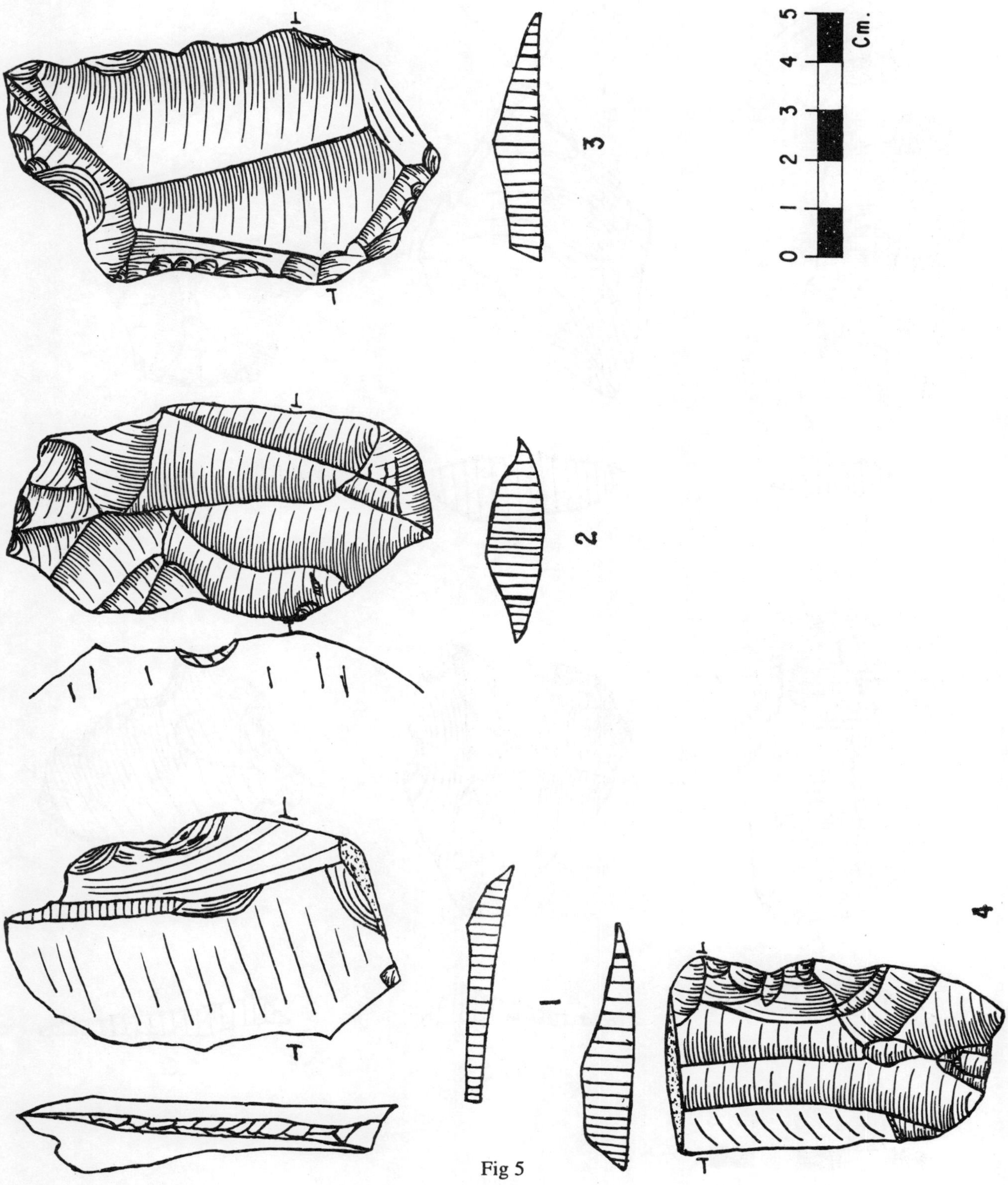

Fig 5

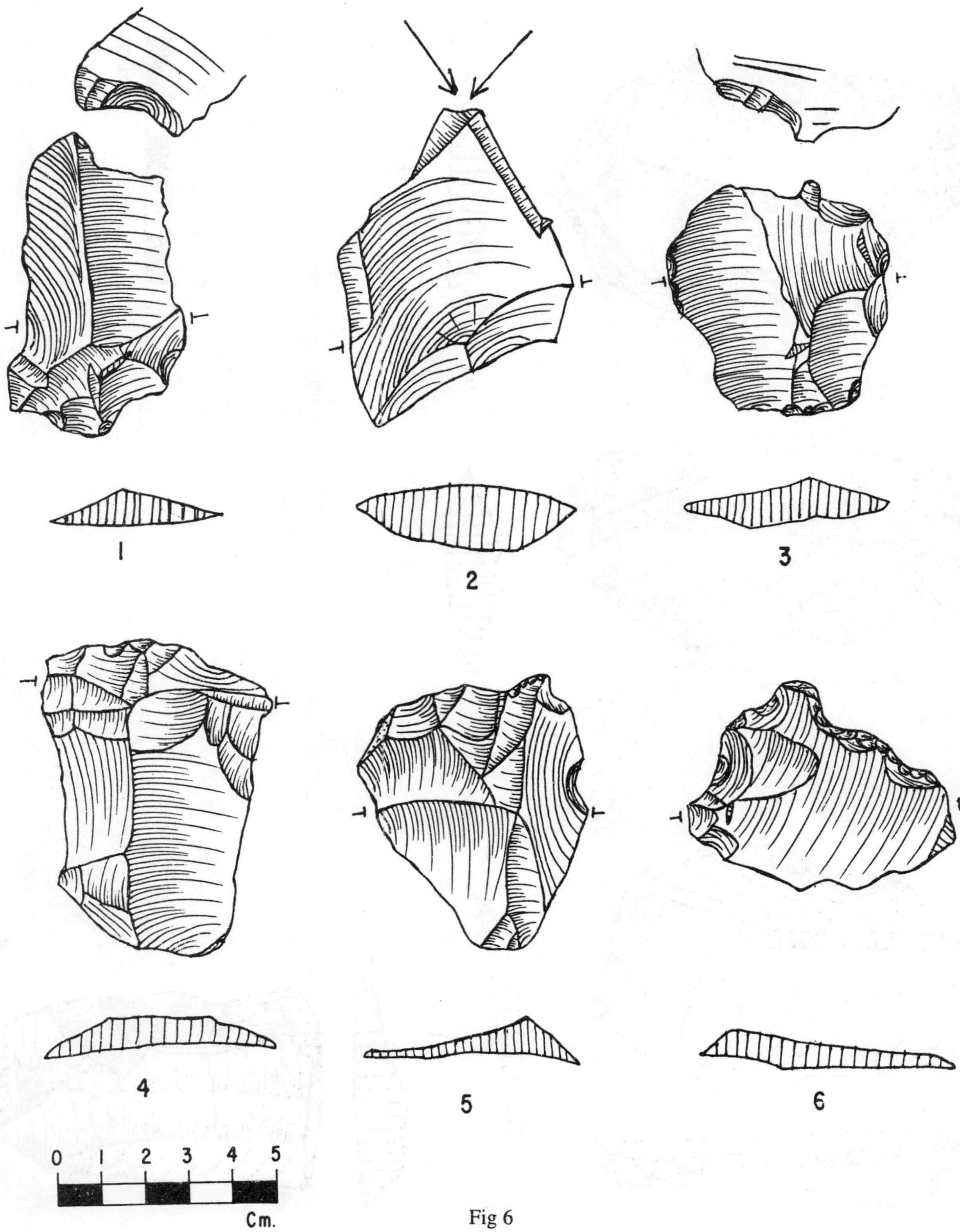

Fig 6

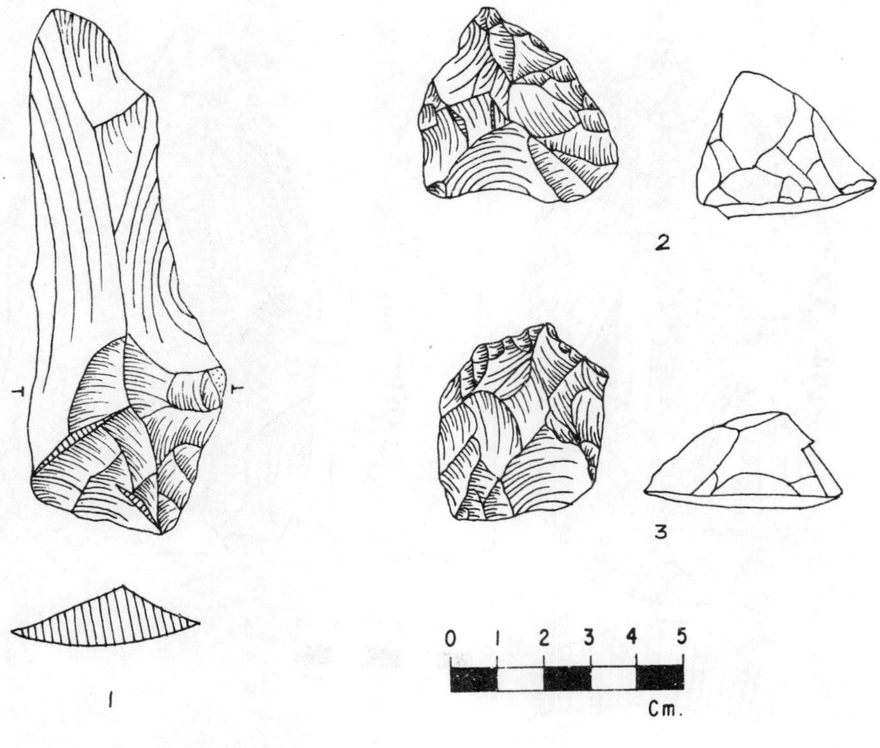

Fig 7

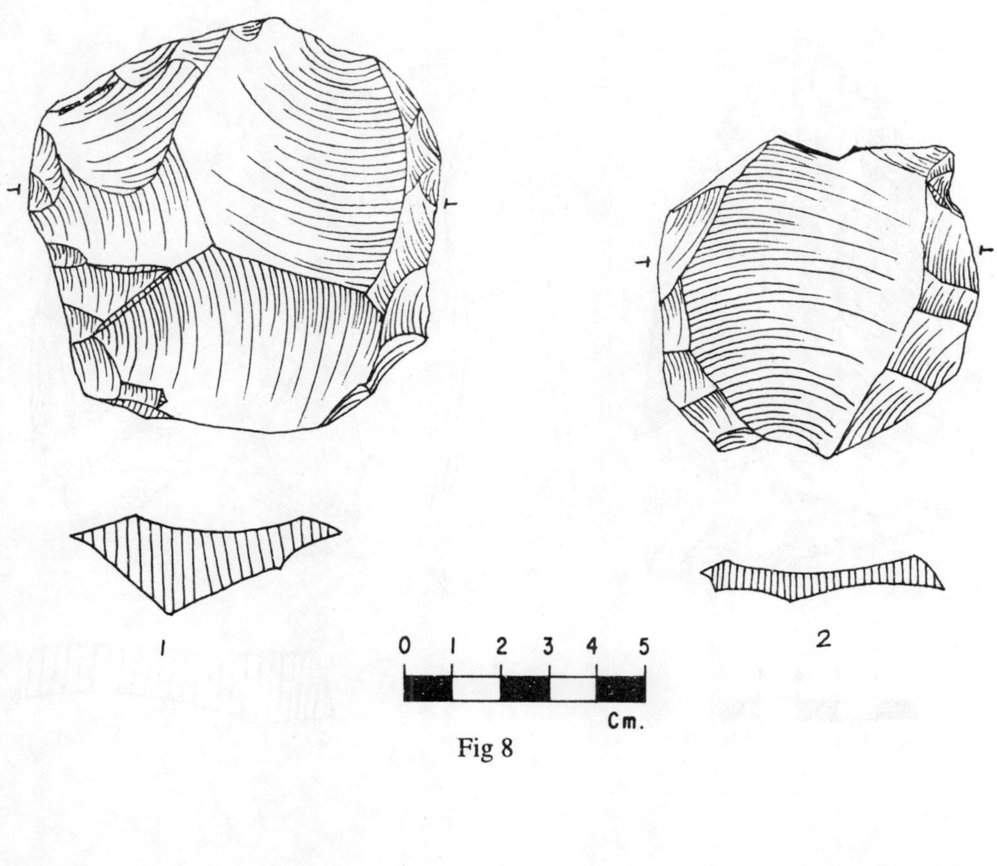

Fig 8

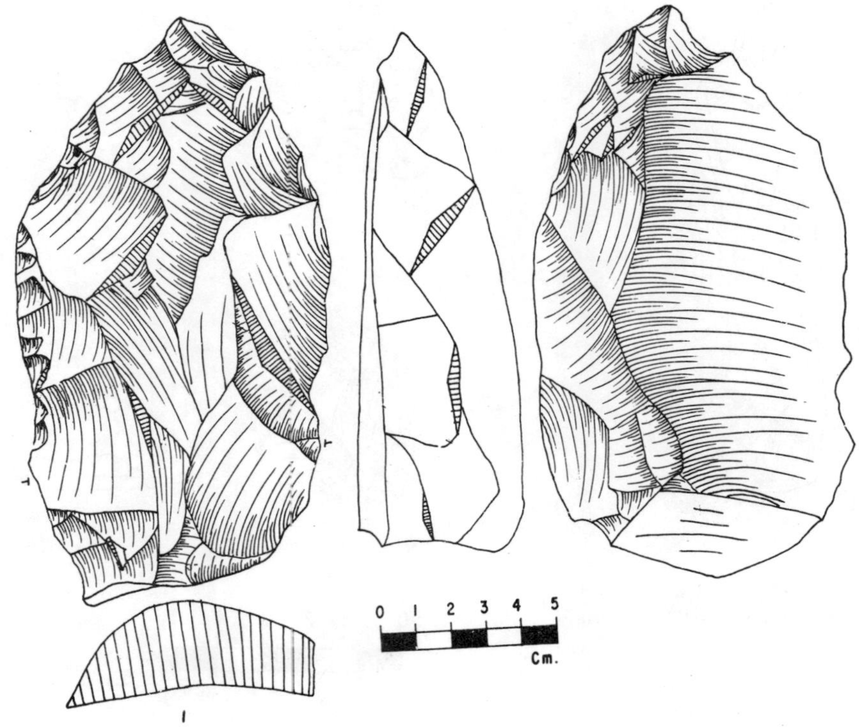

Fig 9

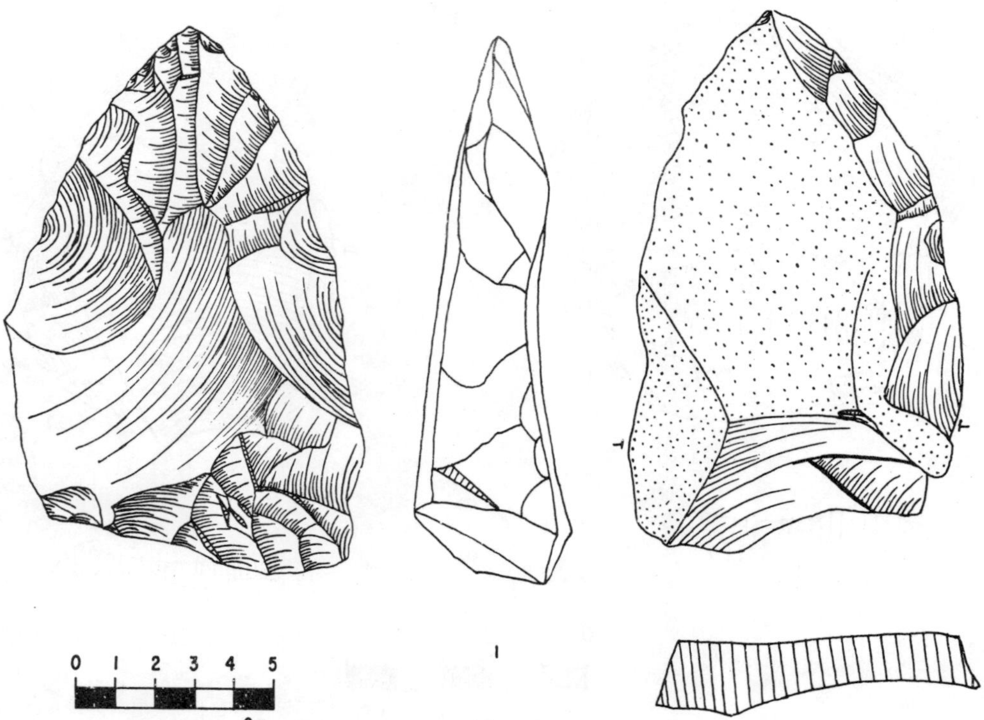

Fig 10

overwhelming influence of biological sciences where rules describe new observations. While in biological sciences transformation are possible on the basis of earlier one which constitute their pre-conditions, in social sciences acquired knowledge at every step of transformation can provide newer choices, and hence there is an urgent need of deconstruction in our methods.

The evidences of Pathalgarwa, as described above, will also demonstrate such a need for much more carefully understanding all our surface evidences with a more open mind. There are numerous examples of isolated Neolithic celts or small clusters of microlithic debitage recorded from Chhotanagpur region found by earlier scholars and they have been faithfully designated with the archaic terms biz., Mesolithic, Neolithic or Chalcolithic culture[10]. Whenever such watertight terms were found uncomfortable newer terms like Neo-Chalcolithic or Ferro-Chalcolithic had to be invented to suit the nature of the antiquities discovered. Even these terms carried precisely no cultural meaning and had to remain as adhoc nomenclatures for the specific region of group of sites.

Conclusion

We feel that the average duration of the various stone ages in diverse ecozones is so vastly different that one need no longer stick to their chronological or typological definitions. It appears that, at least in areas surveyed in Chhotanagpur, the various type fossils of Lower Palaeolithic, Middle Palaeolithic and Upper Palaeolithic are squeezed together within a small time span, mostprobably during the fag end of the Pleistocene. This is more or less comparable to the classical type tools as cultural discriminants might be grossly misleading in this region.

Finally, it will be also important to mention here that Paisra, being more or less occurring in the same physiographic region, also represents a very Late Palaeolithic culture. This is further indicated by the fact that there are no Middle or Upper Palaeolithic culture. This is further indicated by the fact that there are no Middle or Upper Palaeolithic layers occurring before the Mesolithic stratum. The absolute date 7420±110 B.P.(5470±110 BC.)available for this layer leaves no doubt that the Mesolithic at Paisra is from a rather early Holocene deposit. In other words the Palaeoliths of Paisra are immediately preceding the Mesoliths. Being an excavated site the evidence from Paisra can be taken to further confirm our observation for Pathalgarwa open air factory site. The chrono-cultural terms used in archaeology are deeply ensconced in our thinking that to suggest an entirely different set of terms for the various stages of South Asian Stone Age may not be easily acceptable to most of us. Yet, one cannot deny that such a need has been repeatedly felt by many archaeologists from the day of the discovery of Anyathian and Patjitanian. The evidences from Pathalgarwa would again seem to demonstrate that the available terms for archaeological designation are grossly inadequate for many parts of India as well. Consequently what we are proposing here is to free ourselves from the 'straight-jacket' of pre-decided categories to describe the past cultures. The time is not ripe enough to discard the terms in use but surely they need not tie us down to .the meanings originally conveyed when first used.

NOTES & REFERENCES

1. Singh, R.C.P. 1959. Palaeoliths from *Bhimbandh, Journal of the Bihar Research Society*, XLV: 195-203.
2. Bose, N.K., P. Gupta and A. Bose 1960. Palaeoliths from Monghyr District Bihar, *Man in India*, 40 (1):68-75
3. The field work was undertaken with a financial support of ICHR granted to the senior author. The Junior author is working under Junior Research Fellowship (U.G.C).
4. Bhattacharya, D.K. 1978. *Old Stone Age tool types and their techniques*. Calcutta: K.P. Bagchi and Sons.
5. Bosinki, Gerhard. 1967. Die Mittelpalao lithischen funde im Westlichen Mitteleuropa. Koln, Bohlau Verlag. Bosinki terms them as halbeskeil or Faustel in German.
6. Bhattacharya, D.K. 1977. *Palaeolithic Europe*. Netherlands: Anthropological Publications.
7. No. 44 in the list of Francois Bordes (1961). Typologie duk Paleolithic ancien et Moyen. Delmas. Bordeaux
8. Lubbock, John 1865. *Prehistoric Times*. London: Williams and Norgate. also 1867. Primivel Antiquities, *Archaeological Journal* 23: 190-209.
9. Lyell, Charles 1863. *Geological Evidences of the Antiquity of Man*. London: Murray.
10. Chakrabarti, D.K. 1993. *Archaeology of Eastern India: Chhotanagpur Plateau and West Bengal*. New Delhi: Munshiram Manoharlal.

Sindhu and Sarasvati in the Rigveda and their Archaeological Implications

SHIVAJI SINGH*

Out of about twenty-five rivers mentioned in the *Rigveda,* Sindhu and Sarasvati are undoubtedly the most important ones. This is evident not only from the far greater frequency of their occurrence as compared to those of the other rivers in the text but also from their descriptions wherein they are expressedly acknowledged as the foremost of rivers. Though geographically the Rigvedic horizon extends over a very vast area comprising at least the northern and eastern parts of Afghanistan, almost the entire Pakistan, and Jammu & Kashmir, Punjab, Haryana, north-eastern Rajasthan and north-western Uttar Pradesh;[1] the core area of the Rigvedic peoples appears to be the region falling within these two rivers, namely, the Indus and the now dried-up Sarasvati. In view of the importance of this region for the protohistoric archaeology of South Asia, it might be worthwhile to attempt a textual analysis of the Rigvedic descriptions of these two rivers.

Our present analysis is based on the *Rigveda-Samhitā* published alongwith the Commentary of Sayanacharya in five volumes by the Vaidika Samsodhana Mandala, Pune. For the frequency of occurrence of the names of Sindhu and Sarasvati in the text we have depended on the index of the Rigvedic words provided in the fifth volume of this publication. For the English renderings of the passages we have taken help from the translations of the text by H. H. Wilson and R. T. H. Griffith though at a few places we have not been able to accept their renderings.

The River Names Sindhu and Sarasvati, and Their Frequency of Occurrence in the Rigveda

According to Monier-Williams' *Sanskrit-English* Dictionary, the world 'Sindhu' may probably be derived from the root *sidh* meaning 'to go'. Sayanacharya, the famous commentator, interprets the term as 'swiftly moving' *(śyandanasīla).* It is perhaps the only river name in Sanskrit which is grammatically regarded male, a *nada* and not a *nadī.* In the *Rigveda* it occurs both in the general sense of a river as well as in the particular sense of the Indus. We have excluded from our consideration all the cases of its occurrence in plural *(Sindhavaḥ, Sindhubhiḥ, Sindhūbhyaḥ, Sindhushu, Sindhūn, Sindhūnām, etc.)* for they stand for streams in general and not for the Indus exclusively. We have included in counting the frequency of its occurrence all the cases of its use in singular whether nominative *(Sindhuḥ),* accusative *(Sindhum),* ablative *(Sindhoḥ)* or locative *(Sindhau),* though it cannot be said that all the uses of the name in singular necessarily denote the Indus, for some of these may be taken to be a common noun for any river.

The explanation of the word 'Sarasvati' obviously depends on the meaning of the term *'Saras'.* Sāyana takes *'Saras'* to stand for 'water', but since water is the common constituent of all the rivers, this hardly explains the

*Shivala Nagar (East), Mohaddipur, Gorakhpur - 273 008.

meaning of 'Sarasvati'. Monier-Williams takes '*Saras*' to mean 'anything flowing or fluid'. Perhaps like the words *Sarit* (a flowing river), *Saraṇyu* (quickly moving), *Sarapas* (fast-running), *etc., Saras* too may be derived from the root '*sri*', to be in motion.

In the *Rigveda* Sarasvati is the name of a river as well as a deity, but the two are taken to be identical, often mentioned in the same hymn in both the senses. The importance of rivers for human existence was fully realized in the Rigvedic times and all the rivers were revered as deities. The Sarasvati, though a river, was respected as the goddess of speech. We shall come to the sacred nature of the Sarasvati later, but we find no justification in drawing a line of demarcation between Sarasvati, the river, and Sarasvati, the deity; and so we have counted all the references to this name in its frequency estimation.

Another point must also be clarified in this connection. Do all the references to Sarasvati in the *Rigveda* relate to one and the same river ? Has there been any transference of name from one river to another in the case of Sarasvati ? According to Irfan Habib and Faiz Habib[2], three different rivers have been designated as Sarasvati from time to time. The first is the Avestan Harakhvaiti or Harahvaiti, identified by them with the Iranian Helmand above its junction with the Arghandab, the second is the Indus and the third is the present Sarasvati-Ghaggar-Hakra of the Survey of India maps. We have dealt with the issue in detail elsewhere[3], and have shown that the Rigvedic Sarasvati is the Sarasvati-Ghaggar-Hakra, neither the Indus nor the Helmand or Arghandab. Long ago, some scholars like Roth and Zimmer had proposed the identification of the Rigvedic Sarasvati with the Indus simply because in their time one could hardly believe that the modern Sarsuti which is an insignificant channel losing itself in the sands of Patiala was actually the remnant of the mighty Sarasvati of the text described as flowing down to the sea. Objections to the Indus-Sarasvati equation were raised even then for the various peoples known to have lived in the Sarasvati valley in the Rigvedic times could hardly be located in the Indus basin. Now, however, when archaeological investigations and satellite pictures have shown that the Sarasvati-Ghaggar-Hakra was a large river flowing into the sea as described in the text, there is no justification in upholding the Indus-Sarasvati equation. There was, of course, a transference of the name between the Sarasvati of India and Pakistan and the Arghandab of Iran (the latter known as Archaoti to the Greeks and as Harakhavaiti in the *Avestā*. But, as we have shown in our study referred to, it was the people from the Sarasvati area who had reached the banks of the Arghandab and who were nostalgic enough to give the name Sarasvati to the river of their new habitat. The references to the Sarasvati in the *Rigveda,* therefore, may be taken to refer to the Sarasvat-Ghaggar-Hakra alone. The Iranian Arghandab is too small a river to claim the hymns composed in the honour of the mighty Rigvedic Sarasvati.

TABLE SHOWING COMPARATIVE FREQUENCY OF OCCURRENCE OF THE RIVER NAMES SINDH AND SARASVATI

	Early Rigvedic Period Books	Late Rigvedic Period Books
River	II III IV V VI VIII	I VIII IX X
Sindhu	3 4 5 3 0 3 Total 18 (21.69%)	32 6 13 14 Total 65 (78.31%)
Sarasvati	7 3 0 4 14 13 Total 41 (60.29%	8 3 3 13 Total 27 (39.71%)

The bookwise comparative frequency of occurrence of the two river names Sindhu and Sarasvati in the early and late portions of the *Rigveda* is tabulated here. The inner chronology of the *Rigveda* is not very clear. In archaeology, we have certain principles of stratification, and the various strata of a deposit are distinguished on the basis of a change in colour, content, and density, etc. of the layers. Unfortunately, in literature we have no fixed criteria for deciding the sequence of compositions. This creates a major problem while dealing with a text like the *Rigveda* which might have evolved through various stages of long durations involving about a hundred generations. However, it is generally accepted that the Family Books, that is, Books II to VII are earlier than the other books of the text. A sort of relative chronology has been worked out even for the non-family books according to which the eight book and the first fifty hymns of the first book come first followed successively by the nineth and tenth books. The remaining hymns of the first book also belong to the final phase of the text. Though this is considered to be a reasonable stratification of the Rigvedic hymns, it is based on the considerations of the sequence of compilation of the text and not on the deliberations of its composition. Perhaps we will have to wait till some reliable principles of stratification are known for distinguishing various strata in a literary deposit. Here in our analysis of the frequency of occurrence of the two river names, we have confined ourselves to only two chronological divisions: the early represented by the Family Books and the late represented by the other books.

The bookwise frequency analysis of the two river names brings out some very interesting information. We find that out of the 68 references to the Sarasvati in the text 41, that is, 60.29 per cent are found in the early portions of the text. This presents as contrast to the position of the Indus which is more frequently referred to in the late portions of the text. As the Table shows, out of 83 mentions of the name Sindhu in the text 65, that is, 78.31 per cent come from non-family books. Despite the fact that the occurrence of the name Sindhu is comparatively more numerous so far as the whole text is concerned, in the family books, that are considered to be earlier, the frequency of accurrence of the name Sarasvati is more than twice as compared to that of the Indus. What does it indicate ? To the early Rigvedic people the Sarasvati appears to be more familiar than the Indus: this much at last is quite obvious. It is also clear that the region watered by the Sarasvati was the cradle of Aryan ritual and culture since, as we shall presently see, this river had come to be associated with the Vedic sacrifices in a special manner. But, can we go further and see in it an evidence of a migration of people from the Sarasvati area to the Indus region ?

Bhagwan Singh[4] is convinced of such a migration. His thesis is that the Rigvedic people (whom he identifies with the Harappans) were forced to leave the Sarasvati valley not only because Sarasvati became unnavigable due to capture of its two important tributaries Sutlej and Yamuna by the Indus and Ganga systems respectively but also because of an unprecedented flood that submerged the entire Sarasvati area and the concomitant terrible famine. According to him, people living in the Sarasvati valley fled in both the directions, west as well as east, reaching the Indus region and the Tirhut area in Bihar almost simultaneously. His thesis raises many issues involving chronological considerations and archeological evidence, and we are not in a position to prove or disprove his thesis at the moment.[5] However, our analysis of the frequency of occurrence of the river names Sindhu and Sarasvati in the *Rigveda* does support his thesis inasmuch as a shift of population concentration or, to be more precise, a change in the area of human compositions from the Sarasvati to the Indus basin is clearly indicated by not only an impressive increase in the occurrences of the name Sindhu but also by a simultaneous marked decrease in the references to the Sarasvati in the later portions of the *Rigveda.*

In this connection it is also worth recalling that the maximum number of the Early and Mature Harappan sites are located not in the Indus but in the Sarasvati valley. V. N. Misra[6], S. P. Gupta[7] and B. B. Lal[8] have clearly brought this fact to our notice. According to Lal, so far a total of 177 Early Harappan and 283 Mature Harappan sites have been discovered in the Sarasvati valley as against only 50 (144 in Sindh and 6 in Pakistani Punjab) in the Indus valley. Although the Vedic-Harappan identity is still to be viewed in its proper perspective, our frequency analysis of the two river names in the text seems to support the equation.

Our frequency analysis throws some welcome light also on the possible locations of the various core areas of the different Books of the *Rigveda.* The compilation of the hymns was done in several rounds long after their composition for ritualistic convenience. So, while considerations such as the sequence of the deities *(Devatānukrama),* sequence of the composers *(Ārshānukrama)* and sequence of meters *(Chbandānukrama)* formed the basis of compilation, there was hardly any need for paying attention to any sequence of the separate areas of their composition. In such a situation, hymns composed in far separated regions and at different points of time got mixed up with the result that each book of the text came to have hymns of different areas and times. Nevertheless, efforts are being made to locate the core areas of the different books. Let us see what our analysis reveals on this point.

Consider First the position of the family Books which belong to the early phase of the Rigvedic timespan. We find that the maximum number of references to the Sarasvati is met with in the sixth and seventh books, (14 and 13 respectively to be precise) which, together constitute nearly 66 per cent of the total occurrences of this river in the text. It is significant to note that in these very books the Indus finds the least mention, the sixth book does not refer to it at all and the seventh does it only thrice. Does it not show that at the time when the majority of the hymns contained in sixth and seventh books were composed by poets living in and around the Sarasvati valley, they had but little knowledge of the Indus ? At least our analysis provides an important hint which must be taken into notice while investigating the core areas of these two early books. The fourth book is considered to be the latest among the early books and it is this book in which the name of Sarasvati does not figure at all. This contrasts well with the position of the Indus whose majority of the early references relate to this book. This indicates that by the time of the composition of the fourth book, that is, even before the end of the early Rigvedic period the poets of the Indus area had taken a lead in composing the hymns.

As far as the later portions of the *Rigveda* are concerned, the references to the Indus are much more frequent throughout. This is clear from the Table which records[6] references to the Indus against[3] to the Sarasvati in Book IX. It may be noted that while the number of references to the Sarasvati in these two books has remained the same, the frequency of occurrence of the Indus has more than doubled. This lead of the Indus over the Sarasvati reaches its peak in the first book wherein the Indus is mentioned 32 times as against the Sarasvati which is mentioned only 8 times, a frequency lead of four times. R. N. Nandi[9] is of the opinion that the core area of the first book of the *Rigveda* is Sindh, and our analysis clearly supports his stand. So far as the tenth book is concerned, the references to the two rivers are almost equal in number, the Sarasvati occurring 13 times and the Indus 14 times. This also is quite in tune with the opinion of scholars which takes this last book of the *Rigveda* to be a confused mixture of very early and very late hymns.

Description of the River Sindhu in the Rigveda

The well-known River Hymn of the *Rigveda* (10.75.1-9) gives a vivid description of the river Sindhu. Though referring to several other rivers, this hymn is, in fact, composed in praise of the Sindhu. It is interesting to note that the name of the poet who composed it is Sindhukshit meaning a resident of the Sindhu area. The river Sindhu, he informs, 'surpasses all the other streams in strength'. It is 'straight-flowing, white-coloured and bright-shining, and 'the most impetuous of all other streams'.[10] It flows 'roaring like a bull' and 'thundering like the rains issuing from the clouds' on its course which was carved out by the god Varuṇa. The other rivers hasten to join the Sindhu as earnestly and fondly as do 'the mothers their babes' and 'the milch cows their newly born calves'. Then poet is enamoured by the beauty of the river and compares its grace with that of a speckled mare and a charming woman. In an enchanting imagery he perceives the river, with its two flanks of the various rivers on both of its sides, as a king marching on in a battle array with the wings of his army. In this connection, Gangā, Yamunā, Sarasvatī, Sutudri (Sutlej), Parushṇī (Ravi), Marudvṛidhā (Maruwardwan, a tributary of Chenab), Asiknī (Ravi), Vitastā (Jhelum), Ārjīkīyā (Vipās, that is, Beas according to *Yāska's Nirukta,* (9.26) and Sushomeā (Soan or Sohan) from one group of rivers perhaps constituting the east flank of the Sindhu. The other group, forming the west flank of the river, includes Rasā (Syr Darya or, alternatively, Panjsher), Kubhā (Kabul), Krumu (Kurram) and Gomatī (Gomal) besides Tṛisṭāmā, Susartu, Svetyā and Mehatnu which have not been identified as yet. Obviously, the geographical knowledge of Sindhkshit is appreciable.

Important pieces of information about the river Sindhu are provided also by several other hymns of the text. The river is said to be unfathomably deep *(gabhīraḥ,* 3.32.16), agitatingly flowing *kshodaḥ,* 1.65.6; 66.10; 92.12; 2.25.3), bestower of wealth and fertilizer of broad fields (1.122.6). However, no description of the river is as clear and complete as that given by Sindhukhit, who summarizes in a single verse (10.75.8) all the major qualities of the river (or rather of the region of the river) by calling it rich in horses and chariots *(su-aśvā, su-rathā),* abundant in gold and grains *(hiraṇyayī, vājinīvatī)* having fine clothes *(su-vāsā),* plentiful in wool *(urṇāvatī)* abounding in hemp *(sīlamāvatī),* wearing honey-growing flowers *(madhu-vṛidham),* well-made *(su-kṛitā),* auspicious *(su-bhagā)* , and ever fresh *(yuvatiḥ).*

Besides Sindhukshit, there is one more Rigvedic poet who is named after the river Sindhu, and he is Sindhudvipa, the seer of the ninth hymn of the tenth book. While Sindhukshit is called *Praiyamedhaḥ* (son or descendant of Priyamedha), Sindhudvipa is designated as

Āmbarīshaḥ (belonging to the family of Ambarisha). That, both of them figure in the tenth book, is not just a coincidence. This confirms the view that several hymns of the tenth book as, for instance, the 9th and the 75th must be placed along with the majority of the hymns of the first book that were composed in the Sindh area. This conclusion is further strengthened by the cases of repetitions seen in the first and tenth books. Thus, the last four verses of the hymn composed by Sindhudvipa (10.9.6.9) occur in the first book too (1.23.20.23). Sindhudvipa has addressed his hymn to waters *(āpaḥ)* in general and not to the Sindhu in particular. Nevertheless, in the light of its composition in the Sindh area, it may reasonably be expected to have been inspired mainly by the Indus.

The waters, informs Sindhudvipa (10.9.1-9), are sources of happiness as they ensure health, wealth, safety and progeny. They are also the granter of habitations *(kshayantīḥ)* to men. Like affectionate mothers, they give us their most auspicious juice *śivatamo rasaḥ)* They are solicited to flow around and provide good drinking water *(āpo bhavantu pītaye)*. They are called sovereigns of precious treasures (evidently because of their importance for agriculture and trade). The curative value of the waters is specially emphasized by Sindhudvipa who claims to have been informed directly by the god Soma that all medicaments *(viśvāni bheshajā)* as well as Agni, the benefactor of the universe *(viśva-śambhuvam)* abide in the waters. Probably he was suffering from some disease for he entreats: "Waters, bring to perfection all disease-dispelling medicaments for the good of my body, so that I may long behold the Sun" (10.9.7). The purifying capacity of the waters is also underlined when he earnestly requests: "Waters, take away whatever sin might have accrued to me by doing wrong whether knowingly or unknowingly or by pronouncing imprecations against holy men or by speaking untruth" (10.9.8). It is noteworthy that this Rigvedic belief in water-purification exists in the same form even today.

The importance of the Sindhu, specially the prosperity that the river had brought to its region in the Rigvedic times, may be visualized by going through a dozen hymns (1.116.26; 9.74) composed by Kakshivan (spelt variously as Kakhivat or Kakhivant), one of the most famous and reequently referred to poets in the text. He is said to be a son of Rishi Dirghatamas who had married a slave girl, named Usij,[11] and begotten two sons Kakshivan and Dīrghaśravas. The family lived by a mix-up of occupations like cultivation, trade and priestly functions. While Kakshivan was a relative [12] and family priest of the prince Svanaya Bhavya, who dwelt on the Sindhu (1.126.1-4), Dirghaśravas was a trader (as clearly indicated by the expression *vanije Dīrghaśrvase*, 1.112.11). The sons appear to have regularly brought their earnings to their father Dirghatamas, who had grown fairly old and looked after the family praying the Aśvins for granting kine rich in milk, dwellings, prosperity and long life (1.158.1-6). Constrained by the nature of our text, the *Rigveda*, which deals with priestly activities and not trade, we do not get any information about the earnings of Dirghaśravas, the trader, and we do not know whether he was a petty pedlar or a flourishing merchant, but we do have some details about the wages of Kakshivan, the priest, and these are enormous by any standard. For acting as a priest at the sacrifices performed by prince Bhavya as also for marrying his daufgter, Kakshivan was paid in one installment, as recorded by himself, a hundred *nishkas* (metallic pieces of flexed weight used as coins and often threaded to form a necklace), a hundred vigorous horses and a hundred bulls, besides ten chariots drawn by brown or bay horses each carrying a bride *(vadhū)* followed by a thousand-and-sixty cows (1.126.2.3)! All these gifts were soon delivered by Kakshivan to his father who is described as 'the parent of excellent sons, maintaining his progeny and passing life in the enjoyment of affluence' (1.125.1).

The various references to the Sindhu in the text relate to different and far separated localities on its long course. The episode of Indra's miracle of making the river flow north-west (2.15.6), for instance, pertains as rightly inferred by Nandi[13] to Skardu area in the Baltistan tracts of Kashmir. However, as far as the descriptions given by Sindhukshit, Sindhdvipa and Kakshivan are concerned, there are unmistakable hints in the text to show that they relate to the lower Indus region. Sindhukshit, as we have seen, informs us about the reputation of the river for *silamā* plants, which is a kind of hemp of which ropes are made.[14] Today, it is known as jute called *san* or *patasan* in Hindi. The abundance of this plant, as already noted by Nandi, points to the lower Indus area. According to him[15], even the expressions *suaśvā* (rich in horses) and *su-vāsā* (rich in clothes) used for the river also lead to the same conclusion for the province of Sindh has all along been known for its special breed of horses and good quality of cotton products. Similarly, the very name of the other poet Sindhudvipa connects him with the deltaic area of the river. Kakshivan, as we have seen was the son-in-law and priest of king Savanaya Bhavya who is known to have lived on the banks of the Indus *(Sindhau adhi kshiyataḥ,* 1.126.1). He can also be located in or near the coastal area of the river on the ground of his comparatively more detailed knowledge of the legend of shipwreck met by Bhujyu, son of Tugra, who was ultimately saved by the Aśvins. The incident of this shipwreck, though referred to at several places in the *Rigveda,* is described mainly in the hymns composed by Kakshivan (1.116; 117; 119; *etc.*) The tragedy is said to have happened when Bhujyu was on a sea voyage in deep waters 'where' according to Kakshivan, 'there is nothing to give support, nothing to rest upon and nothing to cling to' (1.116.5). The purpose of the expedition, though not clearly stated, might have been trade for which he was sent by his father.[16] When the accident occurred, the father felt, to metaphrase the poet, 'like a dying man parting with his riches' (1.116.3). We are told by a different seer that Bhujyu was abandoned by his faithless friends in the midst of the ocean (768.7). However, both the father and son were great devotees of the twin gods Aśvins. They cried for help and the deities brought back Bhujyu safely to his father using their own ship fitted with a hundred oars and then, after reaching the shore, their three chariots. The rescue operation took three nights and three days, (1116.3-5). Within the limitations of the Rigvedic geography, the coastal home of Bhujyu would be located somewhere in the littoral areas of Sindh or Gujarat[17]. In view of the associations of Kakshivan with Bhavya on the one hand and Bhujyu on the other, it may reasonably be supposed that he was living in the lower Indus region.

The episode of shipwreck met by Bhujyu draws our attention to the twin gods Aśvins who are the real heroes of the majority of Rigvedic legends. These deities have several significant characteristics, three of which are the main. First, they are the divine physicians and in this capacity they replace the cut-off leg of Vispala by a metallic leg (1.112.10; 116.15; 117.11; 118.8; 10.39.8), restore the eye sight of Rijeasva (1.116.16; 117.17-18), renew the youth and virility of old and dilapidated Rishi Chyavana (1.116.10; 117.13; 118.8), and perform many such acts. Then, they are connected with light, early morning, Usha and the Sun of which the references are too many to be quoted, but we may mention a few (1.182.9; 184.1; 3.39.3; 8.9.17; 10.61.4). Lastly and most importantly, 'they are above all succouring divinities, the deliverers and rescuers, *par excellence,* from distress'[18] and like their Greek counterparts, the Dioskouroi, they are famous as rescuers from the ocean. It is this last mentioned feature of the Aśvins which makes them the favourite twin deties of the coastal regions of Vedic India. This explains why these gods were given a share in the 'Soma' ritual rather late[19]. The 'Soma' cult, as we shall presently see, originated in the Sarasvati valley, and it took time to reach the coastal areas of Sindh and Gujarat. The Aśvins, who were deities of those regions mainly, could be inducted in the 'Soma' sacrifices only at a later stage. This also falls in line with our frequency analysis of the two river names which clearly shows an exodus of men and ideas from the Sarsvati valley in all directions particularly in the west and south-west.

Description of the River Sarasvati in the Rigveda

We have dealt with the description of the river Sarasvati elsewhere[20], but as the details are extremely relevant to our present study, we may be forgiven for its repetition.

In the Rigvedic age the river Sarasvati was a mighty river flowing from the mountains to the sea *(giribhyaḥ āsamudrāt,* 7.95.2). The abundance and tremendous force of its waters had an enchanting impact on the minds of the poets who repeatedly described it as 'abounding in waters' (1.3.13), 'flowing rapidly' (7.95.1), 'moving faultlessly' (7.96.3), 'possessing unlimited strength' (1\6.61.8), 'roaring' *(ibid.),* and 'fierce' (6.61.7). The river is said to be 'the most impetuous of all other streams' (6.61.13). 'With impetuous and mighty waves she, the underminer of both of her banks, breaks down the precipices of the mountains like a digger (who breaks the wet clay) in search of lotus stems' (6.61.21). She flows along with her seven sisters' (6.61.10). She is said to be 'the mother of streams' (7.36.6) who has 'seven elements' *(saptadhātuḥ,* 6.61.12). Perhaps this refers to the various tributaries of the river two of which, Drishadvati and Apaya, are named (3.23.4.).

The prosperity that the river Sarasvati and its tributaries had brought to the region in the Rigvedic days is distinctly referred to at various places in the text. One of her most repeated epithets is 'giver of grains' (7.96.3).

She is credited with having increased the welfare of the five peoples (6.61.12). She is called 'the dearest among the dear ones' (6.61.10) and 'praiseworthy like indra' (6.61.5). Her sanctity is undoubtedly rooted in her ability to foster material prosperity, and while all the rivers are deified, she is considered to be 'the purest of rivers' (7.95.2). In fact, to the Rigvedic people the river Sarasvati is 'the best of mothers' *(Ambitamā)*, 'the best of rivers' *(Nadītmā)* and 'the holiest of goddesses' *(Devitamā)*.

From the above description of the Sarasvati in the *Rigveda*, one fact is clearly established and that is that the river was flowing in its full majesty when the 'five peoples' and others were living in its valley. There is absolutely no indication in the text of its drying up. It is not the scarcity but the abundance or excess of its waters that is found to have occasionaly overwhelmed the people living on its banks.

The past glory of the river Sarasvati of the Rigvedic fame has now come to light by the sustained archaeological investigations in the Sarasvati-Ghaggar-Hakra valley[21]. Satellite photographs of the area clearly mark the various courses the river and its tributaries followed from time to time[22]. It is now known that the river did flow down to the sea as described in the *Rigveda*. It is also clear that the Yamuna and the Sutlej earlier joined the Sarasvati and that it was mainly their capture by the Gangetic and Indus systems respectively which resulted into the drying up of the Sarasvati[23]. The protohistoric culture sequence of the Sarasvati valley has also been ascertained. The earliest, the Hakra Ware Culture, goes back to the fourth millennium B.C. [24]. The prosperity of the valley begins with the Early Harappans and is brought to its climax by the Mature Harappans. The sites belonging to these two phases number at least 177 and 283 respectively[25]. A few of these like Ganweriwala and Rakhigarhi are the largest of their kind[26].

The later Vedic literature, namely, the Yajus, Sāma and the Atharva vedas, the Brāhmaṇas, Āraṇyakas and the Upanishads, speak only about the dried-up Sarasvati. According to the *Panchavimśa Brāhmana* (15.10.6) and the *Jaiminīya Upanishad Brāhmaṇa* (4.26), the Sarasvati 'disappears' at a place named Vinaśana which literally means 'disappearance'. The locality is rightly identified with the Patiala area of the Punjab where the river loses itself in the sands of the desert[27]. The drying up of the Sarasvati is, therefore, an important development which may reasonably be taken as a line of demarcation between the Early and Late Vedic periods. However, the drying up of the river was a long process. The investigations of Rafique Mughal[28] show that while the water supply in the upper parts of the river was almost cut-off as early as about the middle of the third millennium B.C., there was enough water in the lower portions, and it was only about the end of the second millennium B.C. that the entire course of the river seems to have dried up.

Thus, though the chronological limits of the Rigvedic horizon seem to vary from region to region, the Hakra Wares Culture and the Early and Mature Harappan cultures may be assigned to the early phase of the river when it was flowing forcefully and the impact of its drying up was not felt. Similarly, the Late Harappan and Post-Harappan cultures may be taken to belong to respectively to the later phases when the river was struggling to survive and when it dried up almost completely. Though the river could not achieve its Rigvedic vitality again, it did rejuvenate partially from time to time to enable the existence on its banks of Painted Grey Ware settlements and sites like Rang Mahal[29].

Several peoples, Aryan as well as non-Aryan, inhabited the Sarasvati valley during the Rigvedic times of which the *Pancha-jātā* (the 'five peoples', 6.61.12), Bharatas (3.23.2), Pūrus (7.96.2) and the Pāravatas (8.34.18) are expressedly mentioned in the text. Who the 'five peoples' were, is not very clear. A collective name for a group of five Aryan families had become a quite common linguistic usage. It occurs in several forms such as the *Pancha-janāḥ* (3.37.9; 8.32.22), *Pancha-krishṭayaḥ* (2.2.10; 3.53.16), *Pancha-krshitayaḥ* (6.46.7; 7.75.4), *Pancha-chārshanyaḥ* (5.86.2; 7.15.2) and *Pancha-mānushāḥ* (8.9.2)[30]. Some of these different forms of the designation may relate to the changing social formation of the 'five peoples'. Thus, while Chārshanyaḥ, from *char* (to move), may point to their predominatly nomadic pastoral condition, *Kṛishṭayaḥ*, from *kṛish* (to cultivate) may indicate to their settled agricultural situation[31]. Similarly, *Kshitayaḥ*, from *kshi* (to possess, have power over), pertains to a still more advanced stage of social formation when the people had developed territorial consciousness about the areas they occupied.

That, the designation 'five peoples' did not stand for

the entire Rigvedic society, is beyond doubt. The *Rigveda* refers to about thirty ethnic units, and these five are said to be 'renowned among the people' (5.32.11) clearly indicating that there were several others comparatively less famous than them. That, all the five were Aryans, is also clear from their close association with deities like Indra, Agni and Aśvins[32]. Besides, Soma is said to be among the 'five peoples' (9.65.231). The generally accepted view that the Anus, Druhyus, Yadus, Turvasas, and Pūrus together constitute the group called the 'five peoples' seems to be correct since they are mentioned together in one verse (1.108.8) clearly and referred to in another (7.18.6) wherein Yadu is called Yakshu, though in none of these enumerations they are specified as the 'five peoples'.

The Bharatas, who were undoubtedly the most powerful ethnic unit residing in the Sarasvati valley, are not included in the group of these five peoples. There appears to be a keen competition and rivalry between the Bharatas and their allies, on the one hand, and these five peoples, on the other, probably for control and exploitation of the available resources in and outside the valley. The famous *Daśarājña*, the 'Battle of Ten Kings', faught on the banks of the Ravi (7.33.2 and 5; 83.8), was the result of this rivalry in which the Bharatas, under the leadership of Sudas, came out victorious. The defeat in the battle met by the five peoples had uneven impact on their future careers. While some lost their glory for ever, others more than compensated their defeat in due course. The Druhyus, earlier famed for their prowess (6.46.8), were badly routed in the battle. They seem to have migrated towards the north-west and have gradually reached the Gandhara area where their presence is noted by the later tradition[33]. The Turvasas, with whom Indra is said to have mostly dwelt (8.4.1), are described to have been deserted by the god (6.27.7), a typically hymnistic style of expressing their earlier rise and later downfall. The Anus were renowned chariot-makers (5.31.4), but their craftsmanship could not save them from passing into oblivion.

The fortune of the Pūrus was, however, totally different. They did face a great setback in the 'Battle of Ten Kings' for their chief Purukutsa was either killed or made captive without leaving a son behind him to take up the leadership. But, Purukutsani, the wife of their chief, is said to have secured the favour of Indra and Varuṇa with the help of the Seven Ṛishis and given birth to an illustrious son named Trasadasyu who was a slayer of foes like Indra and an *Ardhadeva*, that is, a demi-god (4.42.8-9). True to the meaning of his name, Trasadasyu was a real terror to the non-Aryans who made his power felt even in a far off place like the Swat Valley (8.19.37). The Yadus too survived even after their defeat in the battle against Sudas. They seem to have moved towards south and south west finally reaching the Kathiawar area where, according to epic-puranic tradition, many of their lineages flourished. In their journey towards Kathiawar they had to cross large water logged tracts in which Indra is said to have helped them (6.20.12). That, they became large cattle-owners and wealthy, is also attested to by the text (8.1.31; 6.46).

Thus, out of the five peoples, initially located in the Sarasvati valley, only the Pūrus are found to continue in the area down to the end of the Rigvedic age. Others either lost their identity or went out of the valley and occupied different areas. They and their rivals the Bharatas are the two main ethnic unit of the region who lived there when the river Sarasvati was fully alive. Earlier in this study we have noted that the protohistoric prosperity of the valley began with the Early Harappans and was brought to its climax by the Mature Harappans at a time when the river was flowing in its full majesty. Juxtaposing the literary and archaeological pictures, we may not be wrong in infering that the Harappans of the Sarasvati valley may be recognized *mainly* as the Rigvedic Bharatas and the Pūrus. We have underlined the word mainly the emphasize the fact that other ethnic units living in the locality, including some non-Aryan groups, also must have contributed to the development of the material culture designated as the Harappan Culture of the Haryana and Bahawalpur domains[34]. By the same token, perhaps the Rigvedic Yadus might be considered as one of the important ethnic units associated with the Harappans of the Gujarat Domain, though the *Rigveda* does not provide enough details about them to be confident about it. However, the fact that the Harappans of Gujarat had come from the north is quite clear. They were attracted to the region for its rich resources and harbouring facilities that enabled them to become efficient sea traders. Meaningful in this context are also the Rigvedic references to the youthful Indra's good guidance *(su-nītī)* which brought the Yadus from afar (6.45.1) and the god's help to the people in crossing the ocean *(samudram)* and reaching the shore safely (6.20.12).

In the *Rigveda,* the Sarasvati valley is known specially for the rise and perfection of the sacrificial ritual. This is clear from the close connection of the Sarasvati with sacrificial 'Soma' and Agnl. Three verses of the text (8.96.13-15) speak about a river called Amśumati in which a non-Aryan chief named Krishna was hiding with his ten thousand hosts. He was spotted by Bṛihaspati and killed by Indra. The details of the episode are furnished by the *Brihaddevatā* (6.109-15) according to which the river was located in the land of the Kurus, and it was Soma who was residing in it being afraid of Vritra, where he was found by Indra and Bṛihaspati. Suryakanta[34] identifies the river Amśumati with the Sarasvati and takes the words *Amśu, Soma* and *Saras* to be synonyms of each other. If this inference is correct, as it seems to be, it shows the intimate connection that existed between the Sarasvati and the Soma ritual for if *Saras* means *Soma,* Sarasvati would be Somavati. The connection with sacrificial Agni is much more explicit. The two most important ethnic units of the Sarasvati valley, the Bharatas and the Pūrus, are closely connected with it. Agni is repeatedly called *Bhārata,* that is, a descendant of, or belonging to, Bharata, the progenitor of the Bharatās (2.7.1 and 5; 4.25.4; 7.8.4). There are only a few persons, perhaps not more than five in the entire text, who are credited to have lent their name to Agni. We have referred to Bharata. The others are: Vadhryasva (10.69.4 and 101), Divodasa (8.103.2) and Devavata (3.23.3) all of the Bharata lineage, and Trasadasyu (8.19.32) of the Puru family. Sarasvati's special connection with sacrificial ritual is made apparent by yet another fact. There are three goddesses of speech and knowledge who are praised for welfare at a large number of places in the text (1.13.9; 142.9; 188.8; 2.1.11; 3.8) and they are Iḍā, Bhāratī and Sarasvatī. At one place (7.2.8), they are invoked along with deities of different spheres and the context clearly shows that Iḍā, Sarasvatī and Bhāratī belong respectively to the terrestrial, atmospheric and celestial spheres. This information when analysed in the light of the Upanisahadic distinctions of *avidyā* and *vidyā* or *aparā vidyā* and *parā vidyā,* makes it absolutely clear that while Iḍā is the goddess of worldly speech and knowledge which help us in earning our livelihood and Bhāratiī the supremely divine speech and knowledge *par excellence* that lead us to salvation, Sarasvatī is the deity of speech and knowledge needed for *Karmakāṇḍa,* the performance of sacrificial ritual, that leads us to heaven.

In the light of the above observations, when we are told that Vadhrayasva begot his son Divodasa by the grace of the Sarasvati (6.61.1), the meaning is clear that he performed a sacrifice to get the son. Ofcourse, as we have seen, he and several other kings of the Bharata lineage were renowned performers of sacrifices. Two princes of the family, Devasravas and Devata, are described as sacrificing on the banks of the Sarasvati, Drishadvati and Apaya (3.23.2-4). In fact, the Bharatas' location and enthusiasm for sacrifices are so pronounced that we feel tempted to identify their headquarters with the site of Kalibangan in Hanumangarh District, Rajashtan, where fire-altars for both individual household and corporate performance of sacrifices have been found in large numbers (Lal, 1997: 123-24; 227-28). In that case the Pūrus, situated to a little east of the Bharatas in the valley, might have had their headquarters at either Banawali or at Siswal both situated in Hissar District, Haryana. However, unless and untill a few large mounds like, for instance, Ganweriwala of the Cholistan area of Pakistan, which formed the south-western segment of the Sarasvati valley, are sufficiently excavated, the ethno-geographic configuration of the valley shall not be clear and any pronouncement on these identifications would be premature.

Conclusion

The main points brought to light in the present study are :

1. The Rigvedic Sarasvati was a mighty river flowing rapidly from the mountains to the sea roaring, breaking down the precipices of the mountains and undermining its banks. The contexts of its location and associations of peoples living on its banks leave no room for doubt that it is the present Sarasvati-Ghaggar-Hakra of the Survey of India maps, and all the references to it in the text pertain to this very river, neither to the Indus nor to the Avestan Harakhavaiti.

2. There has been a transference of name between the Vedic Sarasvati and the Avestan Harakhavaiti identified with the Iranian Arghandab. This was caused by the people migrating from the Sarasvati basin to the banks of Arghandab who were nostalgic enough to give the name Sarasvati to the river of their new habitat.

3. The river Sindhu has also been depicted as a very

large river which flows roaring like a bull and thundering like the rains issuing from the clouds. A poet named Sindhukshit, meaning a resident of the Sindhu area, draws an enchanting imagery in which the streams to the east and west of the Sindhu are conceived as two wings of an army along with which the river is said to march ahead like a king. Our analysis shows that, excepting a very few, almost all the references to the river in the *Rigveda* relate to its lower course in the region of Sindh.

4. A bookwise frequency analysis of the references to the two river names Sindhu and Sarasvati in the *Rigveda* makes it very clear that while the Sarasvati dominates the scene in the earlier portions of the text, in the later portions centre shifts to the lower Indus area. It is a very interesting piece of information which may or may not point to a migration from the Sarasvati valley to the Indus area. It is a very interesting piece of information which may or may not point to a migration from the Sarasvati valley to the Indus basin, but it does indicate a change in the core area of hymn compositions implying a transference of the focus of Rigvedic activities.

5. Our frequency analysis also highlights the fact that the majority of the hymns contained in the sixth and seventh books of the *Rigveda* was composed in the Sarasvati valley. About two thirds of the total references to the Sarasvati come from these two books. Interestingly, it is in these very books that the Indus finds the least mention. As against this, the core area of the first and fourth books is the lower Indus region. it may be asserted with confidence that most of the hymns of these two books as also a few, like the 9th and 75th, hymns of the tenth book were composed in the area today known as the province of Sindh.

6. The descriptions of the two rivers bring out another remarkable fact to our notice. While the Sarasvati area comes into focus mostly in connection with sacrificial performances, for which it had become quite famous, the Sindhu region is depicted as renowned for its special breed of horses, abundance of jute, fine quality of cotton and woollen products, and coastal activities including sea trade. The transference of the focus of activities from the Sarasvati area to the Indus basin seems to be related to an accelerated momentum of trade in the later Rigvedic times.

7. The sacrificial ritual, which arose and attained perfection in the Sarasvati valley, took time to reach the coastal areas of Sindh and Gujarat. The Aśvins, the twin deities famous mainly as rescuers from the ocean, were inducted in the ritual as worthy of getting a share in 'Soma' offering only at a later stage.

8. Since in the *Rigveda*; the Sarasvati is depicted as flowing to the sea and in the later Vedic literature it is described to have stopped flowing beyond Vinaśana, the drying up of the river may reasonably be taken to be a line of demarcation between the Early and Late Vedic periods. However, the river's drying up was gradual and prolonged and it was only about the end of the second millennium B.C. that the entire course of the river seems to have dried up.

9. Correlating the history of the river Sarasvati with the archaeological sequence of cultures in its valley, it may be said that the Hakra Ware Culture and the Early and Mature phases of the Harappan Culture belong to the duration when the river was flowing in its full majesty as described in the *Rigveda*. Since there is absolutely no indication in the text of the river's drying up or any sign of scarcity of water to show the impact thereof, only these three earliest cultures may be assigned to the Rigvedic time span. On the other hand, chronologically the Late Harappan and Post-Harappan cultures are definitely post-Rigvedic. While the Late Harappan phase pertains to the period when the river was struggling to survive, the Post-Harappan cultures relate to the time when the river partially rejuvenated after having dried up almost completely.

10. Juxtaposing the literary and archaeological pictures, we may not be wrong in inferring that the Harappans of the Sarasvati area may be recognized mainly as the Rigvedic Bharatas and Pūrus. By the same token, perhaps the Rigvedic Yadus might be considered as one of the important ethnic units associated with the Harappans of the Gujarat Domain.

11. The Bharatas' location and enthusiasm for sacrifices are so pronounced that we feel tempted to identify their headquarters with the site of Kalibangan where fire-altars for both household and corporate performance of sacrifices have been found in large numbers. In that case, the Pūrus, situated to a little east of the Bharatas, might be considered to have had their headquarters at either Banawall or at Siswal. However, these identifications

must be treated as tentative till the ethno-geographic configuration of the Sarasvati valley becomes clearer by excavation of a few large sites like Ganweriwala in the Cholistan area of Pakistan.

12. The Vedic-Harappan identity is still to be viewed in its proper perspective. The Harappan and Vedic cultures are 'culture' in a very broad sense. Both have within them several ethnic units often far separated in time and space and materially at uneven levels of development. Chronologically too the two cultures are contemporary but not coterminous, and the Vedic Culture seems to be both anterior as well as posterior to the Harappan. An areawise ethnic-level identifications of the Vedic and Harappan groups of peoples might be more pragmatic and nearer to the historical reality.

Acknowledgement

The present study forms a part of the author's major Research Project entitled 'Vedic Horizon in Archaeology' financed by the University Grants Commission, and he gratefully acknowledges the help received from the U.G.C.

NOTES AND REFERENCES

1. If we believe, what seems to be almost certain, that the Videgha Mathava episode of the Aryan colonization referred to in the *Śatapatha Brāhmaṇa* (1.4.15.17) is an event not of the later but of the early Vedic times, even eastern U.P. and western Bihar must also be included in the Rigvedic horizon. Besides, if the legend of shipwreck met by Bhujyu *(Rigveda,* 1.116.3-5) relates to the Kutch area, as it seems very likely the southwestern limits of the horizon extends upto Gujarat.

2. Habib, Irfan and Habib, Faiz. 1992. 'The Historical Geography of India B.C. 1800-800', *Proceedings of the Indian History Congress,* 52nd Session, New Delhi, 1991-92, pp. 72-97. Delhi: Indian History Congress.

3. Singh, Shivaji 1998. 'Dating the Rigveda Archaeologically', *Pragdhara.* No. 8 (in press). Lucknow. U. P. State Archaeilogy.

4. Singh, Bhagwan. 1995. *The Vedic Harappans.* New Delhi: Aditya Prakashan. pp 497-56.

   ——— 1997. *Harappa Sabhayta aur Vaidika Sahitya,* Third Edition, Delhi. Radhakrishna Prakashan.

   Singh, Shivaji. 1969. 'Vedic Literature on Pottery', in B. P. Sinha (ed.) *Potteries in Ancient India,* pp. 301-13. Patna: Patna University.

5. The identification of the Vedic peoples with the Harappans finds support from several considerations such as, for instance, almost the same geographical horizon of the two peoples finds of fire-altars and horse bones from several Harappan sites the references to some Harappan pottery forms in the Vedic literature (Singh, 1969: 306), evidence of long distance land and sea trade in the *Rigveda* parallelism between Vedic and Harappan town planning Rigvedic confirmations of the recent archaeological discoveries in the Sarasvati valley *etc.* However, in our opinion, a wholesale equation of the Vedic and Harappan cultures would not be proper. Besides being contemporary to the Harappan, the Vedic culture has comparatively an earlier beginning and a later end. Moreover, both the cultures have within themselves different ethno-geographic configurations. The Harappans of the various areas are not alike. 'Current data suggests that the Harappan Culture represents a fusion of Bagor, Hakra and Kot Diji ethnic groups in the Ghaggar-Hakra Valley'. The *Ṛigveda* speaks about over two and a half dozen ethnic units far separated in time and space and belonging to different levels of social formations. Linguistically and ideologically too some are Vedic-speaking Aryans, others non-Vyrans. Any attempt at Vedic-Harappan identity cannot afford to overlook these ethnogeographic pluralities in both the Harappan and the Vedic categories. The areawise ethnic-level literary-archaeilogical correlations, therefore, must replace the rather vague Vedic-Harappan equation.

6. Misra, V. N. 1993. 'Indus Civilization and the Rigvedic Sarasvati' in A. Parpola and P. Koṣkikallio (eds.) *South Asian Archaeology, 1993,* Vol. 2, pp. 511-25.

7. Gupta, S. P. 1996. *The Indus-Saraswati Civilization.* Delhi: Pratibha Prakashan.

8. Lal, B. B. 1997. *The Earliest Civilization of South Asia.* New Delhi. Aryan Books International.

9. Bisht, R. S. 1989-90. 'Dholavira: A New Horizon of the Indus Civilization'. *Puratattva,* No. 20, pp. 71-82. New Delhi. Indian Archaeological Society.

10. The word used is *asasām-apastamā* (Verse 6) which Sayana renders as *vegavatīnām nadīnām madhye vegavattamā.* The same epithet, it may be noted, is given to the river Sarasvati in another verse of the text (6.61.13).

11. Kakshivan is not directly referred to as a non of Dirghatamas in the *Rigveda,* but at several places in the text (1.18.1; 119.9; 122.4-5; 6.4.6; 10.99.11) he is called an *Auśij,* a metronymic, meaning according to Sayana a son (and not just a descendant) of Uśij, and Uśij's marriage with

Dīrghatamas is described in the *Bṛhaddevatā* (4.24-25). Though doubts have been expressed about the authenticity of the legend of this marriage it may not be considered to be wholly unreliable when scrutinized in the light of some relevant verses of the *Ṛigveda* (1.140-164; specially 1.158.5). Dīrghaśravas, also called an *Auśij* (1.112.11), is by the same token taken to be another son of Dīrghatamas by Sāyaṇa and others.

12. The relationship between Kakshivan and Savanaya Bhavya is brought out by the *Bṛihaddevatā* (3..142-50). It is narrated that after completing his education at his teacher's residence, Kakshivan was coming back to his home when, on the way in a forest, he was seen by king Bhavya who happened to be sporting there along with his queen, priest and the councillors. Being impressed by the look of young and handsome Kakshivan, he inquired about his whereabouts and coming to know that he was a son of Rishi Dirghatamas, he brought him to his palace and married his daughter to him. This episode of Kakshivan's marriage seems to be confirmed by the very wording of the gifts that he received from the king. The *Ṛigveda* (1.126.1.3) informs us that when Kakshivan was receiving the gifts of a hundred *nishkas,* a hundred horses and a hundred bulls after having performed the thousand sacrifices for the king, ten chariots drawn by bay horses, each carrying a bride (*vadhū*), stood near him, given to him by the king, and a thousand and sixty cows followed. Clearly the description is of a bridal procession ready to start for the groom's house. Perhaps Kakshivan's marriage was an example of what later came to be known as the *Daiva-vivāha,* a sort of marriage by service in which the bridegroom officiates as a priest at a sacrifice and receives the bride in lieu of that act.

13. Nandi, R. N. 1989-90. 'Archaeology and the Rigvedia', *The Indian Historical Review,* Vol. 16, Nos. 1-2, pp. 35-79. Delhi. ICHR.

14. The commentator Sayana derives the name *silamā* from *sirāni* and informs that ropes made of it were used to tie the cattle to their pegs. H. H. Wilson (1977/90: 6.254) notes: 'Silama plants, according to the satements of husbandmen, furnish cordage for fastening ploughs'.

15. Nandi R. N. 1994-95. 'Aryan Settlements and the Rigveda', *The Indian Historical Review,* Vol. 21, Nos. 1-2, pp. 9-36. Delhi. ICHR.

16. According to Sayana, Tugra was very much annoyed by enemies residing in a different island, and he sent his son Bhujyu with an army on ship board to defeat them. In view of the repeated references to fabulous profit from sea trade in the *Rigveda* Tugra's adversaries might have been either pirates or professional rivals.

17. Nandi 1994:95 opcit 321.

18. Apte, V.M. 1951. 'Religion and Philosophy', Chapter XVIII of R.C. Majumdar and A. D. Pusalker (eds.) *The Vedic Age,* pp. 360-83. Bombay: Bharatiya Vidya Bhavan.

19. That, earlier the Aśvins did not get a share in the sacrifices, is clearly stated in the *Taittirīya Samhitā* (6.4.9.1), *Maitrāyanī Samhitā* (4.6.1.2) and the *Kaṭhaka Samhitā* (27.4.5). According to these texts, the Aśvins were considered to be *amedhya* (unfit for sacrificial share), but later on when they, as physicians, joined the head to the headless Sacrifice *(Yajnasya siraḥ pratyadhattam),* the Devas purified them and made them worthy of partaking Soma at the sacrifices. The legend is described in detail the in *Śatapatha Brāhmaṇa* (4.1.5.1-15). It is said that the *Pravargva,* an act of great mystic significance, is known as the 'head' of the Sacrifice. Earlier the Devas did not know this act and performed, so to say, headless sacrifices. The Rishi Dadhichi knew it, but was threatened by Indra not to disclose it to the Aśvins. However, the Aśvins, having perhaps obliged the Rishi by renewing his yough like that of Chyavana, managed to know the secret formula from him. They, then went to Devas in Kurukshetra and in lieu of getting a share in the sacrifices instructed them in the *Madhuvidyā* containing the secret formula and made the Sacrifice 'headful', that is complete and effective.

20. Singh, Shivaji 1998 op cit.

21. Suraj Bhan and Shaffer, J. G. 1978. 'New Discoveries in Northern Haryana'. *Man and Environment,* 2, pp. 59-68.

21. Mughal, Rafique M. 1982/1993. 'Recent Archaeological Research in the Cholistan Desert' in Gregory L. Possehl (ed.) *Harappan Civilization: A Recent Perspective,* pp. 85-95. New Delhi, Bombay, Calcutta. Oxford and IBH Publishing Co.

22. Thapar, B. K. 1982/93. 'The Harappan Civilization: Some Reflections on its Environments and Resources and Their Exploitation' in Gregory L. Possehl (ed.) *Harappan Civilization: A Recent Perspective,* pp. 3-13 amd Plate 1 Mosaic of Landsat imegery. New Delhi. Bombay, Calcutta: Oxford and IBH Publishing Co.

23. Ibid. p.5

24. Mughal 1982, op cit p. 87.

25. Lal, 1997. op cit p. 90

26. Agrawal, D.P. 1982/93. 'The Harappan Legacy: Break and Continuity' in Gregory L. Possehl (ed.) *Harappan Civilization: A Recent Perspective,* p.449 and Table 38.3 New Delhi, Bombay, Calcutta: Oxford and IBH Publishing Co.

27. Macdonell, A. A. and Keith, A. B. 1912/Reprint 1995. *Vedic Index of Names and Subjects,* Vol. 1 & 2. pp 300. London. Reprint Delhi. Motilal Banarasidass.

28. Mughal of cit p. 94

29. Lal 1997. op cit pp 9-10

31. Giving the meaning of the word *Kṛishti,* Monier-Williams (1899/94: 306) informs that 'originally the word may have meant cultivated ground, then an inhabited land, next, its inhabitants, and lastly any race of men'.

32. Ghurye, G. S. 1979. *Vedic India,* pp. 180-83. Bombay. Popular Prakashan.

33. Macdonell and Keith, op cit. p. 1.385

34. Possehl, Gregory L. 1982/93. 'The Harappan Civilization: A Contemporary Perspective', in Gregory L. Possehl (ed.) *Harappan Civilization: A Recent Perspective,* pp. 15-28. New Delhi. Bombay, Calcutta. Oxford and IBH Publishing Co.

35. Suryakanta. 1956. 'Saras, Soma and Sira', *Bharati, Bulletin of the College of Indology, B.H.U.,* No. 1, pp. 14-31. Varanasi: Bnaras Hindu University.

36. The word occurs as *Pancha-mānavāh* in the *Atharvaveda* (3.21.5; 12.1.15). Yet another from of the term is preserved in the name of the river Panjsher (medieval name Panjshir), one of the affluents of the river Kabul (Vedic Kubhā). *'Sīra'* in the *Rigveda* means 'plough' and brings the designation *Pancha-siraḥ* (five ploughmen) quite close to *Pancha-kṛiṣhayaḥ* (five agriculturists).

Rakhigarhi: A Harappan Metropolis in the Sarasvati-Drishadvati Divide

AMARENDRA NATH*

In th Harappan dynamics, Rakhigarhi (29° 16′ N and 76° 10' E), in tehsil Narnaul, District Hissar, Haryana is next only to Dholavira in Kutch (Gujarat). The site can be approached from Delhi *via* Rohtak, Hansi and Jind. Jind, besides being the nearest railhead for the site on Delhi-Bhatinda section of the Northern Railway, provides the shortest road link through Gulkani or Narnaul. There is a regular Haryana Roadways bus service from Jind and Hansi to Rakhigarhi. Private conveyances are also available from Narnaul. The nearest guest house of the Irrigation department is at Rajthal.

Over the Harappan mounds are the thickly populated villages of Late Mediaeval times, namely Rakhikhas stretching east to occupy the larger area of the mound and the other contiguously situated Rakhi Shahpur covers less. These settlements have largely caused irreparable damage to the site, but due to the timely action of the Archaeological Survey of India, a fairly large and open area of the site could be saved and protected from further damage and encroachment. Three such mounds have been numbered as RGR 1 to RGR 3 while the largest and its eastern extremities are named RGR 4 and RGR 5 respectively.

Acharya Bhagwan Dev was the first to notice Harappan relics here. Subsequently Suraj Bhan confirmed its Harappan nature in 1963-64[1]. Suraj Bhan revisited the site and ascertained that Rakhigarhi (obviously he meant Rakhikhas) contained both Early or Pre-Harappan and Harappan culture horizons; Rakhi Shahpur only witnessed the Mature phase of Harappan[2]. But in an appendix to his report on Mitathal[3], he recorded, Rakhi Shahpur as Rakhigarhi and saw them as 'twin sites'. He missed completely the presence of the other three mounds noted above. In the early seventies, Silak Ram[4] paid a visit to the site and reported, besides other Harappan antiquities, a seal, presently housed in the Gurukul Museum at Jhajjar (Haryana). He too noticed Early or Pre-Harappan and Harappan elements at the site. But in the early eighties a team of archaeologists from the Department of Archaeology and Museums, Haryana noticed late. Harappan elements here[5] which was later got endorsed by Suraj Bhan[6]. Thus the chronological framework of the Harappan occupation at the site got enlarged. R.S. Bisht, observed earlier Pre-Harappan settlement in the north-western locality of Rakhi Shahpur revenue limit[7]. The corpus of Indus seals and inscriptions included three seals from Rakhigarhi, two of them are regular type of seals while the third is a clay lump bearing couple of seal impressions[8]. In recent years, two similar ones have been picked up , one of them, a fragmentary terracotta cylindrical seal, is quite significant. This has now been published[9] but the other fragmentary terracotta sealing is yet to be published. Besides sealing, Bisht collected a large number of steatite beads and other miscellaneous items, all belonging to the Harappan culture. J.P. Joshi and his team noticed 137 Early Harappan and 109 Mature Harappan sites in the region[10], with their main attention

*Director, Institute of Archaeology, Archaelogical Survey of India, New Delhi.

on Rakhigarhi[11]. Incidently, the Allchins consider this site as second grade settlement based on the area of the site[12], whereas as per the calculation of the area marked on Topo sheet (No. 53 C/3), the site extends over 105 hectares and has established the primacy of this site area-wise. Apparently, the status of provincial capital assigned to the site by Suraj Bhan[13] and Lal seems[14] to be well found. Other excavated sites of the region like Mitathal, Siswal, and Banawali[15] are subordinate settlements in the drainage system of ancient Sarasvati-Drishadvati rivers.

The site is in the drainage system of ancient Sarasvati-Drishdvati rivers. Fig. 1 The mean altitude varies from 219 m to 221 m in the surrounding plains extending over an area of 10 km radius. The alluvial plains in the neighborhood, with occasional patches of sands either exposed or occurring at shallow depths, show gentle slope form north-east to south-west. The nature of the soil is mostly alkaline and the ground water is brackish. The source of potable water lies mainly in the existing or old stream courses or near other water sources. For

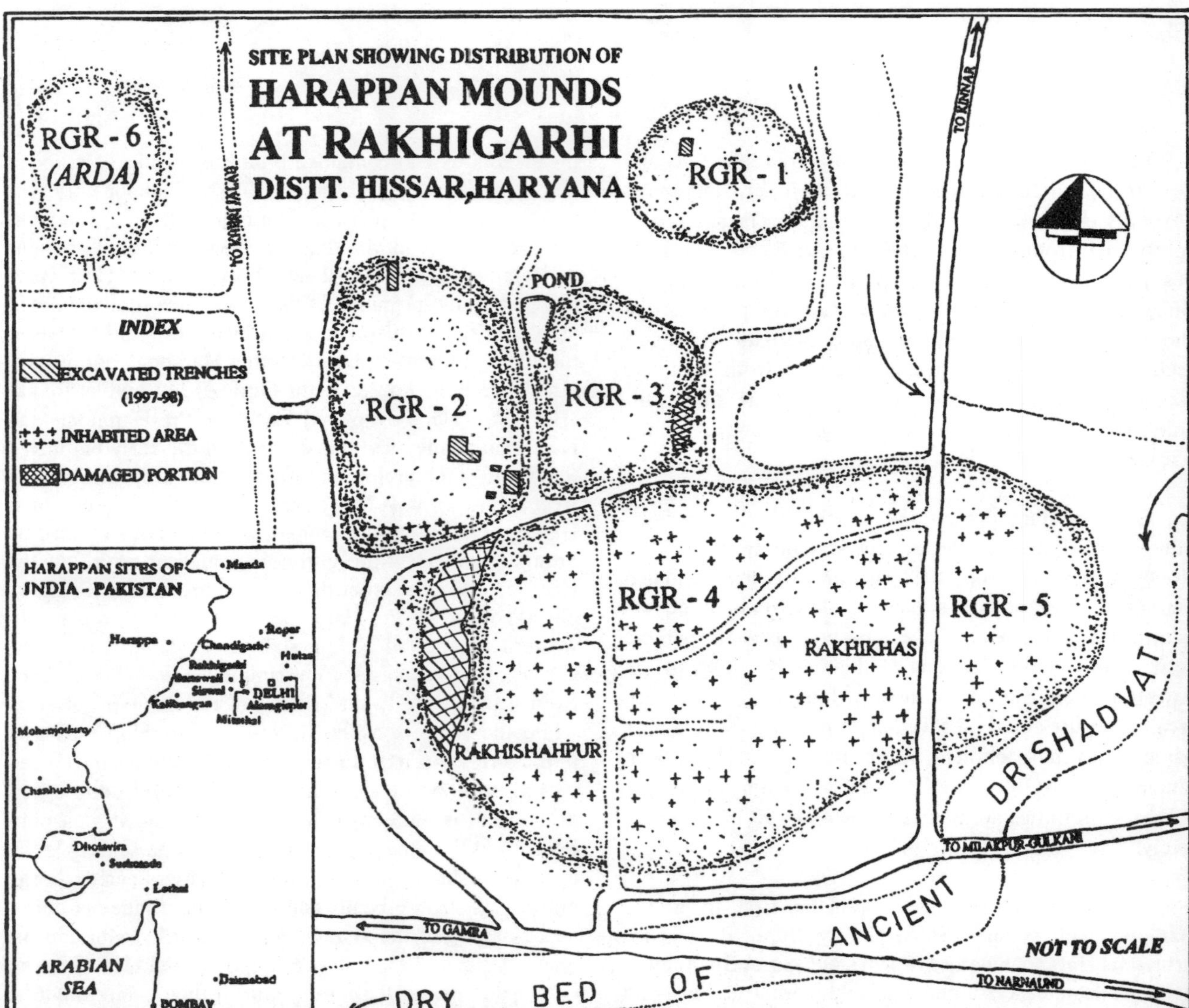

Fig

potable water a few wells in the village can be seen located near the meandering channels of old streams. On the south-western corner of the mound lies a shallow depression or lake-like feature which was watered from both north-west and north-east side, perhaps creating an impression of a confluence in a ncient times. Incidently, on the southern periphery of RGR 4 and 5 lies an elongated watersheet, stretching east-west. These channels, together with those located at intervals in the easterly villages of Gulkani and Milakpur are in alignment and possibly in ancient times a river was flowing along the southern periphery of RGR 4 & 5. As per the existing belief the site was located on the right bank of Drishadvati, we may associate this palaeo-channel with that perennial river of yore.

RGR1, stretching west to east is 6 m high from the surrounding plains and is on the northern extremities of RGR 3. It is ovalish in shape, showing overlapping feature of a twin mound, of which the western portion is higher than the eastern portion and latter merges gently with the surrounding plains towards the eastern side. The surface shows, scanty patches of a rather thin vegetal cover. Intervening barren patches were strewn with tiny red ware sherds; the western and southern slope of the mound were found scattered with *mushtikas* fragments along with terracotta cakes, than with pot sherds. The over all surface features gave an impression of a burial mound. Currently, the villagers use the slope of the mound for raising memorial structures; a couple of them can be seen even now.

RGR 2, larger than 1 and 3 figures on the topo sheet indicating a relative height of 14 m. It is nearly trapezoid in shape(Pl.1). However its ridge, like eastern fringe gently rises from north to south, possibly indicating covering remnents concealed of a fortification wall. The southern and western fringes have been badly encroached upon by villagers of Rakhi Shahpur. The northern portion of the mound exhibits relatively better preserved features of a possible gateway and bastions. The north-eastern corner shows a majestic bastion, strengthened externally by radiating spoke-like earthen buttresses, while the corresponding bastion on north - western side is of low profile, seen merging with other surface features. Between the two bastions lies the residue of screen-walls projecting in opposite directions, giving veiled appearance of skillfully conceived entrance. The artifacts reported from the surface include unfinished beads and burnt patches supporting existence of lapidary and other craft activity areas in RGR 2. Finished products like beads of all representative materials, copper fragments, terracotta cakes and *mushtikas* etc. were collected. The excessive concentration of terracotta cakes including *mushtikas* at the site suggest intensive involvement of the people in their craft activity.

RGR 3, ovalish on plan rises to a height of 12 m from the surrounding plains. The parallel valley-like formation seen on the topo sheet between RGR 2 and RGR 3 have now been partially altered in recent times by raising an earthen barrier across the mound towards the northern slope with the result a pool had formed for sundry usage. As a matter of fact it is going to increase the moisture and create adverse effect on the cultural deposits of the adjoining mounds. Recently, it was desilted and its refuse was dumped on either slopes of the mounds, thus affecting the original contour of the mounds. Further damage is caused by cutting more than knee-deep long trench across the northern periphery of the mound. There on the top exists a grave, under worship, of the late medieval times, maintained by the local Wakf Board. They have further leased out a portion of the mound on the north-western slope and allowed ruthless leveling and scooping of cultural deposits for the construction of subterranean meditation chamber. Similarly, the entire eastern and southern slopes of the mound have been encroached upon by the villagers. Incidently, in one of the central cuttings on the eastern fringe was noticed more than twenty courses of burnt-bricks and equal number of courses in mud-bricks raised side by side; these in all probability could be two phases of construction in the fortification wall.

RGR 4 and 5 contiguously interlocked, are heavily encroached upon by the people of Rakhikhas and Rakhi Shahpur. Streching east-west, the two together, a maximum height of 17 m as with one unit is deceptively ovalish on plan and consists of a number of undations of varying sizes. Towards the south-western portion of the mound an overhanging cliff-like section provides glimpses of cultural deposit. A massive mud-brick fortification wall with successive *mushtika* beddings, overlain by successive mud-floors, occupies a major space in the said cutting. The *mushtika* bedding is reminiscent of what was noticed in the cuttings of a street at Kalibangan excavations[16]. Next to this wall, was noticed a burnt-brick drain.

The evidence of fortification wall from RGR2, 3 and 4 corroborates Harappan phenomenon of encompassing of individual habitation-zones within an integrated network of town planning. Similarly, overwhelmingly rich surface features together with volume and size of the mounds amidst vast arable plains suggest primarily agriculture based subsistence pattern since the days of first occupation at the site. The agricultural waste and vast grazing ground around the site must have given rise to animal husbandry. The agro-pastoral character of the site never got marginalised, other traits of subsistence remained subordinate.

In this backdrop, the excavations at Rakhigarhi was planned by the author in the year 1997-98. Since the excavation was restricted to fifteen trenches, the objectives too were confined to corrobaration of sequence of cultures as known from the explorations, i.e. Early, Mature and Late Harappa, besides understanding a few of the surface features noted in case of RGR 1 and 2. The trenches on both these mounds have been laid separately in north-south orientation with a view to lay bare the site horizontally.

In case of RGR 1 the operation was restricted to six contiguous quardants, i.e. four of G5 and two of G6, laid at the highest point of the mound. The complete sequence of culture could not be determined due to the presence of structures at various levels of the dig. However, in G6/1 the excavation was carried out to a depth of 4.70 m exposing the upper portion of habitation. There five successive phases of structural remains could be noticed, besides a north-south oriented lane of 1.50 m in width. The evidence of series of mud-brick structures did not help to reconstruct a complete house-plan in any one of the phases. However, these were oriented north-south and did not open in the lane. The mud-bricks used were of various sizes but the ratio remained 1:2:4. The brick masonry consisted of alternate layers of headers and stretchers with clay used as mortar. The structure of Phase-1 was in the form of a room (2.60 m x 1.80 m); within this room a built-in platform was noticed (65 cm x 30 cm) in the south-west corner while a *chulha* in the south-east corner, suggest its use as kitchen. It was sealed by layer16. The other three phases of construction were noticed in succession. The mud-brick structure of Phase 2 showed ten courses in the south-eastern corner. Incidently, the mud-brick structure (2.40 m) of Phase-3 had an entrance from east side (80 cm wide). In the western wall 3 courses and in southern wall 14 courses of mud-bricks were noticed. In Phase 4 mud-brick wall of eleven courses was noticed. The structures of Phase 5, sealed by layer 1, were not in alignment with the structures and lane of the preceding Phases 1 to 4. The structure, so far not completely exposed, is stretched east-west showing three cells in a row, devoid of entrance, and an adjoining paved platform. These cells together with massive platform appears to be complimentary to each other and were possibly used for storage purpose and stacking goods. It is to be noted that soon after the desertion of this 'storehouse' complex, the locality was used as cemetry. Such a rare example is reported earlier at Mehrgarh in Baluchistan. The evidence of structural burials has some relevance in the present context as the burial No. 1,3 and 8 at RGR 1 are of a complementing type(Pl.1). Burial No. 4 is in a pit cut identical to the structural ones, but laid in a wooden coffin. All these burials are primary inhumations, laid in an extended position in north-south orientation, head showing west ward tilt. In each case an oblong pit over a metre and half deep was dug in north-south direction. Further, a narrow depth within the pit was made towards the western half of the longer axis of the basal platform, leaving a ledge-like formation and then an oblong cavity of corresponding dimension was scooped out at the base.

This under cut portion formed the actual burial chamber where the dead body was laid and covered by brick work from the level of basal platform by laying header and stretcher courses of mud-bricks–on-edge resting against the overhanging mass of the pit. The dry mud-brick masonry used in the vault like structural burial chamber provided opportunity of reopening of the tomb. This feature was noticed in the burial No. 1,3,4 and 8. In case of burial number 1 and 3 the chambers were left partially open, leaving a few fallen bricks over the skeletal remains in the hollow chamber. In case of Burial No. 4 the courses of bricks were carefully removed but were never reset, otherwise the wooden coffin would have survived as a further testimony. Burial No. 8 was better preserved with all its architectural components. But roughly one-third portion of the obliquely laid bricks on edge along-with couple of supportive header-and-strectcher courses were removed but at the time of resetting a tell-tale mark was left by ignoring the flat courses on the edge and resetting of oblique bricks on edge at a correspondingly lower level. All these graves were bereft of grave goods; however, the skelatal remains were more or less better preserved, at times showing disarticulation of certain joints and shifting of bones under their own weight, besides, fracture due to collapse of bricks at the time of reopening.

At this stage of our knowledge any estimation about the funerary rites would be of a speculatory nature. But, placement of head towards north with a tilt on west may denote some ritual practice adopted by a particular community. Burial No. 4 in coffin appears to be specially devised for an important person. Likewise construction of brick-laid vaulted burial chambers has the ramification of tomb rituals, either proclaiming life after death or denoting status of the deceased.

At RGR 2 a major part of excavation efforts were diverted towards exposing northern gateway and south-eastern extension of the fortification, besides recovering certain structural complexes in southern plain and its adjoining western slope, terminating into a wide rain gully. Excavations on the northern side of mound was located in the central depression with a view to locating structural components of gateway as observed in the course of study of surface features in this particular area. Coincidentaly, the cuttings on the western arm of the entrance revealed a series of cells in north-south alignment, opening towards east. In support of their function as guard cells, a few typical copper and bone arrowheads were picked up from the floor levels of these cells.

The cuttings in the southern locations of RGR 2 highlight tentatively five Mature Harappan occupational levels. Trenches laid across the fortification remains to be verified; hence the present observations would be subject to correction. On plan the wall runs north-south showing narrow steps from east leading half-way to the wall top and there taking a turn to north and after negotiating the guard cells on either side the pathway turns west. Thickness of fortification wall of Phase 1 was 5 m; in Phase 2 burnt-brick buttress was added externally to the wall. In Phase 3 thickness of the wall was increased two times and steps were provided for entrance through climbing the wall top with a turn to the west. In Phase 4 full sized burnt-brick pavement was laid over the wall top with a turn to west. On either side of the brick pavement were noticed guard cells. Finally, in Phase 5 the height of the fortification wall was further raised by laying mud-brick courses over the burnt-brick pavement. Internally, a lane parallel to fortification walls remained undisturbed till the last occupation at the site.

On the corresponding south-western side of the mound revealed other habitational structres of significance. Structural remains of upper levels convey some idea of the poor state of preservation. However, whatever survived shows that there was a street running north-south bisecting the area at right angles, to which there were east-west running lanes joining from either sides. Mud-brick was extensively used in the construction, while burnt-brick with certain exceptions was used in drains. Certain mud-brick structures bore mud plaster as preservative coating. Except a storehouse of granary and craftsman-arcade no other structural complex could be defined for want of complete plan. Certain structures were furnished with elements like pilasters, niches, hearths, fire altars, built-in benches, tiled floors, animal sacrifice pit etc.

Excavations on the south-westerly elevated plain have revealed certain better preserved structures of middle phases. However, the structures in the slope have suffered the onslaught of erosion. In trench R 21, facing street, an impressive pillared corridor was exposed partially with flanking rooms on either side. The pillar, squarish on plan measured 90 cm and on the corresponding western alignment was noticed evidence of pilaster, a rare architectural feature; its floor was rammed with mud brick-bats. It was adjacent to handicraft manufacturing -*cum*- marketing area. There in S21 were located four cells in a row facing the street north-south. In the back wall were noticed brick-lined hearths and their floors retained the evidence of anvil, besides debitage of columellae of *Xancus pyrum*. The evidence suggest intra-regional contacts, besides crafts specialization. A few more traits known to the Harappans of Rakhighari were burning shell for extracting lime, steatite and lapidary work besides preparing terracotta cakes and *mushtikas*. These *mushtikas* were prepared to keep them in cowdung cake fire pans as heat absorbent, thereafter it was reused either in floor bedding or raising levels. A circular potters' kiln was also located which was exclusively used for firing goblets, dishes and terracotta bangles.

A modest granary was located in the cuttings of S2 and T22. It consists of cells, in two segments, with a corridor in front showing built in bench and a guard cell. The accumulated dust and earth from these cells have yielded barley.

Drainage system noticed were of two types, viz public and private. Public drainage system was found from the lower-middle phase and was laid in the centre of a street. A T-shape plan was exposed in T23, besides, terracotta pipe used for drainage was also evidenced. Private drains, possibly connected to bath platforms, were observed from the upper most levels of Mature Harappa in X-25.

From the mid-level of S 22 a couple of structural units associated with religious or ritual purpose have come to light. A floor of tiny bricks-bats on northern side revealed a single-coursed niche facing west. The niche was partitioned in the centre. Originally, the floors and niches were coated with mud plaster. It is quite significant to note that, a terracotta bull figurine was found on the floor abutting the western niche. Perhaps, the structure was a place of worship and the bull was a revered animal. Next to this structure was noticed a T-shaped fire altar with curved ends, the eastern projection may be taken as working end. Further north,in the same alignment, was exposed a brick-lined rectangular pit containing animal bones particularly of bovine family (Pl.2). The pit, oriented east-west, was located in the centre of a walled enclosure with opening towards west. It is conspicuous to note that a terracotta votive tank was found from the north-western corner of the pit. Such type of structural animal sacrifice pit has been reported from Kalibangan-1.

Almost from the same level of T23 was reported three circular fire altars arranged in a semicircular fashion, recalling those from at Banawali[15]. These were found inside the walled floor. (Pl.2) Fine brushing over the surface of altars revealed a few circular white patches of possibly burnt hard shell of fruits offered at the fire altar. Traces of mud-bricks at the base of altar suggest that they were specialy made ones.

The pottery recovered from this excavation mainly falls in two groups viz. red ware and grey ware. Besides these, a few shreds of non-glazed reserve slipped ware, cut ware and cream slipped ware, have been also found, An extremely rare pottrey among Harappan ceramic industry, Barbotino or Pimpled Ware, has also been recovered.

Among these ceramic wares, red ware predominates. This red ware can be divided into following categories :

(i) Red slipped ware.

(ii) Black painted red slipped ware

(iii) Black painted ware.

Important types in red ware included perforated jars, goblets, dish-on-stand vase, jar, ledged rim vessel, fluted vessel, ribbed vessel (*handi*) dish, basin, trough etc.(Pl.3)

The frequency of grey ware with or without black slip is very less as compared to the red ware, the percentage, of which is just 1.17 (of total diagnostic sherds). Though they are limited in shapes and number, yet they are present in almost every level. This ware does not bear any painting. The main shapes in the grey ware are vases, dishes-on-stand, dishes, bowl and lid. Black slipped grey ware is also found in good numbers near by about 10% of the grey ware.

Non-glazed reserve slipped ware is found in a very limited number. It seems that it is the prototype of glazed reserve ware. Its technique of manufacture is almost the same. It had no real slip. Instead of applying double coat of slip, a thick black band is painted on surface with a wash and then on wet smoothed surface of thick black band is simply scrapped by teethed tool exposing the wash surface partly.

One of the distinctive types of pottery is cut ware which has geometrical (triangular, biconvex) cut design, which is cut by a pointed sharp instrument from exterior. The edge of cut is always slanting and there is comparatively smaller opening on the interior than the exterior.

So far decoration is concerned painted and incised decorated pottery has been found in near about 6% of total pottery assembledge (Pl.3). It is frequently found in upper level as well as middle level. In lower level its quantity is less. Paintings are usually found in horizontal or vertical panel mainly on red slipped surface. The important motifs are pipal leaf, palm leaf, triangle, loop, intersecting circles, linear designs, etc.. Besides this, a few sherds with bird (most probably peacock) and fish decoration are also found.

For incised decoration different methods have been used. Important methods are combing, impressing, usually found on the centre of dish of dish-on-stand.

The faunal evidence reported at the site provides reflexes on man-animal relationship, together with their associated food habits. Cattle bones out number other animal bones, including that of wild variety, which indicates existence of highly rich pastoral land in the neighbourhod. Among the cattle, domesticated buffalos were preferred both for abundant milk and meat. Occurrence of rodent bones support the hypothesis of sedentary life style and food habit of the Harappan people at the site, besides storage of foodgrains. Lower percentage of wild animal bones suggest limited hunting activity and more reliability on plant food. The presence of fish bones not only suggest dietry but also fishing as one of subsistence trait; likewise occurrence of bird bones suggest that they formed part of their diet. Among the floral remains only charred wheat and barley could be identified so far.

Remaining samples are under study.

The limited excavation at the site has yielded a variety of objects. The cylindrical seal made of faience, incised with five Harappan signs of Mature phase on one side and an alligator on other, deserves special mention(Pl.). Besides the excavation has yielded two circular terracotta amulets of identical nature depicting an elephant to right and Harappan characters in the upper part, in relief. The cross-section is plano-convex (Pl.4). There are inscribed seals of faience and steatite besides an uninscribed one coming from the lower mid level of Mature phase (Pl.4). Another important seal, upper portion broken depicts composite figure of man, bull, unicorn, elephant and tiger.

Among the terracotta figurines animals find preference over others. Representation of human figurines are few and far between. A preliminary study shows some kind of stylistic development in animal figurines reported from the lower middle phase to upper phase. In the upper levels bovine animals are treated more realistically than lower levels. Among the toy cart wheels both spoked (*sara cakra*) and solid (*paridhi cakra*) varieties noticed were. The solid ones have hub in centre; a few of them are also painted.

Other antiquities of importance are gold fillet and beads, silver, copper and shell bangles, etched and plain beads of siliceous material, steatite and faience beads, weights and measure, gamesman and game-board etc.(Pl.4)

To sum up, the present excavations at RGR 2 have brought to light certain important structures like pillared corridor with flanking cells, granary, places of performing rituals, shopping arcade in a close knitted area; these to identify the mound as 'citadel' mound, as some of these structural components have been reported from the 'citadel' area of other Harappan sites. Again the occurrence only of seals from the excavation at RGR 2 it as a of authority.

As the present excavations were of preliminery nature, more work is needed to finally confirm the results so far arrived at.

REFRENCES

1. *IAR - 1963-64*, p.90.
2. *IAR - 1966-67*, p. 12
3. Suraj Bhan, 1965, *Excavation at Mitathal (1968) and other esplotions in the Sutlej - Yamuna Divide,* Kurukshetra University,Kurukshetra p.95.
4. Silak Ram, Archaelogy of Rohtak and Hissar District (Haryana), PhD. thesis (unpublished) Kurukshetra University, Kurukshetra, pp. 77-78, Pl. XXXIII A&B.
5. *IAR - 1980-81.* p.16
6. A.Ghosh (ed). 1984, *An Ecyclopedia of Indian Archaeology*, Vol.2, p. 366.
7. *IAR* - 1987, 88, p. 27.
8. Joshi, Jagat Pati and Parpola Asko, 1987, *Corpus of Indus Seals* and *Inscriptions*. M.A.S.I, 86, Helsinki, pp. 359-60,375.
9. Bhardwaj Sudarshan, 1997. 'A terracotta cylidrical sealing from Rakhigarhi', *Numismatic Studies*, vol.5, New Delhi, pp.153-55 (with an unnumbered plate).
10. Joshi J.P., Madhubala and Jassu Ram, 1984. 'The Indus Civiliztion: A reconstruction on the basis of distribution Maps' in B.B. Lal and S.P. Gupta, (eds.) *Frontiers of th Indus Civilization*, pp. 511-30, New Delhi.
11. Joshi J.P., 1991, Settlement Patterns in the Third, Second and First Millennia in India, *The Cultural Heritage of an Indian Village,* British Museums, London.
12. Bridget and Raymond Allchin, 1997, *Origins of a Civilization : The Prehistory and Early Archaeology of South Asia.* New Delhi, p.159.
13. Suraj Bhan, 1975; Op. cit., A. Ghosh 1984., op.cit.
14. Lal B.B.1997. *The Earliest Civiliztion of South Asia,* New Delhi. pp. 236-237.

    IAR - 1966-67. p32. Pl. XXIIB. Structural Remains at Kalibangan. In Gupta Sp. etal (ed.) *Frontiers of Indus Civilization,* p.57. Pl.17;
15. Bisht, R.S 1987, 'Further Excavation at Banawali : 1983-84' *Archaeology and History.* New Delhi, p. 150, pl. 25, pp 135-156.

Geomorphic Perspective of Archaeological Sites in the Bhima Basin, Pune District, Maharastra

KALYANI BHAVE AND SUSHAMA DEO*

Introduction

Human culture is always related to the landscape and surrounding environment. Man lives in an area under specific geographical environment. Settlement is man's first step towards adapting himself to his surrounding environment. There are several geomorphological factors which influence the locations and distribution of the settlements. Analysis of distribution of locations of phenomena has been a fundamental theme in geography and one which has been central to the links between geography and archaeology, especially prehistory[1]. This paper mainly deals with the analysis of geomorphic factors and location of the archaeological sites.

Geography and archaeology are concerned with two dimensions of a single field. The primary objective of both is to study the effects of human behaviour relying on physical evidences namely the landscape features and artefacts preserved, respectively[2].

Geomorphology, a tool in geoarchaeology can contribute to archaeology in recognition of terrain types which were significant to the past communities. Geomorphic studies in archaeology deal with, man–land relationship in terms of geomorphic setting of archaeological sites as well as geomorphic agents which play role in preserving or destroying archaeological evidence.

*Department of Archaeology, Deccan College, Pune 411 006.

In this connection the investigations carried out by Rajaguru[3] and Guzder[4] in Maharashtra; Pappu[5], Deo[6], Pappu and Deo[7] and Korisettar[8] in Karnataka; Rajendran[9] in Kerala; Marathe[10] in Saurashtra; and Kale[11] in Goa are relevant to the present study where geomorphic investigations have been used to interpret palaeolithic landscape.

Area of Study

The study area i.e.Bhima Basin in Pune district (between 17° 54′ and 19° 22′ N and 73° 24′ and 75° 14′ E) approximately covers an area of 9644 square km. It is drained by the river Bhima and its tributaries (Fig. 1)

Physiographically, the major hill complex here is the Western Ghats and its transverse off-shoots. The basin can be divided into two relief units; the western hilly tract and plain area in the eastern part of the basin. Geologically, the basin exhibits uniformity i.e. the major formation is the Deccan traps and its varieties.

Aims and Methodology

The Bhima basin in Pune district provides adequate evidence for archaeological research and it is suitable for the interpretation of man–land relationship during different phases of human culture, since the area exhibits continuity from the Palaeolithic phase.

The present study is an attempt to throw light on the geomorphic aspects viz. relief and drainage and their relationship with archaeological site-distribution in the study area. The present work therefore, will identify and explain landform factors and establish the relationship between the archaeological sites and the geomorphic landscape.

This work aims at:

(i) a comprehensive landform analysis of the study area;

(ii) study of distribution of archaeological sites in relation to the landorms, and

(iii) integration of geomorphological and archaeological data towards understanding of man–land relationships during different cultural periods.

Cultural Background

About 26 sites yielding artefacts of the Palaeolithic,

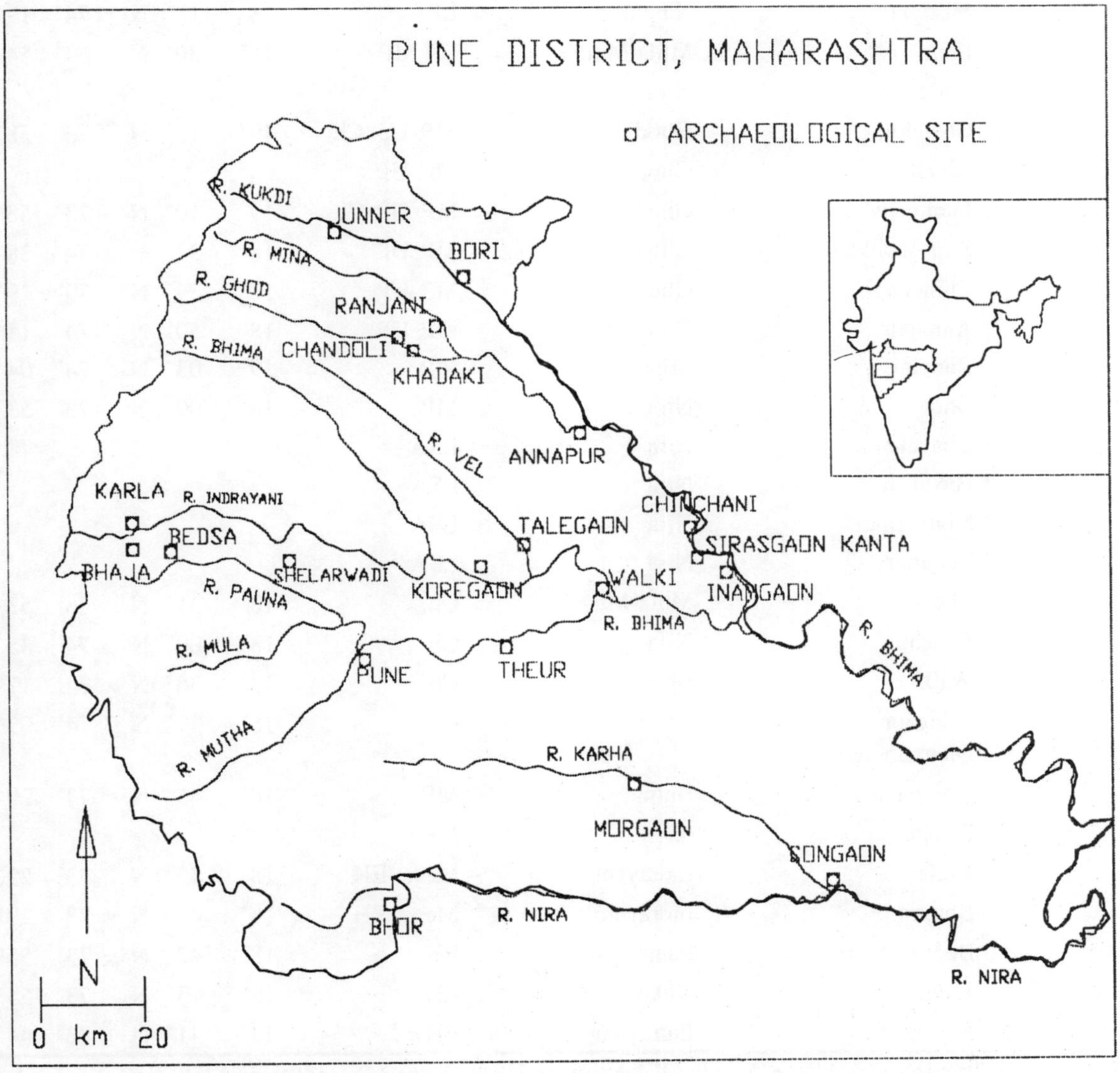

Fig. 1.

Chalcolithic and the early historic periods were located in different parts of the area (Fig. 1). Out of 27 sites, 7 are on the river Nira, 6 on the river Ghod. 3 on river Indrayani, 2 each on the rivers Bhima, Mula-Mutha and Kukdi, and one each on river Mina, Karha, Pauna and Vel.

The evidence for Lower Palaeolithic culture has been found at 4 sites, of Middle Palaeolithic culture from 10 sites. Six sites have yielded Upper Paleolithic tools. Evidence for Mesolithic culture has been found at 2 sites, while that of the Chalcolithic has been found at 6 sites; 4

Table 1-List of Sites in Pune District Source IAR)

S. No.	Site name	River valley	Culture	Geo. co-ordinates
1.	Bori	Kukdi	LP	19° 6′ N 74° 5′ E
2.	Morgoan	Karaha	LP	18° 17′ N 74° 19′ E
3.	Pune	Mula-Mutha	LP, MP	18° 30′ N 74° 54′ E
4.	Shirgaon*	Nira	LP	
5.	Chandoli	Ghod	MP, Up, Ch	19° 10′ N 73° 58′ E
6.	Khadki	Ghod	MP, UP	
7.	Inamgaon	Ghod	MP, UP, Ch	19° 10′ N 73° 58′ E
8.	Sirasgaonkanta	Ghod	MP, UP	18° 37′ N 74° 28′ E
9.	Chinchani	Ghod	MP, UP	18° 39′ N 79° 29′ E
10	Annapur	Ghod	MP, UP	18° 50′ N 74° 18′ E
11.	Ranjani	Mina	MP	19° 03′ N 74° 04′ E
12.	Bhor	Nira	MP	18° 09′ N 73° 53′ E
13.	* Bhavekal	Nira	LSA	
14.	* Hirdoshi	Nira	LSA	
15.	* Nigudghar	Nira	LSA	
16.	* Venupuri	Nira	LSA	
17.	Theur	Mula-Mutha	Ch	18° 31′ N 73° 53′ E
18.	Songaon	Nira	Ch	18° 00′ N 74° 35′ E
19.	Walki	Bhima	Ch	18° 36′ N 74° 17′ E
20.	Talegaon Dhamdhere	Vel	Ch	18° 39′ N 74° 09′ E
21.	Koregaon	Bhima	MP	18° 45′ N 73° 29′ E
22.	* Donge		Meso	
23.	Karle	Indrayani	Meso, EH	18° 45′ N 73° 29′ E
24.	Bhaja	Indrayani	Meso, EH	18° 45′ N 73° 29′ E
25.	Bedsa	Pauna	EH	18° 42′ N 73° 55′ E
26.	Junnar	Kukdi	EH	19° 13′ N 73° 54′ E
27.	Shelarwadi	Indrayani	EH	18° 41′ N 73° 44′ E

LP = Lower Palaeolithic; MP = Middle Palaeolithic; UP = Upper Palaeolithic; LSA=Late Stone Age; Meso = Mesolithic; Ch = Chalcolithic; EH = Early Historical and * = Sites reported in IAR but not sited in the map (Fig. 1) sites have yielded evidence for early historic period. It is significant to note that many of the sites have preserved multicultural material evidence thereby indicating the continuous occupation at the same localities.

In the Pune district, evidence for Lower Palaeolithic culture has been found mostly along the river banks e.g Bori on the Kukdi river[12] and Morgaon the Karha river. The raw material used was the locally available Deccan trap.

The second stage of lithic culture (i.e. Middle Palaeolithic) is represented mostly by surface sites of the Upper Pleistocene period where man adapted himself to a different climate. These sites are found along perennial as well as seasonal streams or hill slopes. Smaller and thinner flake tools and blade-tools are more common types in this culture. Koregoan, Chandoli, Ranjani and Inamgaon yielded such an evidence

In the Upper Palaeolithic phase man lived along the river banks, at the foothills and on the plains. Blades and burins are the characteristic tools of the Upper Palaeolithic. Systematic working of bone, ivory and other various tools are also found in this phase. An important Upper Palaeolithic site was reported at Inamgaon on the river Ghod, where a 15 metre thick alluvium consisted of a series of gravel and silt. The gravel yielded a large number of Upper Palaeolithic tools made on chalcedony; tools being blades, burins, points and fluted cores. Fossilized bones of hippopotamus, horse, buffalo, cattle and deer have been found associated with the Upper Palaeolithic tools.

Earliest evidence of the well studied Deccan chalcolithic culture (2000 - 600 B.C.) is found along the river basin in the semi-arid region of the study area. They are found along the river banks of Ghod, Mula-Mutha and Nira. Inamgaon is the largest and extensive settlement found located on the bank of river Ghod. The extent of the site is 5 hectares where a 3 m thick habitational deposit was found[13]. Other such sites are Walki, Theur, Shastewadi on the Mula-Mutha river basin; Inamgaon, and Chandoli in the Ghod river basin; Songaon in the Nira river basin; and Talegoan Dhamdhere in the Vel river basin (Fig. 1). Early historical Buddhist cave sites are situated in the Western Ghat region of Pune district. These caves are located on the main route of communication at the proximity to natural passes of the Ghat region. Bhaja, Karla, and Shelarwadi caves are in the Indrayani valley, while Bedasa cave is in Pauna valley near Bhor pass and Junnar caves is in Kukdi valley near the Nane pass. On paleographic grounds of inscription found here these caves have been dated between the 2nd century B.C. and the Ist century AD[14].

Landform Analysis

Landform analysis has been carried out by applying methods of numerical systematization of landform elements measured from topographic maps. For this the study area was divided into 1656 quadrants of 1.5×1.5 cm and the process has been based on four parameters Relative Relief, Dissection Index, Stream Ordering, and Stream Frequency for each quadrant.

Morphometric analysis regarding the relief and drainage basin morphology reveals following aspects:

Relief Morphology

Relief is the important aspect of the landform which interprets its evolution and development. The quantitative methods selected to study the landform developments are relative relief, dissection index and altimetric frequency analysis. These are useful for comparison of various relief characteristics.

Relative Relief

Relative relief represents actual variation of altitude in an unit area with respect to its local base level. It is the vertical extent of landscape feature without reference to the absolute relief or the slope[15]. It represents the differences among altitudes in given area, yet it does not show feature of vertical distance from the erosion base. Relative relief is closely related to the slopes and is useful for understanding the morphogenesis, i.e. steeper the slope, higher the relative relief.

The area under investigation has been divided into equal grids of 2.25 sq. km each. The highest and lowest point in each quadrant has been recorded and difference between highest and lowest, i.e. relative relief is calculated for each square. The area is divided into the 5 categories of relative relief as exteremely low, moderately low, low, moderate moderately high and high.

Distribution of relative relief gives a clear idea of the nature and amount of local relief. It shows that the concentration of the extremely low and moderately low relief are mainly confined to the central and eastern parts whereas moderate to high relief is concentrated in the western parts while high reliefs found in the source region of the rivers of Pune district.

The percentage frequency distribution of relative relief of the basin (Table 2) shows that the area of high relative relief represent the smallest area (5.58%) and about 65% of the total area has been occupied by extremely low relative relief. Thus the low relief as its maximum expansion over the basin indicating maturity of the basin.

Table 2 : Percentage Distribution: Relative Relief (Rr)

Rr in m	Percentage	Category
0-30	64.43	Extremely low
30-75	8.57	Moderately low
75-150	7.79	Low
150-225	7.07	Moderate
225-300	6.56	Moderately high
> 300	5.58	High

Dissection Index

Dissection index is the ratio between relative and absolute reliefs. As the relative relief does not allow the vertical distance from the erosion base, the dissection index is useful. In the present study area, spatial variation of the dissection index shows five major categories of dissection (Table 3).

The total area is represented by dissection in decreasing order (Table 3). The extremely low and low dissection categories are mainly confined to central and eastern part of the district while the moderate and high dissection categories are restricted to western part. This spatial variation appears due to differences in local rock type, relative relief, slope, vegetal growth and rainfall distribution.

Table 3 Percentage Distribution : Dissection Index

Dissection in%	Category	Percentage to the total area	Stage of morpho–evolution
0 - 5	Low	64.43	Peneplain
5 - 20	Moderate	8.57	Old age or youth
20 - 40	Moderately high	7.79	Late maturity
40 - 70	High	17.34	Maturity
above 70	Very high	1.87	Early maturity

Altimetric Frequency Analysis

Altimetric frequency analysis is based on the geomorphic principle that hill tops offer the last refuge for vanishing relief[16]. This analysis reveals the existence of erosional surfaces or levels which shows the numerical frequency of certain levels. It is useful to identify the high level erosional surfaces formed by denudational processes.

The altimetric frequency (Fig. 2) drawn for the study area is based on grid method of frequency distribution. It is useful in the area of multiple cycle than in uplifted or structural platforms. The peaks on this histogram represent the remnants of that height of erosional surfaces.

The altimetric frequency graph (Fig. 2) of the study area shows three major surfaces: the high level surfaces of more than 1050 metre and that of 900-1050 metre height occupy least area whereas surfaces between 450-600 dominate the landscape.

Basin Network Analysis

Rivers are one of the most important characteristics of geomorphic system on the earth surface which provides valuable information about the denudation history of the region.

Basin morphometry is defined as the measurement and mathematical analysis of drainage form, character, shape and network which is based on an ordering system applied to the channel network. This analysis deals with various aspects such as stream order, bifurcation ratio and stream frequency.

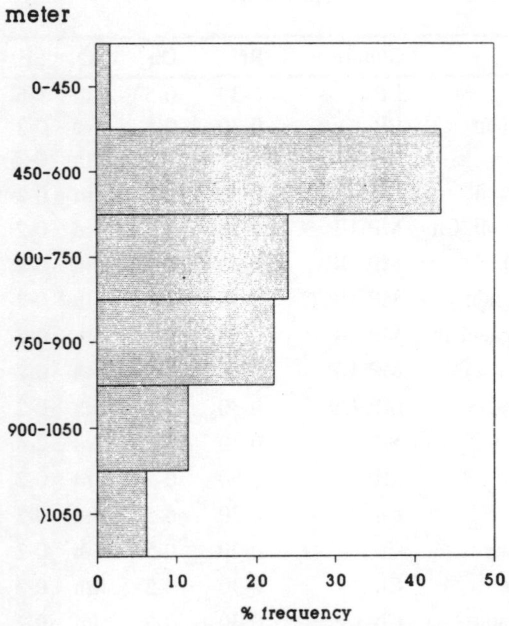

Fig. 2 Altemetric Frequency Graph

The Bhima and its tributaries Ghod, Nira and Mula-Mutha rivers originate in and near the Western Ghats and are bounded by the east stretching spurs, and flow east and south across the district. Dendetric pattern is common in this region which can be attributed to the lithological homogeneity.

Description of stream order is the first step in the drainage basin analysis. Strahler's[17] modified method of stream ordering is followed in this study. According to this method, all finger-tip tributaries (streams which have no tributary) are called as first order streams. When the two first order streams join, they form second order stream and so on with streams of higher order. Thus with this ordering of streams, the trunk streams of any watershed bears the highest order number in the entire system.

Thus the study area follows Horton's[18] first law, which states that the relationship between stream order and stream number is straight line geometric relationship (with an increase in order the number of streams decreases).

The Mula-Mutha river system bears the 4th order system, Ghod river and Nira river system bears the 5th order and the main river of the district, river Bhima bears the 6th order. Number of the first order streams are less in the Mula-Mutha river system than the other three river systems (Table 4).

Table 4 : Stream Ordering for various basins

Stream	Number of streams in the rivers			
order	Bhima	Ghod	Nira	Mula-Mutha
1	281	212	209	148
2	35	23	39	20
4	5	4	5	5
5	2	1	1	1
6	1	-	-	-

Bifurcation Ratio

The ratio between the number of streams of a given order and the number of stream of the next higher order is the bifurcation ratio. This has been calculated for Bhima and its main tributaries Ghod, Nira and Mula-Mutha (Table 5). These values are more or less normal according to Horton's law as they range between 3 and 5 which indicate the maturity stage of the basin. In the study area except Mula-Mutha basin others show the mature stage. This can also be confirmed by applying hypsometric analysis.

Table 5 : Bifurcation Ratio for rivers in Bhima Basin

Stream order	Bhima	Ghod	Nira	Mula-Mutha
1				
2	8.2	9.2	5.35	7.2
3	7.0	5.75	7.8	4.0
4	2.5	2.0	2.5	5.0
5	1.0	2.0	2.0	---
6	2.0	---	---	---
mean	4.14	4.73	4.41	5.46

The variation between bifurcation values are found due to the differences in topography, surface run-off, the degree of the integration of streams[19]. Horton[20] considered the bifurcation ratio as an index of the relief and dissection.

In general, bifurcation ratio decreases with increase in the order. But in case of Nira basin it is not following the rule because only northern part (which occurs in Pune district) of the entire Nira basin has been calculated. This rule is also not followed by Mula-Mutha basin due to the relief which have affected the branching of streams.

Stream Frequency

It is defined as the number of the streams per unit area within the drainage basin. It is a useful supplementary measure of the fineness of the texture of the topography and also the extent of the dissection. The stream frequency depends on the lithology, porosity of the rock, slope, rainfall and the vegetation cover. The values of stream frequency in the study area (Table 6) indicates that major area is covered by stream frequency of less then 2 per unit area. Very few areas show maximum stream frequency of 7 per unit area.

Table 6 Stream Frequency

Stream Frequency	Percentage Area
0-2	67.5
2-4	29.6
4-6	2.7
> 6	0.2

Man–land relationship

Geomorphic analysis is useful to reconstruct the archaeological landscape and man–land relationship in the past. Here an attempt has been made to examine the relationship between the sites discovered so far and in context of their location in a particular landscape. Archaeological sites of varied cultural periods (prehistoric, chalcolithic and few early historical) exhibit a significant geomorphic control in their distribution. Superimposition of site distribution map on the relative relief, dissection index, stream frequency and stream ordering map show interesting man–land relationship (Table 7)

Table 7 : Geomorphic Parameters and site distribution

Site name	Culture	Rr	Dn	SO	SF
1. Bori	LP	0-30	0-5	4th	>6
2. Morgoan	LP	0-30	0-5	3rd	0-2
3. Pune	LP, MP	30-75	5-20	4th	0-2
4. Shirgaon	LP	0-30	0-5	3rd	0-2
5. Chandoli, Ch	MP, UP	0-30	0-5	3rd	0-2
6. Khadki	MP, UP,	0-30	0-5	5th	0-2
7. Inamgaon	MP, UP, C	0-30	0-5	5th	0-2
8. Sirasgaonkanta	MP, UP	0-30	0-5	5th	0-2
9. Chinchani	MP, UP	0-30	0-5	5th	0-2
10. Annapur	MP, UP	0-30	0-5	5th	0-2
11. Ranjani	MP	0-30	0-5	3rd	2-4
12. Bhor	MP	0-30	0-5	3rd	0-2
13. Theur	Ch	0-30	0-5	4th	0-2
14. Songaon	Ch	0-30	0-5	5th	0-2
15. Walki	Ch	0-30	0-5	4th	0-2
16. Talegaon Dhamdhere	Ch	0-30	0-5	4th	0-2
17. Koregaon	MP, Ch?	0-30	0-5	3rd	0-2
18. Karle	Meso, EH	225-300	40-60	2nd	4-6
19. Bhaja	EH	> 300	40-60	2nd	0-2
20. Bedsa	EH	30-75	5-20	2nd	2-4
21. Junnar	EH	0-30	0-5	2nd	2-4
22. Shelarwadi	EH	0-30	0-5	3rd	0-2

LP = Lower Palaeolithic Rr = Relative Relief in metres
MP = Middle Palaeolithic Dn = Dissection Index-percentage
UP = Upper Palaeolithic So = Stream Order
LSA = Late Stone Age SF = Stream Frequency per unit area
Meso = Mesolithic
Ch = Chalcolithic
EH = Early Historic

Drainage network analysis and site distribution

As generally expected, the sites are mostly located close to the streams and rivers. Major sites are concentrated in the basins of Ghod, Kukdi, Nira, Mula-Mutha rivers in the study area. Stream ordering and site distribution analysis revels that Palaeolithic sites are mostly located on the 3rd or 4th stream order. Whereas the

Chalcolithic sites are mostly located on the main river flow i.e. on the 4th or 5th order streams.

Stream frequency and site distribution shows that mostly the sites are located between stream frequency of 0-4 streams per square km. Only the lower Palaeolithic site of Bori is located in the area having stream frequency of 6 (Table 7).

Relief morphometry and site distribution

Five categories of the relative relief in relation to the sites indicate that the existence of more favourable conditions are found below the relative relief of 75 metres. Only early historical cave sites are situated in the high relative relief area of western part of Pune district.

Dissection index analysis shows that the concentration of prehistoric and protohistoric sites is in the range of the 0-20% dissection, and that the distribution of sites is more or less similar to that found in relation to the relative relief.

Conclusions

The setting of the prehistoric and protohistoric sites is influenced by number of environmental factors like availability of the perennial water supply; suitable physiography;favourable climactic condition; availability of raw materials; and plant and animal resources. Early man preferred a particular region for settlement where such environmental factors were suitable.

The hilly rugged terrain of the western part of Pune district perhaps were avoided by the prehistoric and protohistoric people. Palaeolithic and chalcolithic man lived in the plain region of the eastern parts. Only early historical cave sites are located in the hilly region.

Most of the archaeological sites are confined to the riverine environment. Hydrologic analysis shows that the palaeolithic sites are mostly confined to the 3d and 4th stream orders indicating limited exploitation of territory. On the other hand the chalcolithic sites are located on the 4th or 5th stream order i.e. on the main river bank, on the Ghod, Mula-Mutha, Nira rivers. However, Chalcolithic site at Talegaon Dhamdhere is not located near the perennial water source like other sites. This site is located on the 4th stream order of the Bhima river and extends over small area. Perhaps this represents temporary activity of chalcolithic man (personal communication from Sonali Naik and S. Mishra).

Sites that show continuation from the middle Palaeolithic to the Chalcolithic period are also located on the main rivers, on the 4th and 5th stream order and on the flat region of eastern part of the study area. Therefore, it suggests that flat region was relatively more favorable for human activity in the past.

Abundant microlithic scatters have been found all over the denudational surfaces of the study area. Since there are no other archaeological remains associated with these microlithic scatters and since microliths are undatable, the nature of man-land relationship in this context cannot be inferred properly.

Thus this study of the man-land relationship provided evidence of the early man's relationship with his surrounding environment. Detailed morphometric analysis, field-work and relevant statistical analysis may help for better understanding of association of man and land.

This paper is based on the dissertation entitled Landform analysis of archaeological sites in the Bhima basin in the Pune District submitted by the first author in 1996 to the Deccan College, Pune as a partial fulfillment of M.A. degree.

REFERENCES

1. Goudie, 1987. Geograpy and Archaeology: the Growth of Relationship. In J.M. Wagstaff. (ed.) *Landscape and Culture: Geographical and Archaeological Perspective* Oxford: Blackwell. pp. 11-25
2. Wagstaff, J.M. (ed) 1987. Introduction, *Landscape and Culture: Geographical and Archaeological.* Oxford:

Blackwell. pp. 1-10

3. Rajaguru, S. N. 1968. Studies on the Late Pleistocene of the Mula-Mutha Valley. Unpublished Ph. D, Thesis, University of Poona.

4. Guzder, S. 1980. *Quaternary Environment and Stone Age Cultures of the Konkan.* Pune: Deccan College.

5. Pappu, R.S. 1985. The Geomorphic Setting of Acheulian Sites in Peninsular India, In Misra V.N. and P. Bellwood (eds.) *Recent Advances in Indo-Pacific Prehistory.* New Delhi: IBH Publishing Co. pp. 9-12.

6. Deo S.G. 1991. Geomorphic Study of Palaeolithic Settlements in the Ghataprapha Basin Karnataka. Unpublished Ph. D. Thesis, University of Poona.

7. Pappu, R.S. and Deo S.G. 1994. *Man-Land Relationships during Palaeolithic Times in the Kaladgi Basin, Karanataka.* Pune: Deccan Collage.

8. Korisetter R. 1979. Prehistory and Geomorphology of the Middle Krishna, Karnataka. Unpublished Ph. D. Thesis. University of Poona.

9. Rajendran, P. 1980. *Environment and Stone Age Cultures of North Kerala.*

10. Marathe A.R. 1981. *Geoarchaeology of Hiran Valley, Saurashtra, India.* Pune: Deccan College.

11. Kale, V.S. 1983. Neogene and Quaternary Geomorphology of Mandvi and Zuari Basins. Got Unpublished Ph. D. Thesis, University of Poona.

12. Korisetter, R. T.R. Venkatesan, Sheila Mishra, S.N. Rajaguru, B.L.K. Somayajulu, S.K. Tondon, V.D. Gogte, R.K. Ganjoo, V.S. Kale. 1989. Discovery of Tephra bed in the Quaternary Alluvial Sediments of Pune District (Maharashtra), Peninsular India. *Current Science* 58 (10) : 564-567.

13. Dhavalikar, M.K., H.D. Sankalia and Z.D. Ansari 1988. *Excavations at Inamgaon,* Vol. I part I. Pune: Deccan College.

14. Dahejia, Vidya 1972, *Early Buddhist Rock Temples: A Chronological Study.* London: Thames & Hudson Ltd.

15. Evans, I.S. 1972. General Geomorphology, Deviations of Altitude and Descriptive Statistics. In R.J. Chorley) (ed.) *Spatial Analysis in Geomorphology,* London: Methuen and Co. Ltd., pp. 17-91.

16. Miller, A.A. 1953. *The Skin of the Earth.* London: Methuen.

17. Strahler, A.N. 1971. *Physical Geography.* New Delhi: Wiley Eastern Pvt. Ltd.

18. Horton E. 1945. Erosional Development of Streams and their Drainage Basins: Hydrological Approach to Quantitative Morphology. *Bulletin of Geological Society of America,* 56: 275-370.

19. Sidu G.S. and I.G. Pande. 1974. Parametric Analysis of Patalgad Drainage Basin (East of Mussourie). *National Geographical Journal of India* 20 (4) : 223-235.

20. Horton, op. cit.

A Lost (?) Aśokan Edict From Vidarbha

Ajay Mitra Shastri*

Hitherto only one edict of the Maurya emperor Aśoka was known from the Vidarbha region of Maharashtra. It hails from the village of Deotek in the district of Chandrapur, some 80 km south-east of Nagpur. It was first noticed by Beglar, Cunningham's Assistant, in 1873-74 and Cunningham published an eye-copy of the inscription and his own transcript without any translation interpretation in his compilation of Aśokan edicts[2] in 1877. However, the credit of inviting scholarly attention to this inscription goes to the late V.V. Mirashi who presented a paper on it at the eighth session of the All-India Oriental Conference, Mysore in 1935.[3] However, nearly half of this edict was damaged to make room for an inscription of the Vakataka king Rudrasena.

Recently a news item in a local Marathi daily[4] attracted wide notice of the elite of the Vidarbha region as well as other parts of the country. According to it, a gentleman, one Mr. Fernandes, who had come to see some of his relatives at Ghuggus in the Chandrapur district, came across, during one of his morning walks, a stone-slab with some writing on it in the forest near the town. As the exact whereabouts of it or provenance was not given by Fernandes, a number of search parties sent by the Department of Ancient Indian History, Culture and Archaeology, Nagpur University, Excavation Branch of the Archaeological Survey of India located at Nagpur and the Nagpur regional office of the Department of Archaeology, Government of Maharashtra, in spite of the best of their efforts could not trace the stone. Dr. Amarendranath, Superintending Archaeologist, Excavation Branch, at the instance of the higher authorities of the Archaeological Survey of India, made herculean efforts in this direction, but to no avail. He even enquired of the local people and at the weekly Sunday assemblage of the local Christians at the church[5]; but all this proved futile. At Bombay, from where Mr. Fernandes had allegedly written to Shri Shripad Chitale who was the source of the news in the Nagpur dailies, could not be traced[6]. Thus till date the inscribed slab remains unlocated and at the same time we have no means to locate the whereabouts of its discoverer. But that the inscribed slab did really exist is crystal clear from the xerox copy of its impression that Shri Chitale has supplied to me and which is appended to this note. But one point should be made clear in this context. Mr. Fernandes is reported to have seen this inscribed slab during one of his walks. But this does not appear to be a fact. Normally one does not carry a camera on his person while going for a walk. And even if we suppose that an inquisitive person as Mr. Fernandes appears to be may have carried a camera with him even while going for a walk and photographed an interesting object by way of curiosity, what we actually have with us is a xerox copy of an impression taken carelessly and not a photograph from a camera. So Mr. Fernandes (it may as well be a fictitious name) had the stone-slab available to him or had visited the findspot for at least second time with full preparation for taking an impression, howsoever carelessly. We are without any means to ascertain if the inscribed slab was really found near Ghuggus in the

*Prachi, Rana Pratap Nagar, Nagpur.

Chandrapur district or elsewhere; but if there be any truth (or even semblance of it) of the information about it published in the local dailies, it may reasonably be concluded that it was actually located in Vidarbha. There should be absolutely no room for suspicion that the slab in question really exists though its present whereabouts is unascertainable.

Now coming to the inscription itself as it can be made out from the said xerox copy. The slab bearing it measures about 28 cm in breadth and 40 cm in height. No other details about the slab–such as the stone and border, if any, are available. However, as we shall see in the sequel, it appears to represent another copy of the Bairat stone-slab inscription, and it is not impossible that this inscription also might have been incised on a similar slab. The xerox contains only eight lines of writing in Aśokan Brahmi with its characters sharing all the characteristics noticed in Aśokan Brahmi edicts. As will be shown further on, the inscription must have been much larger, and the finder, perhaps deliberately and cunningly, supplied xerox copy of only its upper portion. The letters are inscribed boldly, their height ranging between 2 and 2.5 cm and breadth between 1 and 1.5 cm. The maximum number of letters accommodated in line 2 is 12 and the minimum, as can be made out from the deliberately blurred indication, 7 (line 7).

The language is Magadhi Prakrit as in most other known Aśokan edicts in India. In keeping with the general practice in vogue , *r* is invariably turned into *l* as in *lājā* for *rājā* (line 1), *vihālataṁ* for *vihāratāṁ* (line 3) and *gālave* for *gaurave* (line 6). Nominative singular case with *a*-stem ends in *e*-as in *Māgadhe* for *Māgadhaḥ* (line 1) *vidate* for *vidite* (line 4), *āvatake* for *yāvathkaḥ* (line 4), *gālave* for *gaurave* line 6) and *pasāde* for *prasādaḥ* (line 7). The initial *y* is elided as in *avatake* instead of *yavatke* (line 4). The locative singular words with *a*-stem ends in *si* as in *Budhasi* and *dhaṁmasi* (line 5) and *saṁghasi* (line 6) and conjunctions are normally avoided: at least in the preserved portion we do not come across a single conjunct.

The record commences with the mention of the emperor Aśoka as *Priyadarsi* the king of Magadha. He salutes the Buddhist Order and enquires about its well-being. He next expresses his high esteem for the Buddha, *Dhaṁma* and *Saṅgha*, the well-known Buddhist trinity in the prescribed order. After it is impossible to make out anything from the xerox though there is absolutely no doubt that many more lines must have followed.

That it is definitely an inscription of Aśoka is apparent from not only its palaeography but also form the use of the phrase *piyadasi lājā* referring to Aśoka at its beginning. Looking for comparable Aśokan edicts we find that its contents and even the wording are those of the well-known Bairāt stone-slab[7] or Calcutta-Bairat[8] inscription. Like the latter, it commences with the expression *Piyadasi lājā Māgadhe.* In fact, the preserved matter of the present inscription[9] is almost exactly literally identical with the first two lines of the latter which read

Line 1 *Priyadasi lājā Māgadhe saṁghaṁ abhiva de ta (the) nāin āhā apābādhataṁ cha phāsuvihālataṁ cha*

Line 2 *vidite ve bhaṁte āvatake hamā budhasi dhaṁmasi saṁghasi ti gālave chain prasāde cha*

Hereafter there are another five *aksharas* in the second line, viz. *e kechi bhaṁte.*

Compared to this our inscription reads as follows:

Line 1 *Piyadasi lājā Māgadhe saṁghaṁ*

Line 2 *abhive (vā) [de*] ta (tū)naṁ āhā apaba (bā) dhata (ṁ*)*

Line 3 *cha phāsuvihālataṁ chā*

Line 4 *vida (di) te ve bhaṁte āvatake*

Line 5 *hamā budhasi dhaṁmasi*

Line 6 *saṁghasī ti gā (lave)*

Line 7 *pasāde*

The remainder of line 7 is not legible in the xerox while nothing can be made out of the eighth line. It would be observed that except for *pi* for *pri* in line 1 the entire inscription is completely identical with full first line and a major part of the second line of the Calcutta-Bairat edict. The text that followed in the second line and subsequent six lines, which must have been present in the original text in view of the almost complete identity in the initial portion, as pointed out above, are missing in the xerox. The remainder of the Calcutta-Bairāṭ edict states that the emperor regarded all that Buddha had stated well-said and advised hearing repeatedly and memorising by the Buddhist monks and nuns as well as the lay followers of Buddhism of certain religious texts *(dhaṁma-paliyāyas)* which, he felt, were conducive to the longevity of Buddhism[10]. Our incription also must have said the same, though at present it is not available in the xerox.

This edict is sometimes regarded as an evidence in support of the tradition that a Buddhist Council took place during the reign of Aśoka. It is pointed out that the emperor's description as 'king of Magadha' *(lājā Māgadhe)* is a pointer in this direction. As Buddhist monks from areas even outside Aśoka's empire, it is averred, must have participated in this Council, it was felt necessary by him to refer to himself as the king of Magadha[11]. However, according to the Ceylonese Pali tradition, the Council took place at the Kukkuṭārāma-vihāra at Pāṭaliputra.[12] Had the edict been addressed to the participants of the Council held at Pāṭliputra, it must have been found at Pāṭliputra or somewhere closeby. That it has been found at far off places like Bairāṭ in Rajasthan and near Ghuggus in the Chandrapur district of Vidarbha or anywhere in the region or even in Maharashtra shows that it was in no way connected with the Council. And *Piyadasi lājā Māgadhe* was just another mode of mentioning the emperor like *devānaṁpriya.*

The find of this inscription is of momentous importance for the history of Buddhism. For the findspot must have been a Buddhist centre of consequence where a large number of Buddhist monks and nuns must have lived and lay warshippers must have flocked in large numbers quite frequently. Otherwise there would have been no point in putting this edict addressed to Buddhist monks and nuns and male and female lay followers and recommending religious texts for their repeated hearing and memorising. There must have been monasteries for both monks and nuns there. Unfortunately we are not sure regarding its provenance. It must be pointed out in this connection that during the Maurya period, especially Aśoka's reign, Buddhism had not only reached vidarbha but had come to claim quite prosperous centres. At Pauni (Bhandara district) in particular at least two Buddhist *stūpas* of very large size had been built during the Maurya period[13]. And at Aḍam in the Nagpur district also evidences of a Buddhist establishment have been noticed during recent excavations[14]. All this was evidently due to Aśoka's missionry zeal. There is also no doubt that the findspot of the inscription in question must have been situated on a busy trade route or close to it. It is difficult to understand the rationale for Aśoka's instructions to lay followers of Buddhism to repeatedly hear and memorise the recommended texts.

The inscription is, thus, of great importance for historical purposes and its actual discovery, for which herculean efforts are a must, will be epoch making.

NOTES AND REFERENCES

1. Cunningham 1877, *Archaeological Survey Reports,* VII, p. 124
2. Corpus Inscriptionum Indicarum. *Inscriptions of Asoka,* pp. 124. After this Hira Lal noticed this slab under 'unimportant, incomplete or illegible inscriptions and referred to the inscription in question as 'one in Pali characters of about the same period as Asoka's edicts'. See his *Inscriptions in the Central Provinces and Berar,* 2nd ed., Nagpur, 1932, p.15, no. 16.
3. "New Light on Deotek Inscription", *Proceedings and Transactions of the All-India Original Conference,* Eight h Session, 1935, pp. 613 ff., *Studies in Indology* I, Nagpur, 1960, pp. 109-17; 2nd ed., Nagpur, 1968, pp. 125-34; *Inscriptions of the* Vākāṭakas, CII, V, Ootacamund, 1963, pp. 1-4.
4. *Trauna Bhārata* (Marathi daily) dated 26. 1992, Basing on this news item a correspondent of a local English daily, *Nagpur Times,* approached me for an interview which appeared in its issue dated 16.7.92. The news item in the *Taruna Bhārata* is replete with unwarranted assumptions regarding the purpose and contents of the inscription.
5. Mr. Fernandes is a Christian and is reported to have his relations at Ghuggus. However, nobody knows anything about him.
6. Surprisingly he could not find any person in Bombay to decipher the inscription and at Nagpur also he could con-

tact only Shri Shripad Chitale for this job.

7. Sircar, D.C. 1965, *Select Inscriptions bearing on Indian History and Civilization,* 2nd ed., Calcutta, p. 74. Sircar classifies it, as 'stone-skab edict'.

8. Hultzsch, E. 1925, *The Inscriptions of Aśoka,* CII, I, Calcutta, p. 172. As the inscription (inscribed slab) was deposited in the Asiatic Society (now Indian Museum) located at Calcutta, the city's name was added to the provenance as in the case of Delhi-Topra edicts.

9. We mean, the xerox available to us.

10. There are in all seven such texts.

11. Bhandarkar, D.R. 1955, *Aśoka,* 3rd ed., Calcutta, p. 189-90.

12. For an account of and discussion on 3rd Buddhist Council at Pātaliputra, see Ajay Mitra Shastri, 1965, *An Outline of Early Buddhism,* Varanasi, pp. 56 ff.

13. Deo S.B. and J.P. Joshi, (eds) 1972, *Pauni Excavation,* Nagpur,

14. Information kindly supplied by Dr. Amarendranath, the excavator of the site.

Traditional Bead Making Industry In Tamil Nadu

K. RAJAN*

The art of cutting and engraving hard semi-precious stone, a specialized craft occupies a unique place due to the value of material and its aesthetic appeal. Continuity of the tradition without much change has been noticed in gem cutting. The present study discusses this against the backdrop of the basic archaeological and literary evidences. Skills are studied through field observation in the present day bead-making industry at Kangayam in Erode district.

India's tradition in ancient and medieval gems is authenticated by the archaeological and literary evidences and by travellers' accounts. .*Arthasastra, Ratnasastra, Vishnudharmottara, Brahtsamhita* of Varahamihira, *Yuktikalpataru* of King Bhoja and Sangam literature are replete with references to germs and their qualities. This paper lays emphasis on the data form Sangam literature.

Gems and gem cutting in Sangam literature

The Sangam literature belonging to the early part of the Christian era gives valuable evidence on the existence of gem stone industry in Tamil Nadu. They had knowledge of advance technique of preparing minute stone beads, as small as mustard seeds, out of hard minerals. They made beads by boring and polishing carnelian quartz, garnet, sapphire, beryl and amethyst. This is amply borne out and by literary data of the Sangam works.[1]

The *Patirruppattu* speaks exclusively of Chera kings who ruled the Kongu region (present Coimbatore and Erode districts) of Tamil Nadu. This area is very famous for its precious stones.

The *kovalar* (cattle raising people) used to collect semi-precious stones from the hillock called Cheruppumalai belonging to the Chera king Pooliyar Ko (Palyanai Chelkelu Kuttuvan). This can be identified, contextually, with the Sivanmalai and Perumalmalai located west of Kangayam in Erode District (*Patirruppattu* 21:20-23). They also turnout while ploughing *(Patirruppattu* 58: 12-19; 76:11-15). In one occasion even the nature of occurrence of the gem is noticed. The gems were found in the midst of milk-white quartz and felsper *(Patirruppattu* 66: 16-20). The exposed gem stones sparkled in the evening sunlight falling on the western slopes of the Kolli hill (near Namakkal) belonging to Chera king (*Akananuru* 213:12-15). *Kanavas* (hillock people) also collected precious stones while they dug for roots (*Kuruntokai* 379:1-3). They were also found in the pits dugout by wild boars (*Narrinai* 399:2-4) and also in the pits dug by the *kanavas* (hill people) with the help of elephant tusk to locate gems (*Akananuru* 282:1-10). The gems due to the thrust of the hoofs of galloping deers come to surface (*Purananuru* 202:1-8). The hills, hill-slopes and lands were strewn with the gem stones (*Maduraikanchi* 273-285; *Narrinali* 234:3) and these were found exposed during rains and were also some-

Department of Archaeology, Tamil University, Thanjavur, 613005.

times brought down by the streams (*Akananur* 233:2-4).These precious stones collected by the local people were sold in the markets (*Maduraiknachi* 504-506). Quite interestingly a specialized artisan called *tirumani kuyinar* (*Maduraikanchi* 511 ; *Silappatikaram* 5:46) and *mani vinaiar* (*Manimekalai* 28:45) exclusively worked on the gem stones. The Brahmi inscription of 2nd c. AD found at Archchalur in Erode district mentions about gem-stone trader called *manivanakkan*. The famous anklet story in *Silappatikaram* says that the hollow of Kannagi's anklet was filled with gems whereas the Pandiyan queen's anklet had pearls. The whetstone/lapstone (*sanaikal*) specialist *chirukarotan* prepares the wheel by mixing *payin* (lac) and *kal* and probably *kuruntam* (corundum powder) (*Akananuru* 1;5-6; 359:9-10). The gems to be faceted or polished are fixed in lac and placed at the tip of the rod (*Kuruntokai* 155:3-4).

These references clearly indicate the existence of the gem-stone industry in Tamil Nadu during Sangam age and fetched large amount of external currency particularly Roman gold mostly in the form of coins to Tamil country.

A typical bead making centre, Kangayam, the taluk headquarters, is the hub of stone-industry of the region. There are nearly 250 families working in this industry when the author visited in 1990. But today their number has drastically come down to 50. This is due to the gradual introduction of the mechanical lathe and electrical components in this industry. Presently the bead-making industry is restricted to the Muslim community. But once this place was a bead-making centre involving all communities.

Here in Kangayan are seen three groups of megaliths mostly cairn-circles concealing trancepted cists.

Technology

The present-day artisans of Kangayam region follow largely the traditional methods. Semi-precious stones used here are sapphire (*nilakkal*), beryl (*patchaikkal*), quartz (*palingukkal*) and moonstone (*ennaikkal*). corundum (*Kurundam*) is mainly used for boring and polishing. The bead-workers collect these stones either directly going to the field or buy from the local weekly market where the village-folks bring them for sale.

The methods used for cutting and engraving have not changed much. Firstly the bottom portion of the gem, called *mastam*, is faceted and then the top portion *kutchai*. According to the artisans, faceting (*paṭṭai podaradu*) of the gem's bottom section (*mastam*) is considered much easier.

Process

The first step in the process in the workshop (*paṭṭarai*) is to separate the valuable material from the impurities (*maṇḍakkal*) adhering to after removing cortex. After removing the cortex by chipping a small portion of the surface of the mass was polished and an incision was made at the dividing line between limestone and laurite using micro-blade. Then the gem is removed without much damage by striking the block indirectly at the point of incision.

The second step is to heat the some of the material like carnelian in small pots filled with smoldering sawdust. This causes physical change in the stone which makes the next process, clipping, an easier one. The knapping of the stones is done in two stages, the first of which roughs out the shape of the bead. This is smoothened by finer chipping. In both the cases the technique involves the use of a hammer and a spike (or anvil) driven into the ground. The rough chipping hammer is made of buffalo horn fixed on to a thin flexible bamboo handle. In few cases small chisels are used. The chisels are applied directly on the rough surface by the artisan. They hardly use any hammer on the chisel head. In the case of horn, only of buffalo horn is used and not that of cow. The reason is not known to the present day artisans. By careful chipping all through the final roughed-out bead is produced in no more than two or three minutes. Beads requiring further chipping are taken over by another worker. The chipped blanks are then sorted and sent to be ground to their final shape. This smoothening operation takes place in a separate work-area.

Tools - the wheel

The primary equipment in the bead-making process is the wheel which is fashioned by the artisans. To prepare a wheel, sealing wax is heated to a molten condition and is poured inside a ring formed out of two semi-circular rings which are placed on a flat stone surface. Once the wax reached its leather hard condition the semi-circular rings are rotated around the edges of the sealing was. A stone dabber is used to rub the wheel to get an even surface. The wheel is fusioned with corundum powder or sand. The abrasive wheels, against which the beads are ground, are commercially made today and powered by electric motors. The thickness of the wheel ranges from a quarter to one third inch, and is turned rapidly by a bow and string fitted to the axle similar to the carpenters augur. The gem to be ground is cemented to one end of a small rod (generally in a mushroom shaped stick called *dop stick*). The fixation of bead on the rod top involves a minor process. First the rod is pasted with a thick coat of sealing wax. Then the sealing wax is slightly heated on a slow fire and the bead to be fashioned is fixed. The fixed bead is applied by the lapidary having the means of giving a very rapid rotary motion to the mill-plate. It grinds away the substance of the gem according to the kind of effect required to be produced. The workman holds the gem in one hand and turns the wheel with the other and grinds the gem applying it to the rough surface of the wheel. When the stone is sufficiently worn out, it is polished by another smoother wheel than the first and managed in a similar way. Several individuals usually work at a single machine. The grinding of a single bead never takes more than a minute. Spherical beads are shaped on a specially formed "corrugated" grinding wheel. This wheel is used in conjuction with a simple but specially prepared wooden implement which holds the rough chipped stones in place while they are pressed against the rapidly spinning wheel. It takes only a matter of seconds for rough chipped stones to be transformed into nearly perfect tiny spheres.

For grinding diamonds, sapphires and rubies, the mill-plate is coated with a slight touch of diamond-powder and oil, to give the requisite abrading power. For emeralds, beryls, topazes, garnets and all other softer gems, corundum and water are applied to the plate. The grinding wears away the surface of gem in various parts. But the new surface thus produced is dull without lustre. This lustreless gem is then polished on softer mill-plate with leather and water to produce a shine.

Each side of the gem has to be faceted independantly for the simple reason that one side is always embedded in the sealing wax (*arakku*). The gem has to be held absolutely steady against the spinning lap so that the friction facets the portion of the gem that is being carefully held in a wooden clamp called a *kai-savi* (hand key). This instrument is the primitive ancestor of the modern faceter used on the semi-automatic modern machines.

Perforation

Drilling hole is the most delicate of entire process and in which the probability of wasting pure and extensively processed material is highest. These losses are attested by the numerous partially perforated beads broken during drilling which are found alongwith wastes in the excavations. At Kodumanal a rock-piece with perforation for chipping a bead was unearthed. This may be due to the erroneous drilling angles and flaws in the crystalline structure. From the discarded material it appears that polishing preceded drilling. Even to this day, the rock crystal beads are bored by using simple instruments like steel needle fixed with diamond or corrundum (*kuruṇḍam* in Tamil) point (borer) and bow drill. The corundum stone is available in the region between Tiruppur on the west and Karur on the east. These corundum chips are placed on the drill tip by using an awl to form a cup like thing at the drill point. The bead to be drilled is fixed on to lac and, while boring, water kept in a coconut shell cap to drip on the bead to reduce the heat.

The position of the craftsman is worth observing. He sits on a small wooden plank with right leg in folded posture. The left leg sometimes placed over the bead to be drilled. He holds the drill in his left hand and bow in his right. Sometimes he places a stone dabber below the knee portion of the folded right leg. According to the artisan, the stone dabber helps to keep the body position perfect while giving thrust. The speed at which the beads are drilled is largely determined by the hardness of the material . The Kodumanal beads were bored from both sides to make a single hole of hour-glass section. The same technique is still followed in the bead-making centres of Tiruppur, Kangayam and Tiruchirapalli. The use of simple instruments and the long survival of this tradition in the vicinity of Kodumanal reminds the technology adopted in ancient days.

The final step in this process of bead manufacture is the final polishing which is usually done on a leather or fabric covered revolving horizontal lap, on which very fine, abrasive powder has been sprinkled.

Engraving

Engraving of seals is an operation allied to that of cutting and polishing gems. In hard material the engraving requires the action of a rotating edge to cut it. Generally speaking, it is the softer kind of the gems, such as carnelian, chalcedony, quartz, amethyst and onyx which are best suited for engraving. Diamond, sapphire and ruby are too hard for this operation. Beryl, topaz and emerald are sometimes engraved. Whichever gem is used, it is first ground to proper form by the lapidary, and then engraved by the aid of small and delicately constructed lathe. A small steel cylinder or bar is made to rotate very rapidly on a horizontal axis, and on the one end of this cylinder is fixed a very minute disc or wheel, which forms the cutter or engraving tool. In Tamil Nadu, engravings are not attempted at all. However, on my request an artisan from Tiruppur demonstrated the process involved in engraving. He fixes the gem by a cementing material to the end of a stick.

The gem to be engraved is brought near the little wheel or disc with diamond powder and oil on it and the wheel is set in rapid motion and when the gem is pushed against the surface of the wheel. For bringing about desired design, shape and size can be altered. The engraved portion is generally rough. This rough surface is once again polished as stated earlier.

Decoration

Majority of the carnelian beads in Tamil Nadu were collected from megalithic burials. Most of them are of the etched variety. The carnelian beads no longer are etched now . Enquires made in the local gem industry divulge that no one knows about the technology involved in etching. However, the observation made by Mackey along with N.G. Majumdar in 1930 is worth recalling here. Mackey who was fortunate enough to learn the process from an old man of Sehwan in middle Sindh, named Sahebdino. According to him, the artisan carefully macerated the tips of young shoots of a bush (*capparis aphylla Sindhi: Kirar*) in a glazed pottery bowl with the aid of a wooden stick with rounded end– This maceration was done with the aid of water until a thick pasty mass of olive-green colour was produced. Then he took fine powder of ordinary washing soda and mixed it with water. A small solution is poured on the *kirar* and rubbed on the whole carefully together to a semi-fluid mass. This is again strained through a piece of linen into a large empty mussel-shell and the paste was ready.

The carnelian beads to be etched are fixed in a setting made of clay mixed with cotton wool. This cotton wool prevents the clay from cracking in the process of drying. This setting is evidently intented to protect the bead as much as possible from contact. When the setting is dry, a design is made upon the exposed surface of the carnelian bead with a reed pen dipped in the paint. It is very difficult to see the painting at the time of execution but when the paint is dried it appears very distinctively. These painted pieces are placed on a piece of iron-sheet and laid on the embers of a charcoal fire until the design is perfectly dry. The beads are then buried in the embers and fire slowly fanned for about five minutes. The removed stone from the fire is taken from its clay setting and placed under a small cup to cool down gradually. After the cooling, the bead sparkels once it has been rubbed briskly with a rag.

The foregoing study clearly emphasises the fact that due to the availability of the large amount of semi-precious stones, this region has sustained this technology over a period of time and also played an important role in the development of lapidary industry.

Acknowledgement

I am grateful to the Nehru Trust for extending financial assistance to carry out my exploration in and around Kangayam.

BIBLIOGRAPHY

Arkell, A.J. 1936. "Cambay and the Bead Trade". *Antiquity*, 10(39): pp.292-305.

Biswas, A.K. 1994. "Vaiduriya, Marakata and Other Beryl Family Gem Minerals:Etymology and Traditions in Ancient India". *Indian Journal of History of Scince*, 29(2).

_______ 1994. "Non-Gem Minerals in Pre-modern India". *Indian Journal of History of Science*, 29(3): pp. 389-420.

Chakrabarti, D.K. 1978. "Lapis lazuli in Early India", *Man Environment*, 2: pp.51-58.

_______ 1982. "Long barrel-cylinder beads and the issue of pre-Sargonic contact between Harappan civilization and Mesopotamia" in G.L. Possehl(ed.) *Harappan Civilization— A Comparative perspective*. Oxford and IBH Publishing Company, New Delhi, pp. 265-270.

Gwinnett John, A. and Leonard Gorelick, 1981. "Beadmaking in Iran in the Early Bronze age". *Expedition*, 24(1): pp.10-23.

Habib, Muhammad(ed.)1937. *The Campaings of Alauddin Khilji:Khazaimul Futuh of Treasures of Victory of Hazrat Amir Khusrau*. D.B. Taraporewala and Sons, Bombay.

Kapadia, Karin. 1995. "The Profitability of Bonded Labour: The Gem-cutting Industry in Rural South India". *The Journal of Peasant studies*, 22 (3) : pp. 446-483.

Keene, Manuli. 1981. "The Lapidary Arts in Islam", *Expedition*, 24(1):pp.44-63.

Kenoyer, J.M., M.Bidale and K.K. Bhan. 1991. "contemporary stone bead making in Khambhat, India: patterns of craft specialization and organisation of production as refelected in the archaeological record". *World Archaelogy*, 23(1): pp.143-63.

Mackey, Ernest. 1933. "Decorated Carnelian Beads", *Man*, 33(150): pp.44-146.

Mahadevan, I. 1966. "Corpus of Tamil-Brahmi Insctiption". *Seminar on Inscriptions*, Book India Pvt. Ltd., Madras.

Possehl, L.Gregory. 1981. "Cambay Beadmaking", *Expedition*, 23(1): pp.39-47.

Rajan, K. 1990. "New Light on Megalithic Culture". *Man and Environment*, XV(1): pp.895-102.

_______ 1991. "Iron and Gemstone Industries as Revealed from Kodumanal Excavations". *Puratatva*, 20: pp.111-112.

_______ 1994. "Roman Coins in Coimbatore Region". in S.R. Rao (ed.) *Role of Universities and Research Institutes in Marine Archaeolory.* National Institute of Oceanography, Goa, pp. 117-180.

_______ 1994. *Archaelogy of Tamil Nadu*, Book India Publishing Company, Delhi.

_______ *Archaelogical Gazetter of Tamil Nadu,* Manoo Pathippakam, Thajavur (in press).

Ray Chaudhuri,Tapan and Irfan Habib. 1993. *The Cambridge Economic History of India*, Vol. 1, Cambridge University Press, Reprint Orient Longman Limited, New Delhi.

Roux, V., B.Bril and G.Dietrich. 1995. "Skills and learning difficulties in stone knapping: the case of stone-bead knapping in Khambhat, India". *World Archaelogy*, 27(1): pp.63-87.

Shastri, Ajay Mitra. 1969. *India as seen in the Brhatsamhita of Varahamihira*, Delhi.

Tosi, Maurizio and Marcello Piperno. 1973. "Lithic Technology behind the Ancient Lapis Lazuli Trade". *Expedition*, 16(1): pp. 15-23.

Valentine, B. 1879-80. "A Geologists Contribution to the History of Ancient India". *Journal of Royal Geological Society of Ireland*, V(111) (New series): pp. 215-263.

_______ 1881. *Manual of the Geology of India, Part III, Economic Geology*, Geological Survey Of India.

_______ (ed.). 1889. *Travels in India by Jean-Baptiste Tavernier*, Oriental Books Reprint Corporation, New Delhi.

Archaeological Remains and Further Prospects in Arunachal Pradesh

A.A. ASHRAF*

Arunachal Pradesh, the easternmost region of India lies within 26°28′ and 29°30′ North latitude and 91°30′ and 97°31′. East Longitude, encompassing an area of 83,743 sq km with a density of population of 10 persons per square kilometre (Fig 1). There are 29 major tribal groups belonging broadly to the Indo-Mongolold racial stock speaking Tibeto-Burman dialect sexcept the Khamtis, whose language and script belong to the Tai family. The largest tribal groups with more than 15,000 people are : the Adis (previously known as Abor), Nishis (Daflas), Apatani, Wancho, Monpa, Tansa, Indu-Misimi. In earlier days the people of Brahmaputra valley identified these tribes by various names and accordingly their territory was named as - Abor pahar, aka Dafla pahar and so on and also a few are named after the river of the locality, viz. Lohit (Lohitya), Kameng, Subansiri, Siang etc.

With the advent of British rule in India and till early post-independence period, the entire area had been named variously from time to time as an administrative unit, such as Balipara Frontier Tract, the Lakhimpur Frontier Tract, Tirap Frontier Tract, Sadiya Frontier Tract etc. In 1954, the area was consolidated and renamed as North Eastern Frontier Agency (NEFA).

Arunachal Prauesh adjoins the plains of Assam on the south and east and has a common frontier with Bhutan, Tibet, and China and Myanmar (Burma) in the north, north-west and north-east. Because of its strategic location, right from prehistoric past to till now it has been subjected to waves of cultural traditions and influence both from east, south east Asian parts and is the melting pot for various ethnocultural groups.

Archaeological investigations conducted so far in the densely forested area unravel the ancient past. Though meagre, they are important.

The tribal way of life in Arunachal Pradesh is a distant echo of the movement of people and idea in a most conservative way. The prehistory of Arunachal is a continuous process and its cultures polarise around the land; it was true till the begining of the 20th century. The tools and devices used for getting food were of nonlithic and nonmetallic and were made out of perishable materials like bamboo, wood or bone. This is evident from the unpublished reports of Noel Williamson (Political Officer, 1910) and C.R. Stonor (Agricultural Officer, 1945). In their reports Williamson observed that "if they (Nishis) wore anything formerly, it must have been the skins of wild animals as one can find no traces of weaving amongst them"; while Stonor in 1945, observed that in the *jhum* cultivation the Dafla (Nishis) relied on a bamboo hoe, and a bone hoe made from the shoulder blade of mithan (*bos frontalis*).

Department of Anthropology, Guwahati University, Guwahati.

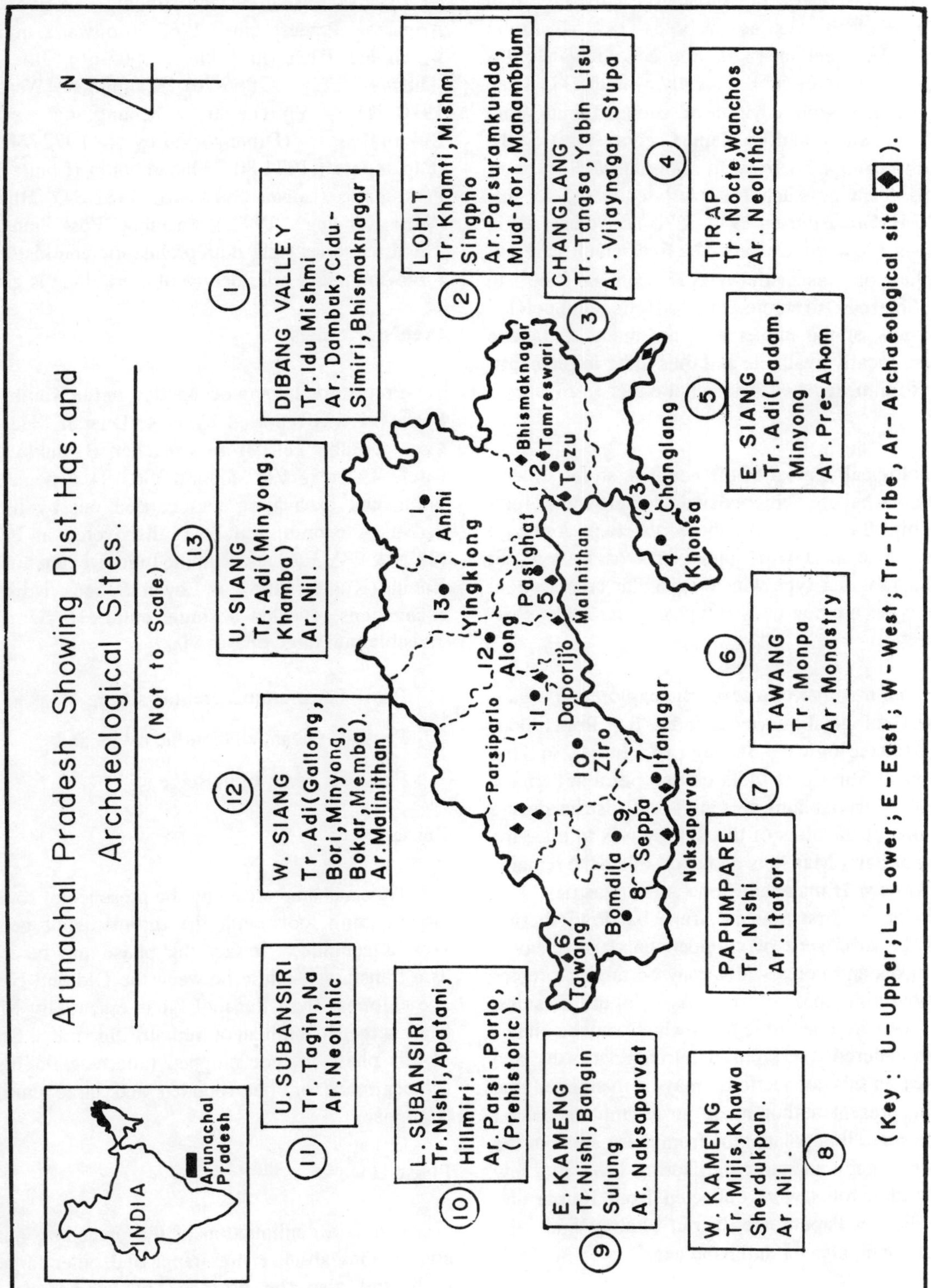
Arunachal Pradesh Showing Dist. Hqs. and Archaeological Sites.
(Not to Scale)
N
INDIA
Arunachal Pradesh
1 DIBANG VALLEY Tr. Idu Mishmi Ar. Dambak, Cidu-Simiri, Bhismaknagar
2 LOHIT Tr. Khamti, Mishmi Singpho Ar. Parsuramkunda, Mud-fort, Manambhum
3 CHANGLANG Tr. Tangsa, Yabin Lisu Ar. Vijaynagar Stupa
4 TIRAP Tr. Nocte, Wanchos Ar. Neolithic
5 E. SIANG Tr. Adi(Padam, Minyong Ar. Pre-Ahom
6 TAWANG Tr Monpa Ar. Monastry
7 PAPUMPARE Tr. Nishi Ar. Itafort
8 W. KAMENG Tr. Mijis, Khawa Sherdukpan. Ar. Nil.
9 E. KAMENG Tr. Nishi, Bangin Sulung Ar. Naksaparvat
10 L. SUBANSIRI Tr. Nishi, Apatani, Hillmiri. Ar. Parsi-Parlo, (Prehistoric).
11 U. SUBANSIRI Tr. Tagin, Na Ar. Neolithic
12 W. SIANG Tr. Adi(Gallong, Bori, Minyong, Bokar, Memba). Ar. Malinithan
13 U. SIANG Tr. Adi (Minyong, Khamba) Ar. Nil.
Anini
Yingkiong
Along
Pasighat
Malinithan
Bhismaknagar
Tamreswari
Tezu
Changlang
Khonsa
Daporijo
Parsiparlo
Ziro
Itanagar
Naksaparvat
Seppa
Bomdila
Tawang
(Key: U-Upper; L-Lower; E-East; W-West; Tr-Tribe, Ar-Archaeological site ◆).

The first discovery of Stone Age artifacts from Arunachal Pradesh was as early as 1871 by John Anderson. E.H. Steel in 1870, noticed a few neoliths made of jade (raw material not locally available) in Tirap district[1]. An axe with curvilinear rounded butt from Dibang valley was found by Capt. Gregory towards the end of 19th century. There is an important collection of stone tools from Arunachal Pradesh collected by J.P. Mills and J.H. Grace during 1933-35° is now preserved in the Pitt River Museum, Oxford. The first scientific report of this collection was made by A.H. Dani in 1960[2]. In 1966 T.C. Sharma also studied this collection and pointed out that a few of the implements are made on jadeite which is not locally available and thus these implements, according to him, reached Arunachal either from Burma or China[3].

Technologically, most of the neoliths, so far collected from Arunachal are : chipped and edge ground or fully ground tools. Typologically, there are two dominant types, viz. stone axes with lenticular crosssection and faceted quadrangular type with rectangular crosssection. The minor types are hog-backed type of celt slender chisel of jadeite[4].

As a team member of a scientific exploration organised by the Geological Survey of India, B.P. Boperdikar[6] of the Archaeological Survey of India of the Archaeological Survey of India carried out a systematic survey in the Daphabhum area of Lohit district during 1969-70. One of the aims of this survey was to trace the habitations of Early Man here and to co-relate the remains with the Western Himalayan Stone Age industries. This expedition for the first time in Arunachal Pradesh succeeded in the discovery of chopper, handaxe, cleaver, scrapers, flakes and cores which may be taken to represent the Paleolithic phase of Stone Age Culture. Besides, they also discovered neolithic tools which may be classified as: shouldered axes, chisels, triangular axes and splayed axes. In this connection it may be mentioned that in 1981 the present author made an attempt to collect information regarding palaeoliths from these area but the result was not much encouraging. During 1983-84 a few more paleolithic tools were collected from Kamla and Dikrong valley of Papumpare district as stray finds; the types are chopper, cleaver and hand axes[5].

Systematic exploration and excavations were initiated by the Research Department of Government of Arunachal Pradesh since 1965-66 onward, important of which are Paya (in Lohit : 1965-66), Bhismaknagar (Dibang Valley : 1966-70), Malinithan (West Siang : 1970-72), Vijaynagar (Changlang: 1970-71) Rukmininagar (Dibang Valley : 1972-74), Itafort (Papumpare : 1974-80), Manambhum (Lohit: 1981-82), Parsi parlo (Lower Subansiri: 1982-84), Bhalumpung (West Kameng : 1997-), Pasighat (East Siang: 1997-). The discoveries were both prehistoric and historic. In the following pages brief details of work done is given:

Prehistoric sites

Prehistoric human occupation in the Kamla valley of Subansiri was reported by D.K. Duarah[7]. He collected three neolithic celts from a teacher, B. Sukla of Damin Circle. Later, in 1982-83 and 1983-84 systematic exploration and excavation was carried out by the present author. A neolithic site was discovered at Parsi parlo (28°N & 93°33′ E), close to the Indo-Tibetan border in the Kamla (Kume) valley of Lower Subansiri district. The excavations revealed a single culture horizon (Fig. 2) divisible into three phases viz.

Phase-I Aceramic Neolithic stage,

Phase-II Ceramic Neolithic stage, and

Phase-III Ferro-lithic stage.

Phase I

This is characterised by the presence of scrapers and large cutting tools with the rudiments of pecked and ground techniques. In fact, this phase may be considered as a transitional phase between the Old and New Stone age cultures. Here the tool kit is essentially Mesolithic bearing the Hoabinhian or Sumatrilithic traits. Other tools of this phase include chipped (alternate flaking) round scraper made on flat rounded and large cutting tools (Chopper).

Phase II

This is a continuation of the preceding phase with conspicuous absence of scraper and other large cutting tools and also the presence of hand-made prottery stamped/cord-impressed ware). The tools in general provide hafting facilities and are mostly for agricultural use as indicated by the presence of constricted hoe blades.

Phase III

This is a continuation of the preceding phase but with the emergence of iron tools. It is not clear whether iron technology was a local innovation or had been brought in from somewhere else. A single piece of iron implement-probably a hoe-blade, along with a lump of raw material has been found and hence it is named as Ferro-lithic stage; the latter penetrated into the former (iron using stage).

The stone implements of this phase are : round butted pecked and ground celts made of serpentine rock and schist. Though no structural remains were found, open fire-places were often encountered. Pottery continued to be same in all respects as that of Phase II.

Raw material Stone Tool

No systematic study on lithic raw material-sources has ever been done in this region. However, most of the raw materials for tool-making were available locally as evidenced in the river sections and stream beds. One common features noticed right from Damin to the foothills region is that the knappers were preferring raw materials from stream beds and in most cases they efficiently exploited the material sandstone, schist, diorite and jadeite were the commonly used raw materials. Jadeite is said to be the only foreign material nearest source being in; northern Burma besides eastern China.

Living Archaeology

Archaeological materials in prehistoric context from Arunachal Pradesh consisting of pottery and stone artifacts bear similarity with that of the material reported from wider context, especially South-east Asia. At the moment stone artifacts do not exist in contemporary situation but a genetic link between the past and the present may be postulated taking present day's non-lithic objects into account. On the basis of material cultural evidence, an attempt has been made to understand the relation of the ethnic groups with that of the past; if there be any. In fact the archaeological problem of this province may better be understood if the existing ethnographical conditions are studied. Here the materials collected from the prehistoric site at Parsi Parlo will be used as basis to evaluate the origin and development of some of the well represented items of the present day tribal groups living in and around the archaeological sites. These localities are situated at an altitude around 1500 metre's near Indo-Tibetan border, some 200 km north-west of Ziro, the headeuartars of the Lower Subansiri district. The land in question as a whole is a humid, rain swept least vegetal with wild environment. It is a zone of difficult hilly terrain, linked up only with footpath or jungle tracks. The region is covered with dense sub-tropical evergreen forest which receives rainfall almost all the year round. In this hostile environment the cultures of both present and past remain encapsulated without showing major changes in the face of modern impact. The traditional way of life is still upheld to a great extent by the tribes of Arunachal Pradesh; among them the Nishis are numerically the most prominent and the dominent tribe of the locality.

The Nishis are basically agriculturalist supplementing their subsistence by gathering wild edibles and rearing semi-wild animal known as Mithun (*bos frontalis*) and also pig, dog and fowls. They are traditionally expert hunters and their mastery over bows, traps, snares and posioning is remarkable. Till recent past the Nishi-subsistence economy was solely based on *jhum* cultivation where paddy, maize and millet were principally cultivated. Without going into details a tentative relationship in agricultural operation carried out during the neolithic age and the present can be visualized from diagrams below :

The agricultural economy like that of the hunting too involves limited number of implements which include a hoe or a scraper *(lowdap)*, a digging stick *(Sangnik)* and a iron chopper (Auriow). The staple food of the people is rice but the production is insufficient and hardly lasts for three to four months. For rest of the period they have to depend upon other cereals, specially maize, millet and ofcourse *tase* (wild sago).

No culture develops from vacuum; it comes from the pre-exsisting ones. Over the time, changes are expected to occur, but technology works within a given ecological condition. The same thing happens the this area under study. Transition to metal from the lithic tools does not bring about any quantitive change in economy as tool types remain same. This is being supported by the currently used items that may be taken as replicas of prehistoric ones. Here the culture may chronologically be called modern; but when the technology related to the produc-

STAGE AND IMPLEMENTS USED

Stg. Jungle cutting, burning and clearing Imp. Aurlow (iron chopper)	Stg. Preparation of the field and sowing. Imp. Lowdap/tabup(scraper/hoe), Sangnik(digging stick).
Stg. Harvesting. Imp. Grains are pulled out of the stalk by hand.	Stg. Clearing of weeds. Imp. Lowdap

1 2
4 3

Fig. Contemporary Agriculture (Jhum)

Stg. Jungle cutting, burning and clearing. Imp. Aleng-ahey (stone axe)	Stg. Preparation of the field and sowing. Imp. Constricted stone blade. (necked/waisted) as lowdap, digging stick(?)
Stg. Harvesting. Imp. By hand.	Stg. Clearing of weeds. Imp. Constricted blade.

1 2
4 3

tion is taken into account it may well be placed in prehistoric state. We are not in a position to say precisely whether the people under study have any genetic link with that of Stone Age people; but the tribe has some elements strickingly common with that of prehistoric. A comparative analysis of the materials available from the past and present is discussed below; but most briefly.

Pottery from archaeological context

Pottery forms small part of the archaeological materials from Kamal valley. Except for fragmentary potsherds not a single complete pot was found. On the basis of colour, texture and surface treatment or decoration of the sherds the whole collection is divided into four classes viz.

Class A

1. Plain coarse ware
2. Cord-impressed coarse red ware
3. Ṣtamped coarse brown/red ware

Class B

4. Stamped (square grid) buff ware
5. Grooved coarse/fine buff ware

Class C

6. Plain brown ware

Class D

7. Plain coarse thick red ware.

Types 2 and 3 of class A in prehistoric context are found to be associated with the stone artifacts consisting of polished axe at Parsi Parlo. Typo-technologically this cultural assemblage is comparable with that of Late

Neolithic period of China[8]. Apart from Kamla valley, stamped coarse red ware has also been reported from the other parts of North-east India. In Daojali Hading (North Cacher Hills, Assam) it occurred as dull red stamped ware. In South-east Asia this type of pottery has been found in Kuei-chou, Lower Wushan gorge and Kao-wei-tzu in China. The lower Wushan gorge specimen is a replica of Parsi Parlo sherds. Pottery class A and B are also reported from Manchuria, Malay peninsula, Indo-China and Burma and probably it dominated the entire

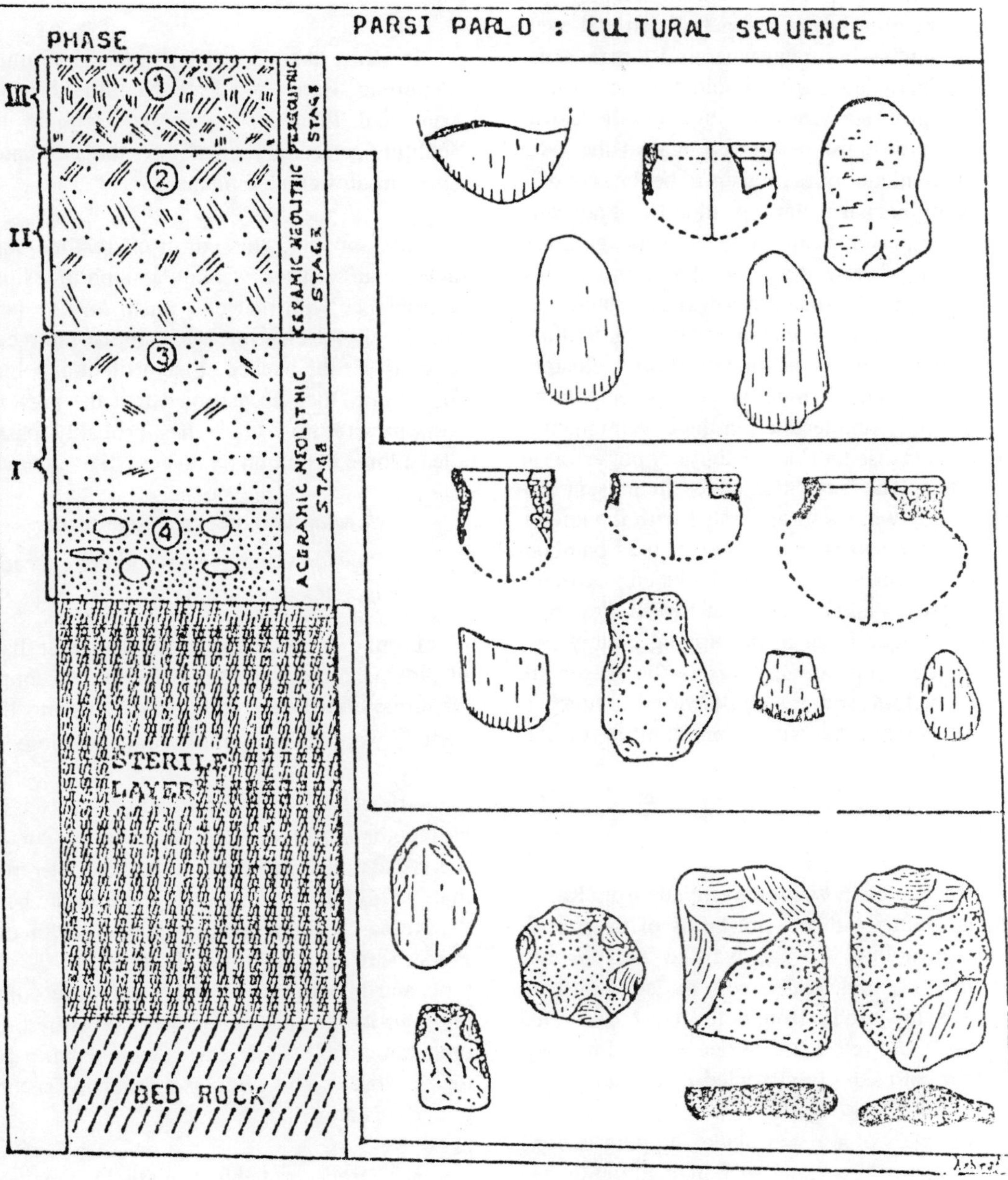

region during late Neolithic times.

Interestingly, the stamped coarse red ware in historical period is found among certain north-east Arunachal tribes. In this respect the Nishi *Takam pachang* (handmade earthen pot) may be considered for analysis.

To say something of pottery, it is imperative to give an idea of the situation where it exists. Each and every artifact has its own environment wherein it operates and the accumulated knowledge of technology which ensures its survival. The prolificacy or restriction and the distribution of pottery type must be viewed against the given environment. As a matter of fact this is to be thought of as to how the idea of this particular type of pot-making came into the mind of man some thousands of years ago. From geographical point of view, it appears that during prehistoric period it was more isolated and less accessible than it is today; but what is more amazing is that the tradition is still upheld by the Nishis, absolutely in its prehistoric form. In this connection it must be mentioned that the Nishis are apparently uninterested in the development of pottery industry because they never consider pottery as an indispensible item. The fact it that under the present ecological setting they were well aquianted with the knowledge of using other natural resources, such as bamboo-tubes, gourd sheel, plant leaves, tree barks etc. as a container. These easily available items at low energy input must have discouraged them in developing pottery as a fullfledged industry and perhaps this is the reason for which the production and development of pottery is extremely low among the tribal communities of this region.

Associated finds

Stone artifacts such as waisted axe/blade from Kamla valley is found along with the potsherds of Class A at Parsi parlo excavations. All the waisted axes or hoe blades are made on pebble flakes with retouches at both ends and notch at the middle from both sides (constricted waist blade (fig.) and retouched at one and and notched at the neck from both sides (constricted-neck blade (fig.)

In both the types of waisted blade chipping is done on the inner surface while the other remained untouched with its original pebble surface. These implements were definitely hafted and used as an agricultural implement.

Waisted axe has been found in Japan in several neolithic sites associated mostly with Yoyoi pottery type. In Siberia, the waisted blade has been found at Laddeiki, in Ynisei valley; in Manchuria at Fu-Shn, Fentien and in Jehol; in Formosa, at Koto-shoe; in Indo-China, at Bac Son and Malaya Peninsula at neolithic site of Ulu, Kalantan and Cina, from Yangtses at Wu-shan and Yun-yeng[10].

In East Asia, waisted aze is found in upper Paleolithic, Early and Late Neolithic periods. Here in Arunachal Pradesh it can be assigned to the Late Neolithic period as indicated by the associated finds and other circumstantial evidences.

Like pottery, the constricted stone-blade (necked rather than waisted) from Parsi parlo exhibits a close resemblance with that of a Nishi *lowdap* (scraper) used exclusively for clearing weeds in the jhum cultivation. If we consider the necked stone artifect as a blade for *lowdap,* it may then be assumed that the present-day Nishi *lowdap* with iron blade has probably passed through atleast three evolutionary stages, (fig.), namely-

1. *lowdap* with necked stone-blade.
2. *lowdap* of bamboo/wood/bone (scapula)From
3. *lowdap* with iron blade

From the available data it is apparent that the culture of Arunachal began right from the Paleolithic and the Neolithic and then gradually merged into the historical period by abruptly adopting iron technology[10].

Arunachal has its historical heritages as revealed the by records left by the Britishers and Indian scholars during pre and post-independent period. There is a lull after that. To fill this gaps vigorous attempts are being made by the Research Department of Government of Arunachal Pradesh. It resulted in the discovery of 21 sites (prehistoric and historical) of which some are continuation of previous works and some newly discovered. Between the prehistoric and historic stages there exists a gap protohistoric is absent. This remains a problem for the archaeologist of this area.

The earliest probable date of which material evidence is available goes back to the 10th century AD Legends of Parasurama, Bana, Bhaluka (grand son of Banasura),

Vidarbha, Rukmini, Sisupala, and Bhismaka are linked with historical ruins and places. These ruins are the testimony of the fact that how people and ideas migrated from one end of the country to the other and how it was assimilated in a new soil and environment to represent the Great Indian Culture in an integrated form.

The following is a brief of account of archaeological sites and monuments in Arunachal Pradesh.

Malinithan

Malinithan at the foothills of West Siang district is a very rich archaeological site. It is situated on a hillock, overlooking the plains and the river Brahamaputra. Numerous relics unearthed from the site have great historical value and significance.

The living temple of Malini is of recent origin but from the archaeological point of view what servives is the platform (pitha) with three components, unearthed at the site. The existing pitha is 2.44 m in height. The basement has five mouldings in Orrisan style. Numerous sculptures of Brahmical images, dvarpalas, dwarfs, yakashas, flying vidyadharas, various motifs like gajavyala, lion and pitcher kirtimukhas etc. were found. The existing pitha and other ruins indicate that "the temple had a shrine superimposed by curvilinear *sikhara* with square astylar *mandapa* presumably having a pyramidal roof of horizontal tiers".

Among the sculptures so far collected from Malinithan five specimens are regarded as masterpiece. They are Indra on his Airavata, standing Ganesa, Surya on chariot, Kartikaya on peacock, and the Nandi Bull. Except these five sculptures which are of granite, for all other purposes sandstone was used. It is not clear to what deity the original temple was dedicated.

The relics of Malinithan give definite evidence of contact between various peoples, of contributors, sculptors and masons who came to Arunachal and Assam from time to time from the neghbouring states. Malinithan serves as a symbol of cultural confluence.

Tamreswari

The roof of the temple was originally covered with copper sheets, and hence the name. In 1848, when Dalton visited the site, he found only the stone structure (plinth) without any roof. In 1956, Debla Mitra visited the site and according to her (IAR, 1956) the temple was originally chaturayatana i.e. having four shrines, built of sandstone and granite. The compound wall which is rectangular on plan was made of bricks about 1.25 m wide and 2.45 m high with a stone gateway on the eastern side. An inscription in Sanskrit and old Assamese script of 15th century A.D. was found inside the temple. It records the construction of a boundary wall around the temple of Dikkaravāsinī (Tamreswari) by Muktadharmanarayana, probably beloing to the Chutiya dynasty of Assam. The inscription dated Saka 1364 (A. D. 1442) was published by D.C. Sircar in the Journal of Ancient Indian History, vol. I, 1968 : [illegible]-21.

Very little information is available on Tamreswari temple located on the right bank of the Paya river and the Siva linga temple on its left (1 km apart) in the Dibang valley district.

Siva Linga

The Presence of a Siva temple on the bank of the river Paya in Dibang valley is represented by the remnants of two brick-built edifices. A linga was unearthed in 1966. Taken into consideration of shape and size of the bricks (40 × 38.10 × 8 cm) the temple can be ascribed to the 15th century.

The Buddhist monuments in Arunachal Pradesh are mostly confined to the westernmost part of the state inhabited by the Monpas and Sherdukpens. They are represented by a number of Mahayana monasteries, stupas and other structures under the cultural influence of Bhutan and Tibet. All these belonged to the 17th-18th century A.D. Of them, the most important are the Tawang Monastry and the Gorcham Choten; both built in 17th century A.D.

The Tawamg Gonpa is a large fortified complex covering an area of 135 square metres. There are 65 residential buildings, ten other structures, lanes and by lanes. The complex is enclosed by a compound wall. The institution is a store house of old scripts (mainly *kanjur tanjur*) and is rich in other records and antiquarian wealth.

The Buddhist chorten at Gorcham is said to be one of the largest of its kind in Asia. It is built of stone and mud plaster the monument needs to be studied in detail.

Vijayanagar Stupa

The Khamti and Singhpho area of Lohit and Tirap districts is the Hinayanan zone where the influence of Burma and Thailand is visible. In 1971 a *stupa* was excavated at Vijayanagar. It had an octagonal platform in relief designs with a companulated super structure. It was built during 18th century.

Forts and Settlement

Six forts and one fortified settlement datable between 10th and 16th centuries have been exposed. They are : Bhaluk pung (East Kameng), Bhismaknagar, Ruknini nagar (Dibang valley), Itafort (Papumpare). Mud fort, Manambhum (Lohit) and Naksaparvat (East Kameng).

The forts of Arunachal Pradesh may hardly be called a fort as compared to the contemporary strongholds in the rest of the country. But the have their own character and a class by themselves. These are actually strategic spots or hideouts intelligently fortified for defence purposes by exploiting the environment. Besides using stones, bricks and also mud in fortification, they often left open deep natural gorges etc which provide protection by them selves. All forts are situated along the foothills of Arunachal Pradesh and bear great significance as as they conform to textual stipulations found in the various Sanskrit texts on defence architecture, viz. *Vana Durga* (forest fort), *Giri Durga* (hill fort), *Ishtika Durga* (brick fort), *Panka Durga* (mud fort), etc. Here in Arunachal, it is interesting to note that a single fort often exhibits more than one feature. For instance, Bhismaknagar is a *vanadurga, panka durge* and also a *ishtika durga,* while the Naksaparvat is a *giridurga, vanadurga, inshtikadurga, siladurga,* and a *pankadurga* too.

Bhalukpung

The fort was situated at the foot of Aka hills in East Kameng district. Unfortunately no remains of this fort exists today. B.C. Allen[12] has mentioned that the fort was located on a hillock overlooking the Kameng river. Except for a portion where the hill slopes which served as a natural defene; other sides were surrounded by brick walls. The fort is ascribed to tenth-twelfth centuries AD but due to paucity of data it could not be confirmed.

Itafort

Itafort, where the capital of Arunachal Pradesh is now located is a monument of significance. There are many legends connected with the foundation of the fort. The fort was built on a vast area without any definite shape. Its brick ramparts are constructed to conform to the broken contour of the landscape. The western rampart runs for 1.40 km in length and has two gates; the eastern rampart is more than half a kilometre long with only one gate through it. The average thickness of the wall is 1.75 m and the original height could have been around 5 m, depending on the terrain. The briks are flat but are of varied size. The three gates of varying designs are built at strategic points. The eastern gate overlooks Doimukh in the Dikrong valley. It is mostly of stone masonry. The southern and western gates are largely brick-built. This fort could be assigned to the 14th-15th century AD

Bhismaknagar

Located 24 km east of Roing in Dibang valley the fort here is a flat land merging with the northern hills. Legend attributes this place to the mythical monarch Bhishmake Excavation at the site reveled relics of two gates and the plinth of a palace. The area enclosed by the ramprts is oval in shape and is about 10 sq km. An earthen rampart of 4.5 m high and 6 m wide runs for a about 5 km intermittently.

The main residential complex is now exists only in the form of a plinth built of bricks. Plinth area is 1860. 52 sq. m, having three halls, two extension rooms and six entrances altogether. The building faces east and is enclosed by a rectangular stone wall (287 m × 193 m) The floor is made of rammed earth.

The fortress has two magnificent brick-built gateways. Western gate is larger with two attached rooms, whereas the eastern gate has only one. Access through the gates is restricted by a curtains and left turn ensures entry.

Rukmininagar

Situated at the foot of Mishmi hills in the Dibang val-

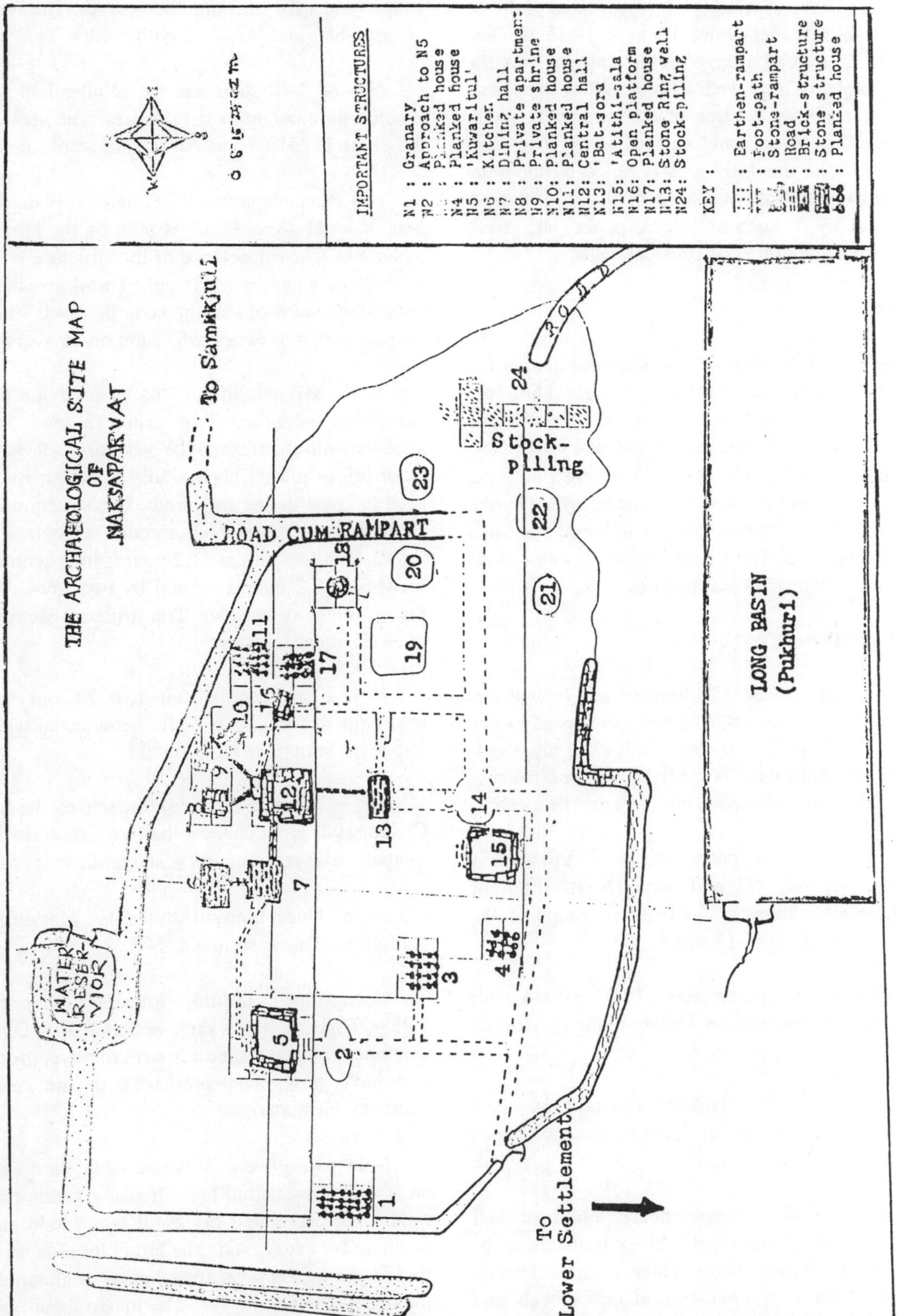
THE ARCHAEOLOGICAL SITE MAP OF NAKSAPARVAT
ROAD CUM RAMPART
Stock-piling
LONG BASIN (Pukhuri)
WATER RESERVIOR
To Lower Settlement
IMPORTANT STRUCTURES
N1 : Granary
N2 : Approach to N5
N4 : Planked house
N5 : 'Kuwaritul'
N6 : Kitchen
N7 : Dining hall
N8 : Private apartment
N9 : Private shrine
N10 : Planked house
N11 : Planked house
N12 : Central hall
N13 : 'Bat-jora
N15 : 'Atithi-sala
N16 : Open platform
N17 : Planked house
N18 : Stone Ring well
N24 : Stock-piling
KEY :
Earthen-rampart
Foot-path
Stone-rampart
Road
Brick-structure
Stone structure
Planked house

ley, excavations here during 1973-74 revealed ruins of two brick structures measuring 10 m × 10.25 m. The brick-built fort, covered a large area extending over the two Idu villages—Chidu and Chimri. After the great earthquake of 1950, the portion of the rampart at Chidu was completely destroyed and washed away. The remnants scattered over this hilly area is called by the local tribe-Indus-Rukmini Nati, meaning bricks of Rukmini. Archaeological finds, such as bricks, pottery etc. from this site are identical to that of Bhismaknagar.

Noksaparvat

Noksaparvat at the foot of east Kamen hills, on the left bank of the river Borgong belongs to the 15th-16th century A.D. Two settlements— one for the royals and the other for the common people are located at a higher terrace (T^8) and lower terrace (T^1) of the river Borgong respectively. The upper settlement is distinguished by the presence of a fortification and a large number of stone and brick structures-Fig. 3. The lower settlement exhibits no distinct planning and structural features.

The Upper Settlement

This covers an area of 2.76 hectares and is well fortified by ramparts and moats. The rampart is partly earth (620 m in length) and partly stone-built (380 m). Sandstone blocks and slabs were lavishly used in constructing the plinths of houses, footpaths, platform and ringwell.

Every archaeological spot within the fortification is identified by N1, N2, N3 and soon (N standing for Naks'a); there are altogether 24 features. Some of the important ones are described below :

N. 1. Granary : A rectangular (16.75 m × 6.9 m) wooden structure standing on twenty-eight cylindrical stone pillars.

N-3, 4, 10, 11 and 17 : Planked house built on raised platform, similar to Granary - N-1. Working space varies from 49 sq.m to 81 sq.m.

N-5 Kuwari tul (Ladies apartment) : plinth of well dressed stone blocks built on the block-on-block technique to a height of one metre. Three layers of stone-blocks are used for it. Short biconical iron dowels and straps were used in fixing the courses. The floor is made of brick-bats and plastered with mud.

N-6 & 7 Kitchen and the Dining hall: Brick-built plinth with a height of 0.45 metres. The area covered by the plinth is 231.05 and 201.4 sq.m respectively.

N-8 Private apartment : Square on plan, covering an area of 88.11 sq.m. Plinth is built on the block-on-block technique. The importance of the structure is manifested in its floor which is made out of well dressed thick and large stone slabs of varying size (0.70 × 0.70m to 1.40m × 88m) with a thickness of 18 cm on an average.

N-9 : Privite Shrine. The plan of the structure is somewhat peculiar. Two arms (alcove) have been attached with the rectangular structure. Atleast ten courses of bricks placed horizontally in two rows have been used in constructing the plinth. The structure is connected with the Central Hall through a footpath made of bricks. The footpath is 31.2 metres long with an average breadth of 2.2 metres, bound by two rows of vertically placed bricks in its sides. The structure occupies an area of 31.85 square metres.

N-12 : The Central Hall; It is 20.36m × 18.90m in area built like that of N-5. It is connected with all other important structures by footpaths.

N-13 : Bat-sora (Portico) Situated on the south of the Central Hall this connects the two structures by a stone footpath. The construction is same like that of N-6 and Z.

N-15 : Guest house : Athiti-sala : Measuring 14.60m × 14.40 m. This is similar to N-5.

N-16 : Open Platform : Stone structure of 8.40 m × 5.35 m. Construction is same as that of N-8. During fifties a number of stone sculptures were removed from this spot and have now been preserved in the Assam State Museum, Guwahati.

N-18 : Ring-well : It is one of the best examples of an archaeological find here. It is a gigantic ring well of sandstone blocks and bricks. It was found silted when taken up for excavation. The last cultural layer of deposition of the well is layer (6) which is contemporaneous to the occupation of the site. The materials unearthed from this layer include only seed and a few pieces of potsherds. The seeds are identified as *Rudraksha (Eloeccarpus janiarus)* and *Kanchan (Bauhinia spp.)* Interestingly, the inhabitants of Naksaparvat had shown interest in wearing this as a chaplet around the neck or upper arm by both male and female as shown in a number of human figures which has been engraved in low relief on some of the stone columns.

The inner circumference of the well from its top to bottom is the same, measuring 3.05 metres in diameter i.e. 9.57 metres on circumference. Fifteen courses of well dressed, perfectly curved stone blocks has ben found. The well was dug into a depth of 4.71 metres, which has been revetted by curved stone blocks in the form of a gridle of rings.

The Long Basin

Just below the Royal settlement there lies a large oblong basin *(pukhuri)*. The tank measures on an average some 262 metres in length (east-west) and some 38 metres wide (north-south) and perhaps 4.50 metres in depth. The tank is provided with two openings in its shorter arms. The most interesting feature of this basin is the presence of a soak-pit or sedimention tank (antechamber) attached near the mouth of the inlet to act as a filtering device for the inflowing muddy water.

Stone Sculpture

There are eight columns of fine grained sandstone, each of them bearing one to three engraved naturalistic figures, representing human, plants and animals (birds and reptile) on its facets. The figures are in relief, yet they are quite bold. They are somewhat crude but realistic in form representing a purely indigenous forms. Most of them are not proportionate—primitive,looking in its balance and elegant, or they are quite simple, lacking in many details they are quite appealing in their own way. The human figure reflects a sort of socio-cultural as well as religious life of the people. They were influenced by Tantric Buddhism. All the figures are depicted in action and mobility of expression. They bear tribal facial characteristics.

The Stone Inscriptions (!) (Markings/Symbols)

The dressed stones used in any structure of the site often bear some engraved symbols or markings. More than forty type of symbols have been detected at Naksaparvat, which represent geometric, non-geometric and pictographic forms. It may be mentioned that more or less similar symbols were also found at Malinithan, some 200 km east of Naksaparvat. While Malinithan is a temple complex and has been dated to 13th-14th century AD Naksaparvat is a residential complex and is dated to 15th-16th century AD. So, within a gap of 200 years or so, same type of symbols were found in a different types of structural complex, which needs further intensive study.

Conclusion

Archaeologically Arunachal Pradesh occupies an important and crucial position from the historical and cultural point of view. The inaccessibility is more or less geo-cultural in origin. But this area has its rich and vivid ethnic, archaeological, cultural and linguistic heritages. Such a rich heritage is a product of interaction among different ethnocultural traditions that took place over a period of time . The data that has come to to light are sporadic in nature and constitute a tiny part of the whole; hence it is not possible to give concrete idea of the sequence at the moment. Further work in future promises rewarding results.

Prehistoric archaeology of Arunachal Pradesh may be divided into—Paleolithic and Neolithic and in between there remains elements of Hoabinhian with the intrusion of neolithic element into the meagre metal using culture. This is important as it denotes its contact with iron using cultures. This also means the begining of metal-using culture is an intrusion in the neolithic economy and also exists till today. The very technology does not bring the economy of the indigenous population beyond its subsistence level excepting a few as is evident from the present ethnographic study. The population density remains extremely low and are distribute. A study of lithic tools reveals that during prehistoric past at this area there had a blending of both indigenous and Southe-east Asian elements.

Proto-historic tradition is absent. this needs confirmation and historical period succeeds. This is evident from the presence of historic sites that flourished along the foothills of Arunachal Pradesh, starting from *c.* 10th-12th centuries AD.

For material and economic necessity, the two traditions from the hills and another from Brahmaputra valley came closer to each other and the process of cultural exchange and infusion between them started taking place through the different contact points. Such contacts did not limit to the material or economic spheres only, it transcended the economic barrier and merged into social-religious spheres also; this is evident from the building of temples and forts bearing testimony to Indian tradition and this is reciprocal which is evident from the existence of animatic elements in stone sculptures discovered at Naksaparvat.

The historic tradition suffered a set back with the collapse of Indianthat imperialism developed in the floodplain of the Brahmaputra valley; the relation between the hills and the plains came to a halt.

This province has entered into a stage of rapid transformation from simple to complex with the development of communication networks that touches the interior areas as well. This opens up the chances of discovering more and more archaeological sites which remained so far unnoticed.

Acknowledgement

I owe a great debt of gratitude to Dr. Sankar Kr. Roy, Curator, Department of Anthropology, Gauhati University for going through the manuscript carefully and suggesting many changes.

REFERENCES

1. Dani, A.H. 1960 *Prehistory and Protohistory of Eastern India,* pp. 1 60-62.
2. Ibid.
3. Sharma, T.C. 1980. Prehistoric Archaeology in North Eastern India-A Review of Progress: *Eastern Himalaya:* 114-115, New Delhi.
4. Ibid.
5. Ashraf, A.A. 1990 : Prehistoric Arunachal, Directorate of Research, Itanagar.
6. Bopardikar, B.P. 1972. Prehistoric Investigations-Daphabhum Scientific Survey Expedition (NEFA). *Arch. Cong. & Seminar paper*, Nagpur Univ. : 1-8.
7. Duarah, D.K. 1979. Neolithic celts from Subansiri district, *Arunachal News,* August, Shillong.
8. Cheng Te-K'un 1967. *Archaeological Studies in Szechwan.* Camb. Univ. Press, New York.
9. Ibid. Pl 11.7.
10. Allen, B.C. 1905. Assam District Gazetteers, Darrang vol. V : pp. 67-68, Allahabad.
11. Raikar, Y.A. and Chaterjee, S. 1980. *Archaeology in Arunachal Pradesh,* Directorate of Research, Itanagar, p. 17.

Archaeology of the Settlements of The Kshatrapa Period

Atusha G. Irani*

Introduction

Present Gujarat is not only a compact unit geographically, but the settlements and material culture are also distinct from the other areas of India. Even within Gujarat, the three regions of Kutch, Saurashtra and east Gujarat show differences in topography, geology and natural resources. These differences are reflected in the settlement characteristics, material culture and the character of the inscriptions.

After surveying the inscriptional information from Gujarat, and the published and unpublished material on Gujarat; the sites of Saurashtra and east Gujarat had been documented and explored to a large extent. Therefore, Kutch was chosen as the area of fieldwork.

Aims

An attempt was made to provide a database for the early historical period in Gujarat. It has been called the Western Kshatrapa period because of the presence of numerous inscriptions of the Kardamaka, Kshatrapa rulers from Gujarat. The purpose of the study is to throw light on the character of the sites, settlement patterns and material culture of Gujarat during the Western Kshatrapa period; to draw attention to the differences in settlement character and material culture of Kutch, Saurashtra and east Gujarat; and to obtain a general idea about the life of the people Gujarat during the Western Kshatrapa-Kardamaka rule. This enables the researcher to highlight certain problems which need to be worked on.

History of Research

Literature, both published and unpublished, as well as fieldwork were used to study Gujarat. However, for Kutch, the major source of information was fieldwork. Fleeting references to early historic sites of Kutch were made by Joshi[1]. Other minor sources like Postans[2] and Thakkar[3] referred to place-names and cultural material. The material on Saurashtra was based on explorations carried out by Bhan[4] and Jairath[5] and sites documented in *Indian Archaeology : A Review* and Ghosh[6]. Inscriptional data was available from numerous journals mentioned in the course of this paper. Various excavation reports like Rao[7]; Mate and Ansari[8] Nanavati et al[9] were also used for Saurashtra. Numerous sites like Devnimori[10]; Vadnagar, Nagara, Shamalaji, Dhatva, Timbarva and Vadodara or Akota[11] and the relationship between east Gujarat and the western world has also been documented by Mehta[12], Momin[13] and the Panchmahals district by Sonawane[14].

*Flat No. 190, Sector A, A.W.H.O. Colony, Gunrock, Secunderabad-9.

Geography

Kutch is basically a sandstone region. The main agricultural area is the southern coastland. Nakhatrana taluka practices agriculture on a marginal level. Major portion of the region is rocky and extremely barren. The river courses are deep and have water only during the rainy season and are susceptable to flash floods. All the streams and rivers of Kutch are estuarine.[15]

Saurashtra has three geographical zones. The western end of the peninsula is cut off by the Okha Rann which in ancient times was a sea[16]. The Okhamandal peninsula located west of the Rann, is barren and is made up of limestone. The area from the Barda hills to the Gir hills contains black soil along its river banks, but like Kutch is dependent upon the monsoon for its rivers to flow. However, the Bhadar river contains water for the most part of the year. The fertility of the soil and agricultural

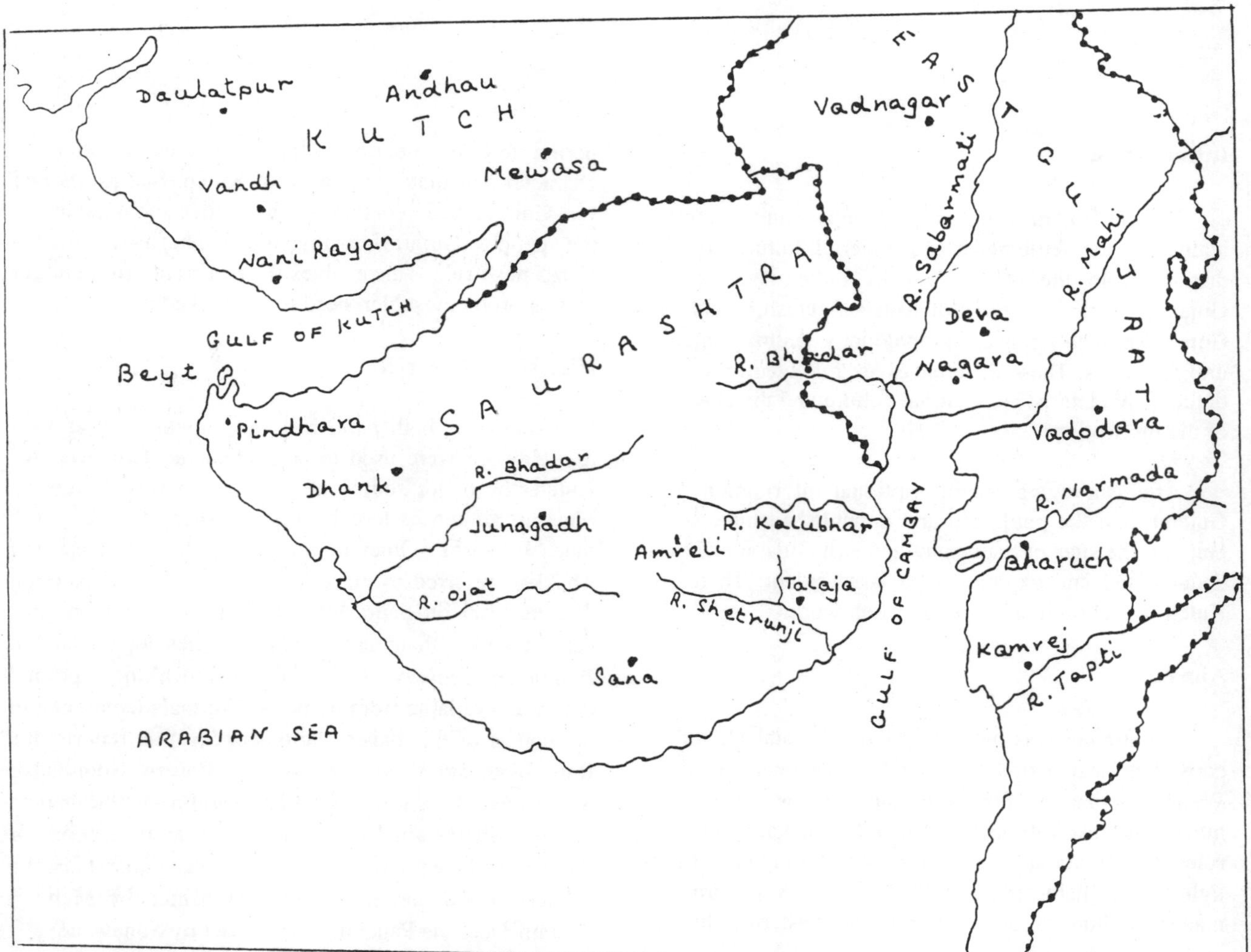

Fig.1. Gujarat showing the early Historic Inscription and sites.

intensity increases as we move east. The rivers of Saurashtra are fertile and provide sweet water in the middle course. The upper parts are rocky and the water is fast flowing. The lower courses of the rivers are salty and useless for agriculture. The area east of the Gir hills is sufficient in rainfall since it borders the Gulf of Cambay and east Gujarat. Both Kutch and Saurashtra have a radial system of drainage[17].

East Gujarat is a flat alluvial plain, rich in agriculture. However, its northern part forms the residues of the Aravalli range and is undulating. The rivers of north Gujarat, therefore, originate in the Aravallis and are dry for most part of the year. Agriculture is dependent upon irrigation. The rivers flow from north to south. South Gujarat is wetter and is dominated by the Narmada and Tapti rivers which are perennial. The rivers flow from east to west. Therefore, the direction of the slope of north Gujarat is different from that of south Gujarat[18].

Description

Of the 18 Kardamaka-Kshatrapa inscriptions found in Gujarat, 10 are in Kutch (Fig 1); 7 in the vicinity of Andhau. One inscription each was found in Daulatpur (Lakhpat taluka), Vandh (Mandvi Taluka) and Mevasa (Rapar taluka). The site of Andhau is located in barren surroundings. The size of site is 50 by 100 m. Black on Red ware, white and black on red were found from here. All the sites of Kutch exhibit these characteristics except for Nani Rayan. No other material besides pottery was recovered from these sites. Neither are the mounds visible. Since mounds are formed by the debris of accumulated habitation, sites of Kutch are therefore, considered to have been occupied by pastoral and semi-nomadic people. People on the move carry only the bare necessities and throw away very little. Hence the discard rate is low[19]. The site of Nani Rayan, located on the southern coast of Kutch opposite to island of Beyt, Jamnagar district, Saurashtra has been discussed in an earlier article[20]. No Red Polished Ware is available from Kutch. The Black on Red Ware found from each and every site in Kutch is also found in the Jamnagar district of Saurashtra (Fig 2). This pottery may have got into Saurashtra from Kutch *via* Nani Rayan and Beyt. Red Polished Ware is also found from the sites not only in Jamnagar district but also all over Saurashtra, albeit in small quantities. The material culture and settlement patterns of Saurashtra differ from area to area. However, in spite of this diversity there are some similarities, like the availability of Red Polished Ware and the rural character of the sites.

Saurashtra can be divided into three parts on the basis of material culture and settlement size. Because of its proximity to Kutch and the aridity of the land, the sites in Jamnagar district are small and rural. Some sites like Chachlona, Khakharda, Bharana, Godavari and Dhrafa are large in area measuring approximately 1 sq. km. These sites generally yield terracotta or stone sculpture. No amphorae was found. One of these sites needs to be excavated to know the character of these sites. The material culture consists mainly of pottery, terracotta discs and shell debitage. However, coins and amphorae sherds have been found from certain sites. This is an indication of trade, an activity practiced by non-urban centres as well. Except for bangle-making from shell there is no other manufacturing activity. Lots of discs without holes have been found from Saurashtra. These discs, according to Rhyd[21] were used to cover the hole in the *hukka,* a smoking device still use in most parts of India. A few stone discs are also found[22]. The speciality of the Saurashtra sites is the presence of decorated spouts and handles of pottery. These were fashioned in the form of animal and human heads, and have been found from Nagarabad (Haryana) and Sambhar (Rajasthan)[23].

The sites east of the Alech hills upto the Gir hills, and south of the Barda hills and north of Porbandar have been dubbed as Red Polished Ware sites[24]. No information about the associated material has been given. Nothing is known about the size of these sites. Based on their geographical situation these sites have been considered as agricultural sites. The sites north of Porbandar are located on salt flats. Perhaps these were salt producing. And pottery making sites. However, conclusive evidence is lacking. Kaolin is present in Babia Dungar and Jarderra Dhar located nearby. Until further information on the material culture and the size of site is available, the role of this area in the settlement patterns and functions cannot be postulated with certainty. However, a number of Kshatrapa coin hoards have been found from Junagadh and Rajkot districts[25]. Stray coins occur at Pindara and Dhrafa[26]. Amreli excavations have revealed a number of Kshatrapa coins of silver and base metal[27]. Near the site of Amreli, from Lathi a coin hoard has been found[28]. Therefore, this area seems to be an important trading area.

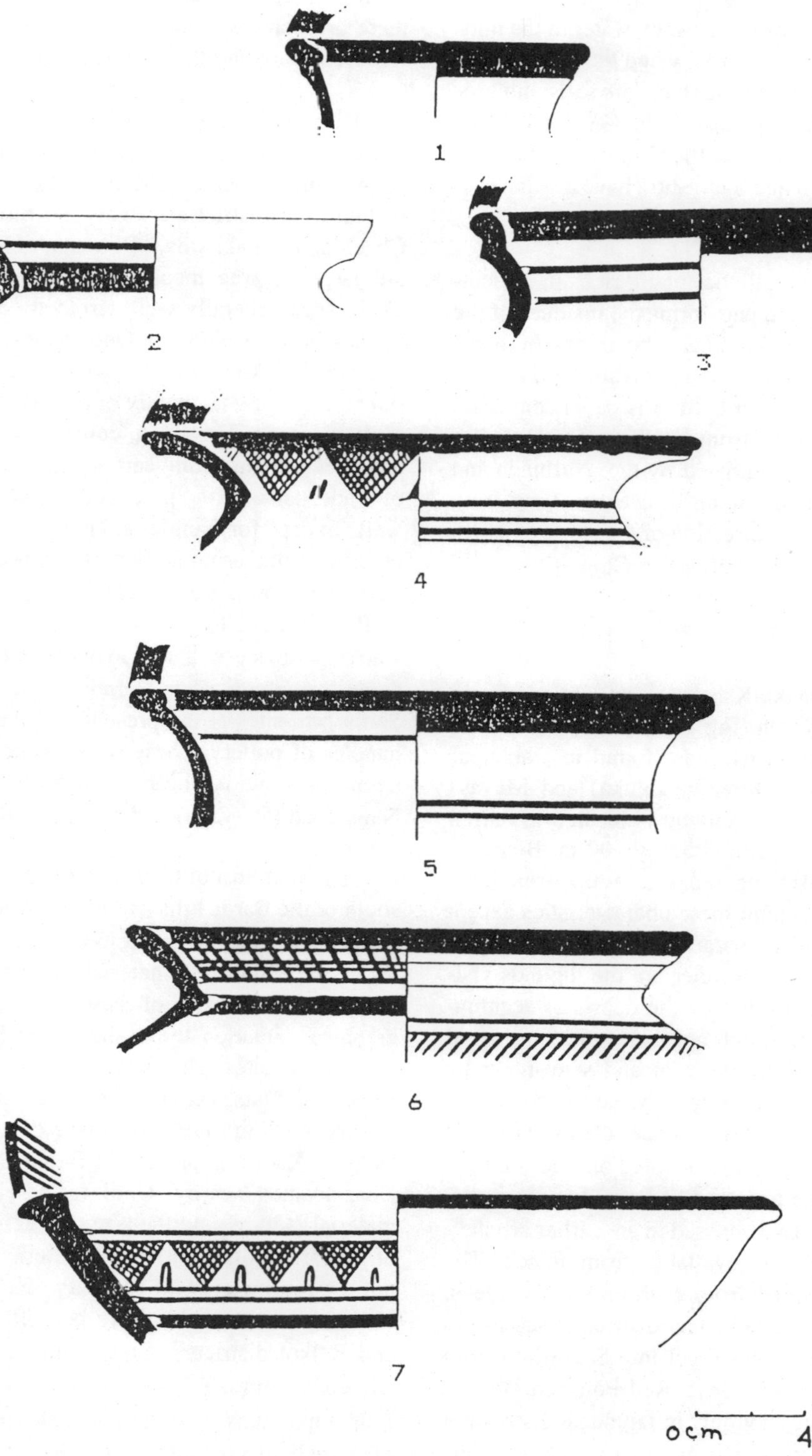

Fig.2. A Few shapes of Black on Red ware.

Small artifacts are however, absent in majority of the sites.

Buddhist caves of Dhank[29], Sana[30] and Talaja[31] have revealed Red Polished Ware (Fig 1). *Stupas* and monasteries have been found and some were excavated viz . Intwa monastery[32] and Boria *stupa*[33] located near Junagadh. A brick *stupa* was found at Harmatala, Junagadh district. Vestiges of structure from the Amreli excavation has also been identified as a monastery[34]. The importance of the Buddhist connection is highlighted by the number of caves near Junagadh and the Khambalida caves along the Bhadar river. In spite of all this there is no record of donations or land grants made either by the Kardamaka rulers to the monastic congregation or by the merchants who must have been present in the area. Nowhere in Gujarat has a record of donation to monastery in Gujarat ever been found. Therefore, Saurashtra must have been a prosperous zone of Gujarat during the Kshatrapa times. The site of Amreli marked the eastern end of this zone and Somnath on the south. Both these sites are located north and south of the Gir hills which is interesting.

The site of Somnath, unlike Amreli, does not have a substantial amount of early historical debris. Almost the entire site of Amreli pertains to early historical period. If the site of Bhavnagar to the east of the Gir hills and those inland yield amphorae then it may considered that to the flow of goods to Amreli was from Okhamandal (where amphorae sherds are found from the coastal sites) right across Saurashtra : Amreli is located on the cross roads of communication during Kshatrapa times. From here goods reached north to Bhavnagar district. The port of Hathab mentioned in the *Periplus*[35] as Astakapra, probably functioned as a trading post for southern Bhavnagar district which is dominated by the Shetrunji river. The north Bhavnagar coast line not only borders the Gulf of Cambay, but is also marshy. Therefore, trade may have been carried out from the west and south. Nagara is another port at the head of the Gulf of Cambay which served the north Gujarat sites and Rajasthan[36]. The northern Bhavnagar district explored by Jairath[37] show material culture similar to Saurashtra sites—remains of structures are found, but some pottery like micaceous ware, painted ware which are found from east Gujarat are available from these sites. The Bhavnagar sites unlike most other Saurashtra sites are large. On an average sites are 0.5 x 1 km.

In contrast the sites of east Gujarat, (Fig 1) the major sites like Bharuch, Vadodara, Nagara, Vadnagar were engaged in bangle manufacturing from shell or *chank,* making beads from precious stones, glass, paste and glass smelting. Trade was an important part of the economy of east Gujarat. Coin hoards have been found from Kamrej, Deva etc. Smaller sites like the larger ones reveal brick structures, coins, pottery etc.

The sites of east Gujarat when compared with the sites of the Deccan are poor as manufacturing centres. However, compared to the other areas of Gujarat, east Gujarat appears to be the meeting point of material culture and economy between the Deccan, north India, south India and the maritime Gujarat. Goods from all over the world as well as India were transported through Gujarat. There may not be any archaeological confirmation for this trade because here a was transit trade and in raw materials which were mainly perishable. Further, numistmatic evidences may be lacking since the coins are likely to be melted and remade into other coins. Though the people in the settlements of east Gujarat practiced crafts, each site specialised one craft only, except for Nagara which produced beads and practiced glass smelting. Therefore, east Gujarat was more urban than the other parts of Gujarat and was the transitional point between the Deccan and the rural areas of Saurashtra and Kutch.

Conclusion

The basic points that stand out after surveying the archaeological material of Gujarat are :

1. There is a geographical pattern to the pottery distribution of Gujarat, which is also reflected by the character of the settlements found in each area. As described earlier, Kutch and western Saurashtra reveal Black on Red ware. This ware is not available from the area east of the Alech hills. Saurashtra and east Gujarat form another separate enclave since they reveal Red Polished ware.

2. There is a relative paucity of small artifacts from the sites of Kutch and Saurashtra compared to the finds from the domains of the Satavahanas comprising the Deccan plateau and the east coast of India; the northern boundary was provided by the Godavari delta.

3. The three regions of Gujarat: Kutch, Saurashtra and east Gujarat had affinities and contact with different areas and also with each other. Since the majority of the Saurashtra sites are small and the meagre artifactual evidence lead to their description as rural. However, large areas of Saurashtra have not been explored thoroughly. As a result, a full picture of the settlement patterns of Saurashtra cannot be ascertained at this juncture. A study of the sites of Junagadh, Amreli and Rajkot districts are being made in terms of size, material culture, soil, hydrology etc. This applies to the southern areas of Bhavnagar district as well.

In fine, the three areas of Gujarat were within different spheres of influence. Kutch and western Saurashtra form one group; the connecting link being Black on Red ware found at Mardan, Montegomery, Lahore and Rawalpindi. A more detailed description of the sites from Sind is needed to know the connections between Kutch and Sind. From this it will be possible to gauge the depth of Sind's cultural and economic involvement with Kutch. Central Saurashtra needs to be explored thoroughly before an opinion can be formed. Eastern Saurashtra is within the sphere of influence of east Gujarat as revealed on the basis of pottery.

REFERENCE

1. Joshi, J.P. 1972. "Explorations In Kutch and Excavations at Surkotada", *Journal of Oriental Institute Baroda,* Vol 22; also 1990. *Excavations at Surkotada and Explorations in Kutch.* Memories of the Archaeological Survey of India. New Delhi, p. 98

2. Postans, (Mrs) 1839. *Cutch or Random Sketches of Western India.* Smith Elder and Co. London. p. 17.

3. Thakkar, D.P. 1877. *Report on the Architectural and Archaeological Remains in The Province of Kutch.* Archaeological Survey of Western India.

4. Bhan, K.K. 1983. Archaeological Explorations In Jamnagar District, Unpublished Ph. D. Thesis. M.S. University, Baroda.

5. Jairath, V.K. 1981. Archaeological Explorations in Bhavnagar District. Unpublished Ph.D. Thesis. M.S. University, Baroda.

6. Ghosh, A. (ed). 1989. *Encyclopaedia of Indian Archaeology,* Vol 2. Munshiram Manoharial Publishers, Delhi.

7. Rao, S.R. 1966. "Excavation at Amreli", *Museum and Picture Gallery Bulletin,* Baroda. Vol 18.

8. Mate, M.S. and Z.D. Ansari, 1966. *Excavation at Dwarka.* Deccan College. Pune.

9. Nanavati J.M., R.N. Mehta and S.N. Chowdhary 1971. *Excavation at Somnath or Prabhas Patan.* M.S. University. Baroda.

10. Mehta, R.N. and Chowdhary 1964. *Excavation at Devnimori,* M.S. University, Baroda; Mehta R.N. and A.D. Patel 1967. *Excavation at Shamalaji.* M.S. University, Baroda; Mehta R.N. D.R. (Smt) Shah 1968. *Excavation at Nagara.* M.S. Univesity, Baroda. Mehta R.N. and S.N. Chowdhary 1975. *Excavation at Dhatva.* M.S. University, Baroda.

11. Mehta, R.N. and B. Subbarao 1955. "Excavation at Vadnagar", *Journal of M.S. University.* Baroda.

12. Mehta, R.N. 1983. "Urban Centres of Western India and the Western World in Joachim Deppert (ed.). *India and the West.* Manohar. New Delhi. pp 139-147.

13. Momin, K.N. 1981. Archaeological Explorations in Kheda District. Unpublished Ph. D. Thesis. M.S. University, Baroda.

14. Sonawane, V.H. 1979. Archaeological Explorations In The Panchmahal District. Unpublished Ph. D. Thesis. M.S. University, Baroda.

15. Patel, G.D. 1971. Gujarat State Gazetteers. Kutch District. Ahmedabad.

16. Mehr, S.S. 1992. "Quarternary Sea Level Changes Along The Indian Coast", *Proceedings of the Indian National Science Academy,* Vol 58, A. No 5. P. 465.

17. Spate, H.K. and Learmoth 1972. *India, Pakistan and Ceylon.* Methuen and Co. London.

18. Deshpande 1991 India. A Regional Interpretation. North

Book Centre, New Delhi. pp 122-23.

19. Chang, C. and Koster, 1986. "Beyond Bones, Towards an Archaeology of pastoralism" in M. Schiffer (ed) 1986. *Advances In Archaeological Method and Theory.* Vol 9. 97-148. Academic Press, New York.

20. Bharucha, A. 1995. "Explorations In Kutch : A Prelimnary Study of the Material Culture of Kutch". *Bulletin of the Deccan College Research Institute.* Vol Deccan College, Pune 6.

21. Rhyd, Hanna. 1959. *Rangmahal. The Swedish Archaeological Expediton To India,* 1952-54, CWK Gleerup Publishers, Lund, Sweden.

22. Bhan. op. cit.

23. Agarwal, R.C. 1970. "Human Figurines on Pottery Handles From India and Allied Problems" *Museum and Picture Gallery Bulletin,* Baroda.

24. Ghosh op. cit.

25. Jha, Amiteshwar and D. Rajgor 1994. *Studies in The Coinage of the Western Kshatrapas,* Indian Institute of Research in Numismatic Studies, Anganeri, Nasik District.

26. Bhan op cit.

27. Rao. op. cit.

28. Jha. et al op cit.

29. *IAR 1964-65.* p. 73

30. Mehta and Subbarao, op cit

31. IAR *1964-65* p. 73

32. Chhabra, B. Ch. 1949. "Intwa Clay Sealing", *Epigraphia Indica,* Vol 28.

33. Cousens, H. 1891. "Bora Stupa of Junagadh", *Journal of Royal Asiatic Society of Bengal,* Vol 60.

34. Rao. op cit.

35. Schoff, W.H. 1912. *Periplus of the Erythrean Sea.* Longman Green and Co. London.

36. Mehta 1983. op cit.

37. Jairath, op cit.

Acknowledgement

Special thanks are due to my mother for drawing the map and for her suggestions on the article.

Underwater Exploration off Poompuhar and possible causes of its Submergence

ANIRUDDH SINGH GAUR AND SUNDARESH**

Introduction

Poompuhar also known as Kaverippattinam, one of the most notable ancient Chola ports played a vital role in the maritime history of Tamil Nadu, especially during the Sangam period. It is located at the confluence of river Kaveri with the Bay of Bengal. Sangam period texts such as *Pattinappalai, Ahananaru* and the two epics *Silappaikaram* and *Manimekhalai* vividly describe Poompuhar as the capital port-city of the early Cholas.

Manimekhalai mentions that the Chola king had lost his son and in his great grief he forgot to celebrate the annual Indra festival. This enraged the goddess Manimekhalai who caused the city to be swallowed up by the sea. Though the reference is only to a supernatural incident, it may be taken as an echo of some actual sea erosion of high tidal wave that lashed out on the city.

Previous work

Surface exploration at Kilaiyur, a part of Kaverippattinam, in the years prior to 1963 had yielded square copper coins with tiger emblem which was the royal crest of the early Cholas. Other finds include beads of semi-precious stones and amphora pieces. The most significant discovery was an 'I'-shaped brick structure, exposed in the ancient channel of Kaveri at Kilaiyur which is now completely silted. This brick structure with a drain for the flow of water and platform and wooden posts for handling cargo, served as wharf[1]. The joint offshore exploration in 1981 by the Department of Archaeology, Tamil Nadu and National Institute of Oceanography, Goa revealed some conspicuous features[2] off Poompuhar. They could not be identified as no underwater exploration followed immediately.

Since 1989 underwater explorations have been carried out in Tranquebar-Poompuhar waters[3]. The successive investigations in the inter-tidal zone as well as offshore region in 5 to 8 m water depth revealed a number of ring-wells and brick structures in the inter-tidal zone and submerged stone structures along with early historical pottery in shallow waters and two other objects in deeper waters[4]. On of them was identified as a shipwreck which was carrying lead ingots dated AD 1791-92[5].

Description of the area of Survey

Poompuhar in Nagai district of Tamil Nadu state (11^0 08′ 33″ N and 79^0 51′ 31″ E.) is situated on the east cost of India (Fig. 1). The onshore and offshore exploration area extended from Vanagiri to Nayakkankuppam, about 7 km along the coast and about 5 km in the sea. Two rivers namely Kaveri, south of Poompuhar and Palayar, north of Poompuhar join the sea here. Apart from these rivers a few nullahs join the sea on the north of Poompuhar.

*National Institute of Oceanography, Dona Paula, GOA.
**Paper presented at the Annual Conference Archaeological Society 403 004.

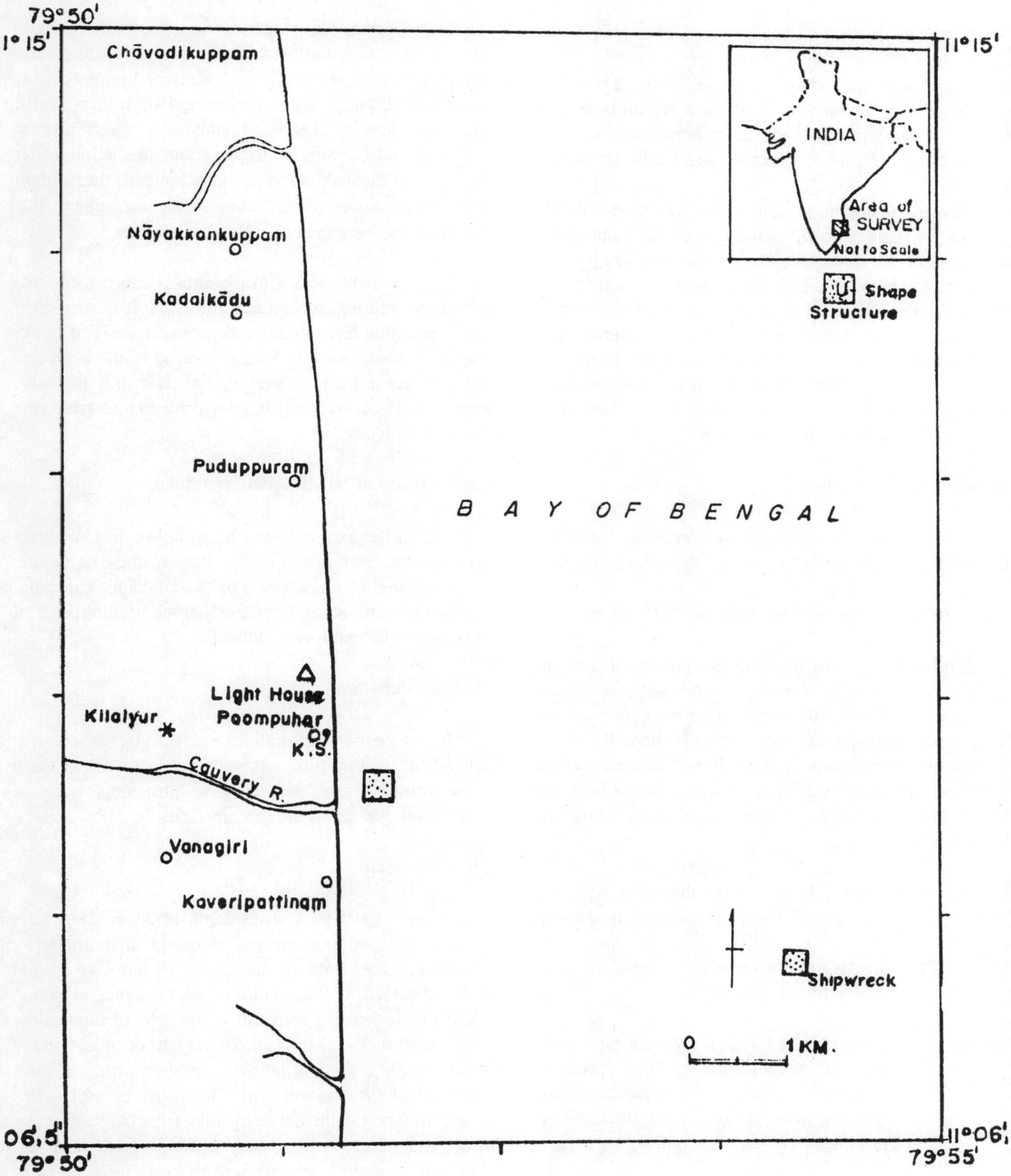

Fig.1. Location Map showing the Survey Area.

Methodology

Four places were identified for geophysical survey as also for diving. These are : 1. Shallow region between 6 to 10 m water depth; 2. Water depth between 11 to 15 m; 3. The area of U-shaped structure; and 4. Shipwreck site.

The diving operations initiated at the located site was gradually extended to the adjoining areas. Each diving team roughly covered an area of about 50 m radius in a circular search pattern. Two places were selected for diving in shallow water where depth varied from 5 to 8 m. Subsequently airlifting work was also undertaken to expose objects buried in sediments. In deeper waters three places, namely a shipwreck, horse-shoe shaped structure and two small structures in 19 m and 23 m water depth respectively were selected for diving.

Results and Discussions

Underwater explorations were carried at 3 different places (fig. 1). These are divided on the basis of depth.

Near the shore area– Water depth– 6 to 10 m

Explorations were undertaken opposite the Kaveri mouth about 600 m offshore. A few dressed-stone blocks were located. One of them measured 90 x 40 x 15 cm. This is semi-circular in shape with a L-shape cut on it's surface. Apart from this there are lots of irregular blocks. All these are sandstone. The area is covered with fine black sand. Airlift operations in this area resulted the following stratigraphy :

Layer (1) is about 10-20 cm in thickness with fine black sand. A few marine organism are seen.

Layer (2) consists of sticky black clay which is about 20-30 cm in thickness.

Layer (3) a very compact yellow clay appears in this layer with a few potsherds. The thickness of this layer is 15-20 cm. A few patches of this types clay also appear of in intertidal zone of Poompuhar and in the neighbouring areas.

Layer (4) White coarse sand with stone-blocks a few potsherds appear in this layer.

This suggests that stone was also used for construction but whether it was used for habitational or other kind of building is still not confirmed. Sangam literature mentions that buildings were constructed of bricks. Airlift operation suggests that habitational site was buried at least 1 m under sediment. Explorations in shallow water also suggest that habitation extended towards the north of present Kaveri river. The ceramic evidences suggest that the habitation belonged to early Christian era.[6]

Up to a depth of 8-9 m the area is much more disturbed by high waves, currents and tides. It is very difficult to presume that some structures particularly of bricks that were mostly used in Sangam period would have survived in tact in the high energy zone. It is only the stone structures which are likely to give a clue to understand the shape of structure.

Explorations at 'U'-Shaped Structure

The earlier explorations carried out in deeper waters revealed the presence of 'U'– shaped stone structure, located at about 5 km seaward off Kadaikkadu. The structure lies in north-south direction. On the northern side of the object an opening was noticed.

Diving operations

An extensive exploration and documentation was carried out at this place. In previous exploration three stone strutures were located. The structures lying in north-south directions are described below :

Bigger Structure

It was located at a water depth of 23 m. Side Scan Sonar records suggest an oval shape for this structure[7]. The maximum length of this object is about 40 m and width about 20 m. The centre of the structure, which is about 1 m deep, is covered with a thin layer of sand below which hard rock was noticed. The height of object on the outer edge is 3 m. The height of eastern arm is greater than that of the western arm. The width of arm varies from 3 to 6 m. On the northern side of the object an open space was noticed, where some rubble was found. A section of the structure was exposed by chiselling and hammering which suggest that a heavy growth of barnacles above the structure. The section is highly porous. At a few places two/three courses were noticed. Airlifting near this structure suggest a huge coarse sand deposition at least up to 2 m.

Smaller structures :

These are lying about 40 m north of bigger structure. These two objects are lying in east-west direction. These structures are heavily disturbed and broken in several pieces. The distance between two objects is 10-12 m. They are covered with the fishing nets. Presently, extensive fishing is taking place here. A few blocks are approximately 2 m in length 1.5 m in breadth and 1 m in height.

Shipwreck–Water depth–, 19 m

Shipwreck was relocated and an extensive airlifting and diving was carried out at this place. A cannon measuring 2.1 m in length was noticed. Five gun-powder boxes were also found. A 5 cm thick barnacles growth was noticed on these objects. Cannon seems to be of iron and is fixed on an iron platform which makes difficult to lift. A large area of surface of wreck was exposed by airlifting near the cannon area. Wooden planks with copper nails were noticed. Airlifting up to a depth of 1 m suggests that ship was mainly made of wood. Surface wooden planks were affected by wood borer while lower planks were in tact. While airlifting three square holes were also noticed. eight lead ingots were retrieved. A new type of ingot was noticed. Now a total five varieties of ingots have been recognised.

(1) Long oval boat-shaped with inscription 'W : BLACKETT' and bearing date 1792 on reverse and symbol of VOC;

(2) Oval-shaped but flat with the same inscription as above;

(3) Long oval-shaped with a crown symbol and below that the alphabet 'D' and the same symbol in smaller size in the reverse side;

(4) Rectangular in shape, without inscription or symbol in obverse while in reverse VOC symbol is seen; and

(5) Long oval boat-shaped without any inscription or symbol on obverse. One of the ingots of this type has a heart symbol on reverse.

Coastal Erosion

The explorations at Poompuhar and Tranquebar clearly demonstrate that sea has gradually encroached the land to a greater extent since the last 2000 years.

It is worth mentioning here that in 1973 the Kannagi statue was installed on the shore of Poompuhar about 200 m away from the high water line, and in 1994 it was shifted about 150 m inward because the structure was destroyed by the sea. Similarly, other monuments at Poompuhar were also destroyed by the sea.

A mid-17th century map of Tranquebar has been displayed in the Dansborg Museum at Tranquebar. It shows a complete plan of the town along with the then shoreline (Fig. 2). A careful study of the map suggests: i. that Tranquebar town was well protected by a seaward fort wall, and ii. the Siva temple was sufficiently landward within the fort wall. It is estimated that during the 17th century AD shoreline was at least 50 m away from the fort wall and temple located around 250-300 m from the shoreline. This observation unequivocally suggests that the shoreline has transgressed about 300 m in the last 300 years infringing at an average rate of one metre per year.

Another example of coastal erosion may be mentioned here at North sea, where a 12th century city called Dunwick[8] got submerged in the sea and the deepest point of finding is 16 m about 1.5 km from the shore. Study of map revealed that between 1702 to 1754 about 160 m shoreline had advanced while between 1754 to 1973 it was about 120 m. So there was no constant rate of erosion.

Factors responsible for the land erosion may include the construction of several dams along the course of river Kaveri since AD 1900 for irrigation and hydroelectric power generation. The rivers discharge significant amount of land-derived detritus to the sea thus maintaining a dynamic balance between the coast line and sea. The influx of sediment to the sea by Kaveri has been reduced to negligible amount due to the construction of several dams resulting in a disturbed natural balance. This human induced disturbance appears to have withdrawn the natur-

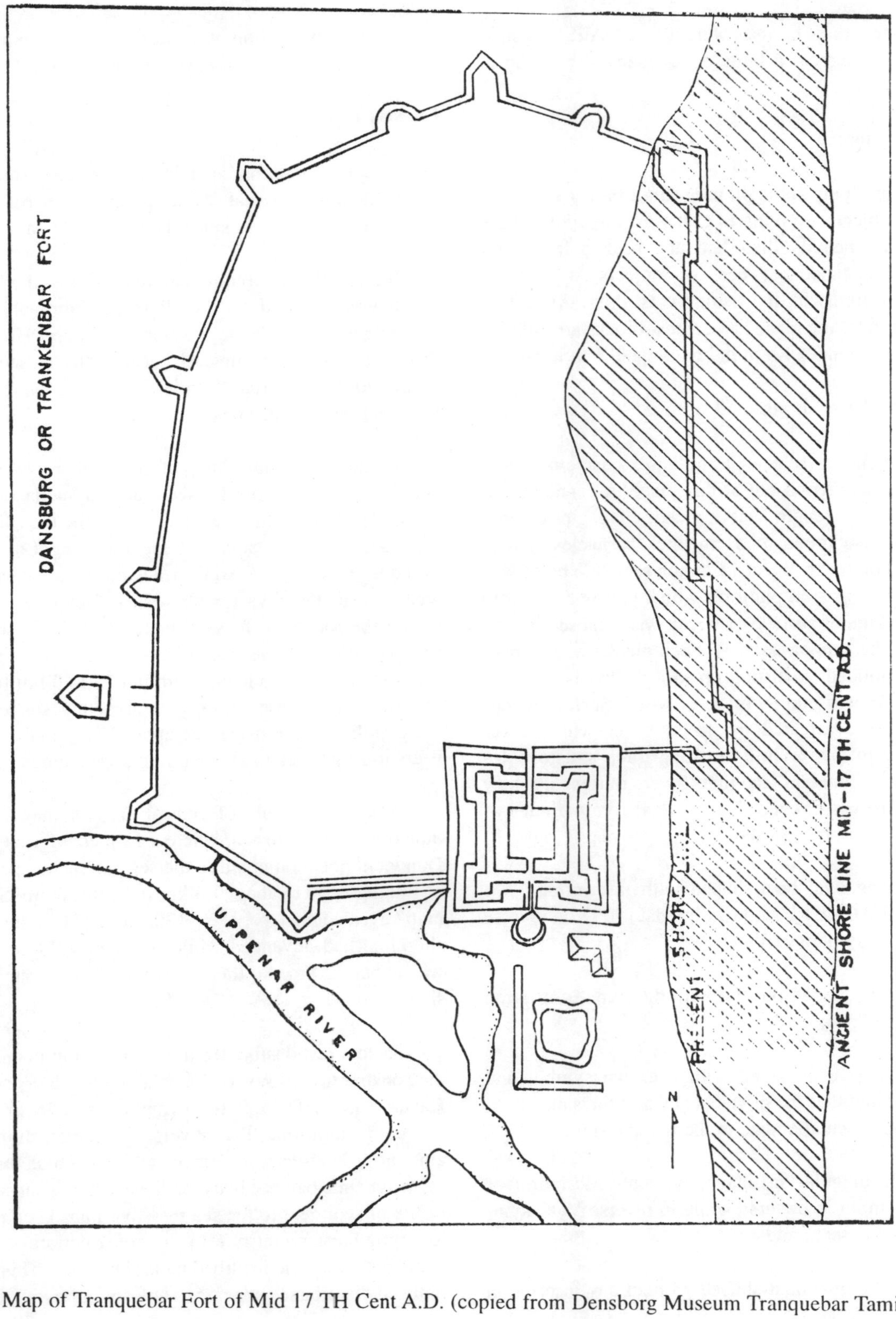

Fig.2. Map of Tranquebar Fort of Mid 17 TH Cent A.D. (copied from Densborg Museum Tranquebar Tamilnadu).

al resistance to the waves. Subsequently, the sea began to erode the coastline leading to the submergence of several ancient coastal structures of Poompuhar.

While the immediate cause of coastal erosion is the removal of sand from the beaches that results in destabilization and destruction of coastal structures, the ultimate causes need to be addressed.

The Bay of Bengal, whose western boundary is formed by the east coast of India, is a rather unusual sea. The Bay of Bengal is subjected to a large number of high intensity cyclones as compared to the Arabian sea. Cyclones, are short-lived phenomena capable of causing immense destruction when they cross the sea and hit the coastline. The destruction power of cyclones at present and in the past along the coast of Madras, Andhra, Orissa and Bangladesh is sufficiently well documented in horrifying details.

The next geological peculiarity that can contribute to the coastal erosion is the narrowness of the eastern continental shelf[9]. This shelf is mostly less than 50 km in width, in contrast to the western shelf which is a few hundred kilometres wide. Wave propagation over a narrow shelf results in low frictional loss of energy and thus expends much of the energy on the coastline causing a great degree of coastal erosion.

Besides these factors is the net rise in global sea level. Recent evidences from the west coast of India[10] and from widely scattered regions such as Florida[11] in the Atlantic indicate episodic and rapid rise and fall of the sea level. The rates reported are about a metre per century over a time period of 500 to 1000 years. These findings have now dispelled the notion that sea level is a stable and unchanging datum. The inference drawn from the above is that during a period of rising sea level the zone of erosion shifts land ward (submergence), and during a fall in sea level, the zone of erosion shifts sea ward, resulting in seaward progradation of land. An example of this is the location of ancient ports at Korkai and Algankulam on south Tamil Nadu coast far inland but which were patently designed and located to be on the shoreline.

Conclusions

Ceramic evidences along with these structure suggest that they belong to the Sangam period. Explorations also confirm that habitation extended further north of river Kaveri. There is a serious problem of coastal erosion at least between river Palayar on the north to Tranquebar on south. This is confirmed by the presence of several brick structures, ring-wells of historical period in intertidal zone and 10th-11th century stone and brick temples in coastal area. The study of mid-17th century map in the Tranquebar Museum suggests that about 300 m advancement of shoreline occurred in 350 years with an average of little less than a metre per year. If the same rate continued in the past 2000 years in this area then one should not be surprised that the ancient city of Poompuhar extended far in the present off sea.

Acknowledgements

The authors are thankful to the Director, National Institute of Oceanography, Goa for permission to present the paper at the Annual Conference of the Indian Archaeological Society. They are also thankful to Shri. K.H. Vora Scientist-in-Charge, Marine Archaeology Centre of NIO for his suggestions. Thanks are also due to my colleagues in the Marine Archaeology Centre for their active cooperation in field trips to Poompuhar. Thanks are also due to S.B. Chitari and Bandodker for their assistance in preparing drawings and photographs.

REFERENCE

1. Rao, S.R.1965. "Excavations at Kaveripattinam. *Transactions of the Archaeological Society of South India* Madras. —and Raman, K.V. 1968. "Excavations at Pumpuhar". *A Handbook of II International Tamil Conference,* Madras.
2. Vora, K.H. 1987. "A note on the geophysical explorations for marine archaeology of Tamilnadu coast, India." *International Journal of Nautical Archaeology,* 16, pt 1.
3. —— 1993 Marine Archaeological Explorations Off

Poompuhar, Goa, *National Institute of Oceanography,* Technical Report, No. SP/13/1993. Gaur, A.S. 1997. Ceramic Industries of Poompuhar S.R Rao, : *An Integrated Approach to Marine Archaeology* National Institute of Oceanography, Goa pp. 127-132. Gaur, A.S. and Sundaresh, 1997 and *Marine Archaeological Explorations off Poompuhar, Tamilnadu.* Goa :, National Institute of Oceanography, Technical Report no. SP/13/1997. Gaur, A.S., Sundaresh, M. Saxena, S. Tripati, and P. Gudigar, 1997. A Preliminary Observation on an 18th Century Wreck at Poompuhar, East Coast of India'. *International Journal of Nautical Archaeology*, 26.3:118-26

4. Rao, S.R., T.C.S. Rao, A.S. Gaur, Sila Tripati, Sundaresh and P. Gudigar. 1995-96. "Underwater Explorations off Poompuhar-1993. *Journal of Marine Archaeology,* Vol. 5-6 (1995-1996) NIO, Goa. pp. 7-22". Tripati, S., A.S. Gaur, Sundaresh and P. Gudigar, 1996. "Marine Archaeological Explorations in the Kaveripoompattinam Region : Fresh Light on the Structural Remains". *Man and Environment* XXI (1) : 86-90.

5. Gaur et. al 1997 *op. cit.*

6. Ibid.

7. Rao, T.C.S. and Mohan Rao 1991. "Geophysical and Magnetic Survey for Marine Archaeological explorations off Tranquebar (Tamil Nadu)" in *Recent Advances in Marine Archaeology,* Goa National Institute of Oceanography, pp. 127-129.

8. Bucon, S.R 1978. "Ancient Dunwick, Suffolk's City" in J.C. Gamble and R.A. (-elb) Yorke *Progress in Underwater Science* in London Plymouth.

9. Sundaresh, A.S. Gaur, and R.R. Nair, 1997. "Our Threatened Archaeological Heritage : A Case Study from Tamil Nadu Coast". *Current Science* 73.7:193-97.

10. Nair, R.R., N.H. Hashimi, R. Nigam, M.C. Pathak, K.L. Kotnala, 1997. "Rapid Submergence During Historic Times Evidence from Submerged Wall of Vijaydurg Fort". (Abstract) Presented at the First International Conference on Marine Archaeology of Indian Ocean Countries held at Chennai, 21-22 February, 1997.

11. Locker, S.D., A.C. Hine, L.P. Tedesco, and E.A. Shinn. 1996. "Magnitude and timing of episodic sea-level rise during the last deglaciation." *Geology,* 24.9:827-30.

Construction and Structure of Step-wells

PRABHUBHAI K. PATEL

Introduction

Water has always been one of the most important elements in shaping the human civilization and human settlements. Planning of water reservoirs came into being with the stablization of human settlement. Water resourse development was needed not only because there were some dry months in a year but also because of occurrence of floods and draughts. In hot arid zones the need to economise the use of water is a must. Human effort took several directions in this field depending on local conditions and technology available. Step-well *(Vapi)* is one such endeavour in Gujarat.

A step-well is a structure which allows one to descend upto the water's edge in a well. The descent is through stepped and inclined shaft, the bottom end of which touches an ordinary well. This type of approach allows one the use of water directly and without much effort. The gradual inclination of the approach reduces the strain of water-fetching as against a straight or spiral-stairs descent. The inclined shaft allows light from the top to every step and landing.

The openings in the shaft also help to keep the step-well dry and clean. The ingenuity of constructing galleries to balance the side thrust from deep walls is a masterpiece of function and structure. The galleries cover the landing at their lowest level and at intermittent levels they provide numerous places for rest, work and worship.

The step-well serves several functions of life with easily accessible drinking water even at a low water-table area, water for irrigation fields from the adjoining but interconnected draw-well, a place to bathe, clean and worship near the water on landing platforms etc. No wonder it became an act of charity to construct a step-well near a village or on the highway.

Structure

Construction of water-reservoirs in Gujarat region have to overcome certain basic problems, viz., high rate of evaporation due to arid climate; low water-table in summer; negligible development of cementing materials; high permeation of water in soil (porous); and unfavourable soil conditions (black cotton soils, sandy soil); need to develop a universal water-reservoir that can be used by public, cattle and for agriculture; and lastly non-availability of hard building materials like stones in most of the areas. The vagaries of monsoon demanded that reservoirs must not solely depend on monsoon for feeding. Thus subsoil water was the most reliable source.

Water-tables in summer are at the lowest. So, a reservoir must be deep enough for use in summer and also for use in a period following the dry monsoon. It meant that reservoir-construction, atleast in some parts, must be carried out below the usual 'sub-soil water-table'. The dug out pit must be kept dry. Moreover the schedule of construction had to be time-bound to prevent monsoon prematurely filling up the intended reservoir.

Among other problems one that most important was

finance and patronage. Structures like tanks not only required a great labour-force but some patronage–royal, religious and community. In Gujarat most of the reservoirs were acts of charity. It was only after the 15th century that reservoirs for recreation came into vogue.

The step-wells – the types of reservoirs found in Gujarat were developed for a variety of reasons (functional needs) under a variety of conditions (availability of water, existing water-level and quantity available) and at different locations, soil condition and position with respect to village road etc.

Functional needs were defined by the use of water by passers by, farmers, cattle, inhabitants etc. Cattle and agriculture needed a distinctly different type. This decided the nature of the reservoir and the method of approach to the water. The type of soil at the site of reservoir was the most important factor for the enclosures and the approach to the water. This, combined with available building material-stone-produced variety of enclosures. Step-well construction involved proper diggins providing adequate gradient and good maintenance so that easy access is available. This was done cleverly by the arrangement of terraced steps sometimes in continuous rows, sometimes in ramps and sometimes in steps and platforms together.

In cutting it can be easily seen that if the sides are left vertical, they will collapse hence one has to adopt a certain slope as defined by natural angle of repose or angle of internal friction of the soil. Thus, the question of stability of earthwork arises. The unprotected earthwork gives way by slipping or sliding. In the diagram below the volume ABC has tendency to slide over the plane AC.

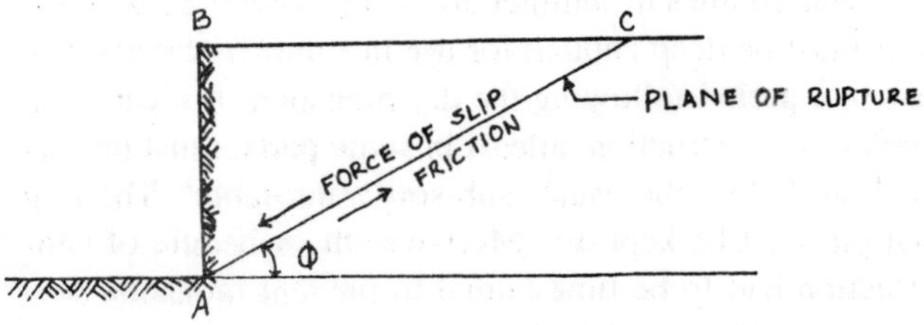

Fig. 1

The forces which try to stablilise it are the frictional forces along the surface AC. The cohesive force directly in proportion to the moisture content of the soil helps it to remain along the plane AB, but as the moisture reduces, the forces reduce and the soil is free to slide down. These frictional forces differ with the quality of soil and also with moisture content in it. If the soil has moisture, a vertical side of a fresh cutting may be quite stable temporarily. Soils consisting of dry sand or gravel, can never remain vertical. The ordinary *murrum* soil, can remain in vertical position even upto a height of 16 feet when freshly cut. The cohesive forces are more in natural undisturbed soils and it is for this reason that the sides of a cutting can be given a steeper slope than those of an embankment. Thus, if the side slope of cuttings are made equal to the angle of repose the earth work will be quite statable.[1]

However, the angle of repose is directly affected by the moisture content that varies with the seasons and this necessitates the pitching of sides, embankments, vertical retaining walls etc. (care has·to be exercised in case of highly porous soils to remove the excess amount of moisture present in it by way of draining it out). To the medieval builders to whom concrete and cement were unknown in Gujarat; stone was the only available material that can fulfil the structural demands of this nature for reservoirs.

Step-well-type of structures are most suited where the following conditions prevail:

Fluctuating sub-soil water–table: High in winter and low in summer; water levels are easy to negotiate in such structures.

High evaporation: Covered and protected structure prevents evaporation of water during arid climate.

High permeation of water in soil: The body of water being small and compact possibilities of permeation are reduced.

Reservoir and subordinate activities: The structure by itself provides manifold resting places, doing away with the need to provide special umbrellas.

However, a step-well does not provide a large area for activities like bathing, cleaning, etc. like a tank, If provided the well becomes unhygienic.

The step-well is a well-framed structure. The frame fixed smugly inside on inclined pit bears the thrust exerted by the sides from the soil, other than its internal self-load distribution system. That means the structure of the step-well has several type of loads:

Dead load: self-load of the structure itself.

Lateral forces from the earth: As discussed before, the vertical cuts in the earth create the thrust in the retaining wall-structure. These forces increase as depth of the cut increases.

Live loads: The people approaching the water, resting on its terraces etc. add to the loads. These, however, are very negligible in the total consideration.

The step-wells are usually at depths that vary from 7.62 m to 30.77 m where the water is available. The approach should be through a system of terraces–steps etc. These are usually built with stones—by nature a heavy material. Stone-walls and monolithic columns built one on the top of another in order to reach from ground level to the water level create varying degree of vertical loads on their foundations. As the height is increased, the loads are more and to balance this the builders had stones fixed with metal clamps (dowels) within (Fig. 6). The sketches in Fig 2 and 4 illustrate the forces and the transfer of these forces, upto the foundations. The transference is mainly due to the friction obtained between various elements. Since stone was the only available material, its proportion of rigidity and monolithic quality had to be used.

The friction between the joint increases with the increase of compressive forces. This helps to achieve a better bondage and as a result a higher resistance to side horizontal or inclined thrusts (Fig. 1)

The rigidity of the structure is created by a beam and column system in the entire structure of step-wells. These frames formed the continuity of structure and helped to distribute loads over the entire system. In this transference the important problem to be solved was that of shear at different joints.

As explained in the sketch 1 on Fig. 3 the post and beam system that uses the beam to transfer loads to the columns, by shear and bending. The use of bracket on top of the column forms wider base for beam and column junction, and in the process provides: (1) greater depth where shear is maximum and (2) reduces the clear unsupported span between the columns to minimise the bending moments and deflection in the beams.

The frame structure in the step-well is a hollowed box. It has openings in its horizontal as well as vertical direction. Horizontal openings in the unit of well arranged post and beam structure systems, while vertical openings are made by separating groups of post and beam structure units. The group of post and beam structure units are connected by thick walls at extreme ends.

The thick stone walls are under the action of direct thrust of the soil which is acting at certain angles (the angle depends upon internal friction of the soil). So it has horizontal as well as vertical components. The vertical component is transferred to the foundation, and horizontal component acts on the wall. The wall distributes lateral thrust by acting as one-way slab supported on the system of beams and columns. This behaviour is illustrated in the Fig. 2.

The ratio between length-breadth is greater than 1.5, so the lateral thrust on the wall is transmitted to the columns by one-way action of the slab. The load in turn is being transmitted to beams through vertical movement and balanced by opposite forces acting at two ends of the beam. The other two sides of the one way slab are ties, which carry negligible thrust, but reduce the length of the column, thus helping in reducing (avoiding) the possibility of buckling. These beams are also useful, for completing the frame, (post and beam system), to resolve the forces for attaining a state of equilibrium.

The horizontal and opposite forces acting in the beam are larger as the depth increases and this tends to cause buckling. The buckling forces become the important criterion in selecting the bay width between columns (Fig 3). The same is then carried on till the top for reasons of simplicity. The same is applied to the selection of bays along the cross section of the step-well so that buckling in the beams does not take place.

The easiest solution to the problem of supporting a side section of a earth would be to provide a surface by itself in equilibrium. But since the step-well depth is substantial such a structure would not be possible. Moreover, a step-well has two side walls, so it is very easy to balance the horizontal components of the thrust of soil, acting on the walls of the step-well, by connecting the walls by some means (in post and beam system, beams are balancing horizontal components of the thrust of soil). As vertical component of the thrust of soil goes to foundation vertically, wall thickness is reduced considerably.

The step-well structure where horizontal components are balanced has been formed by a frame of posts and beams of stone. The area between the two levels of horizontal beam framing was supported by the thickness of the wall, and the half-projecting-out columns (Fig. 2) helped to buttress the wall, and beams helped to balance the horizontal component of the thrust of soil.

The wall, in the cut-out (opening for light) are not supported directly. Possibly the thrust of soil is resisted by increasing thickness (section) of wall, (Mata Bhavani's step-well, Ahmedabad) or by their method of reducing the cut-out (opening for light) zone in size (Bai Harir's step-well, Ahmedabad), with increase in the thrust of soil, Figure 5, explains the actual relationship of depth to the reducing size of cut-out.

Construction

The construction of a reservoir needed a great deal of foresight and coordination of manifold activities. The excavation was one such, where they had to coordinate their activities very precisely with seasons. Excavations usually begin just after monsoon, i.e. in the months of *'Ashwin'* (Oct-Nov.) according to Hindu calendar; during *'Kartik'* no new work of building was started as it was forbidden in the *Sastras*. The excavation was finished before the following April or mid-May. At lower depth the builders had to encounter subsoil water. Atleast one fifth of excavation was always through such zones. This necessitated constant emptying of water. Summer months provided a little respite as the subsoil waters were not as pressing. So, the builders had an opportunity to finish excavation by mid-May and start on with raw structuring of the foundations and lower part of the structure before the on set of monsoon. During monsoon construction work was abandoned and restarted again in winter. Throughout the next season the tempo was a little bit slower as the problems and schedules were not so urgent.

The excavations were supported as and when necessary in various manners.

The second problem was water-proofing. The stones were laid without any bonding materials. There was a great deal of seepage of water. However, the problem was not acute in step-well because it is fed by subsoil waters. In step-wells the bottoms were remade by removing all settled mud and refilling it with fine sand. This helped the bottom volumes of soil more porous, which in turn allowed sub-soil water to come freely upwards.

The materials of construction were bricks for raw structure and Dhangadhra (Saurashtra) and Lalpur (near Himatnagar) sandstones for all the major work. Metal clamps were used to secure blocks of stones.

Excavation of step-well was carried out with the help of lowering wooden log boxes. Square boxes of wooden logs were lowered as the excavation furthered. A series of boxes at varying depth formed the total channel. Extra water was taken out manually. At the correct depth raw masonary was started by removing bottom logs one by one. On this rough masonary fine stone work was carried.

The construction of a step-well always followed the construction of adjacent ring-well. The ring-well was undisturbed all through construction. When the step-well was about to be finished, the ring-well was connected at atleast two places in the shaft, one at the bottom-most level and the other at the upper galleries.

Figures 6, 7 and 8 show the details of joints.

Conclusions

The effort required for digging a step-well varies from soil to soil; hard soil obviously requiring more labour. Hard soils are usually impervious and therefore, easier to store water as contrasted .

If the water-table is high in monsoon and low in summer in a given area then deep structures like wells or step-wells are preferable.

Step-wells are possible in harder soils and stone or

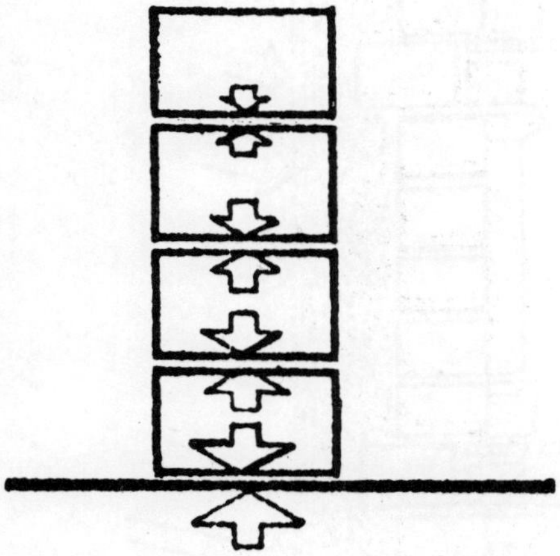

1. Increasing compression in lower stone

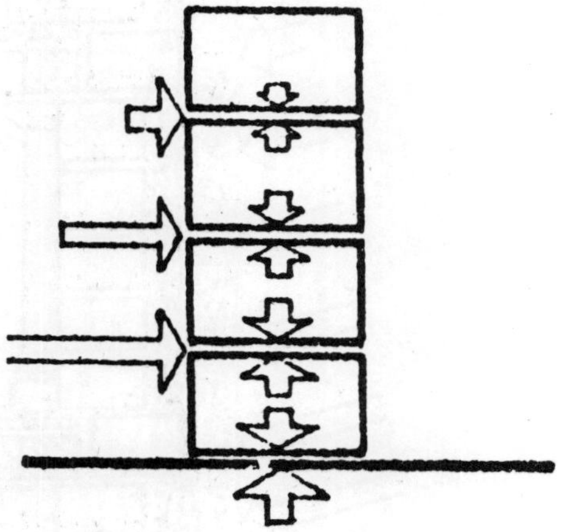

2. Friction Between the joint increases with increase in compression. This helps to achieve higher thrust from sides at lower blocks level.

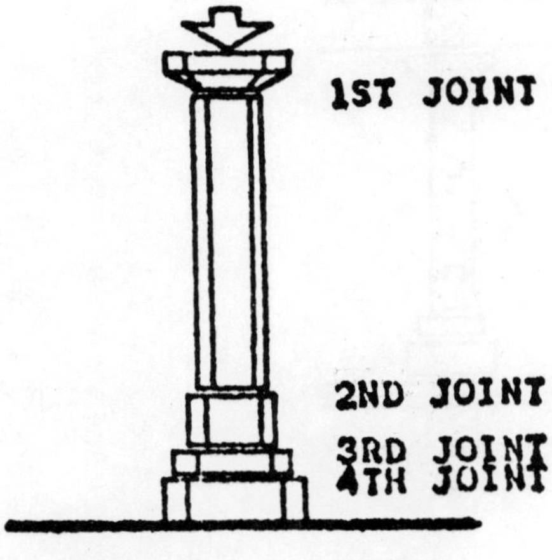

3. Joints where a better bondage is must for the stability of the column.

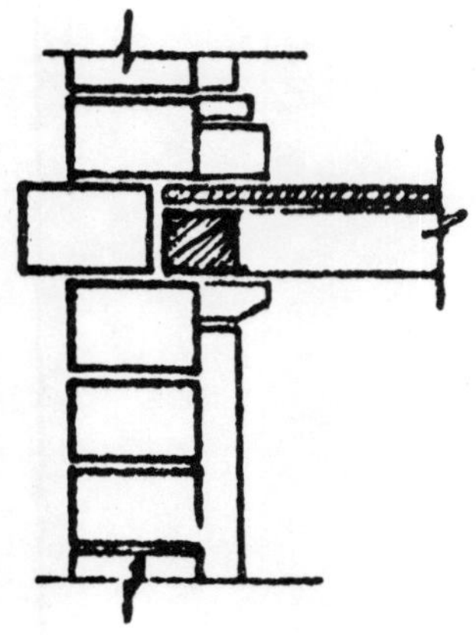

4. Stones of the wall are self bondage because of heavy loads from above.

Fig. 1

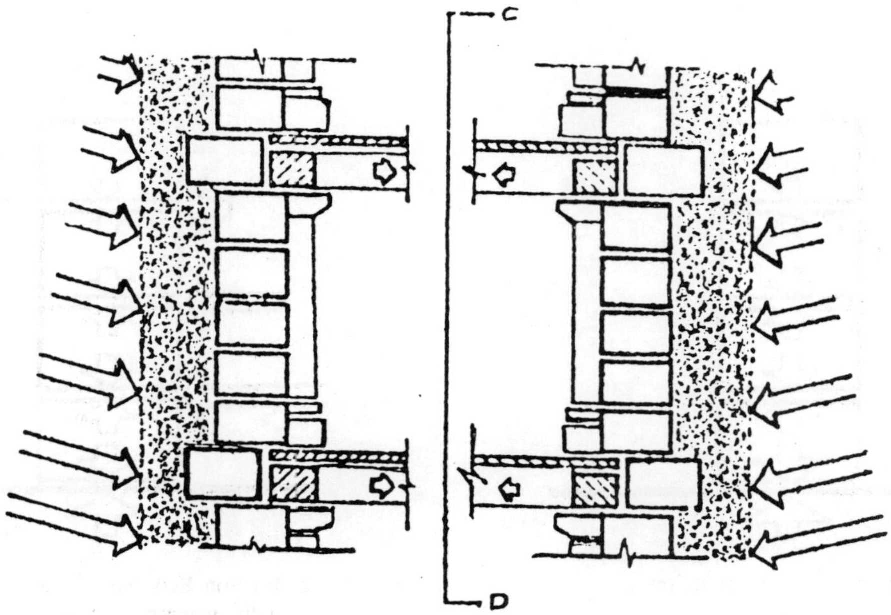

1. Section at C-D
L/B>1.5. So panel enclosed by beams and columns acts as one way slab and transfers forces (as shown in Fig.) exerted by thrust of the soil.

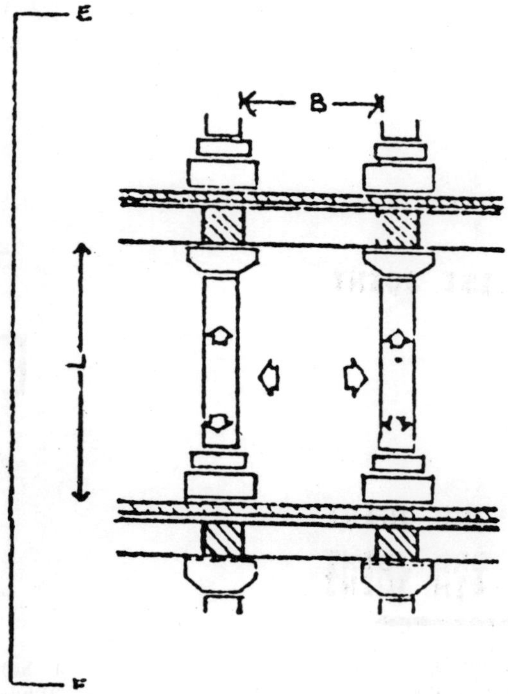

2. Section at E-F
Thrust of the soil acts on walls of Stepwell. vertical component goes to foundation. Horizontal component is balanced by opposite horizontal component.

Fig. 2

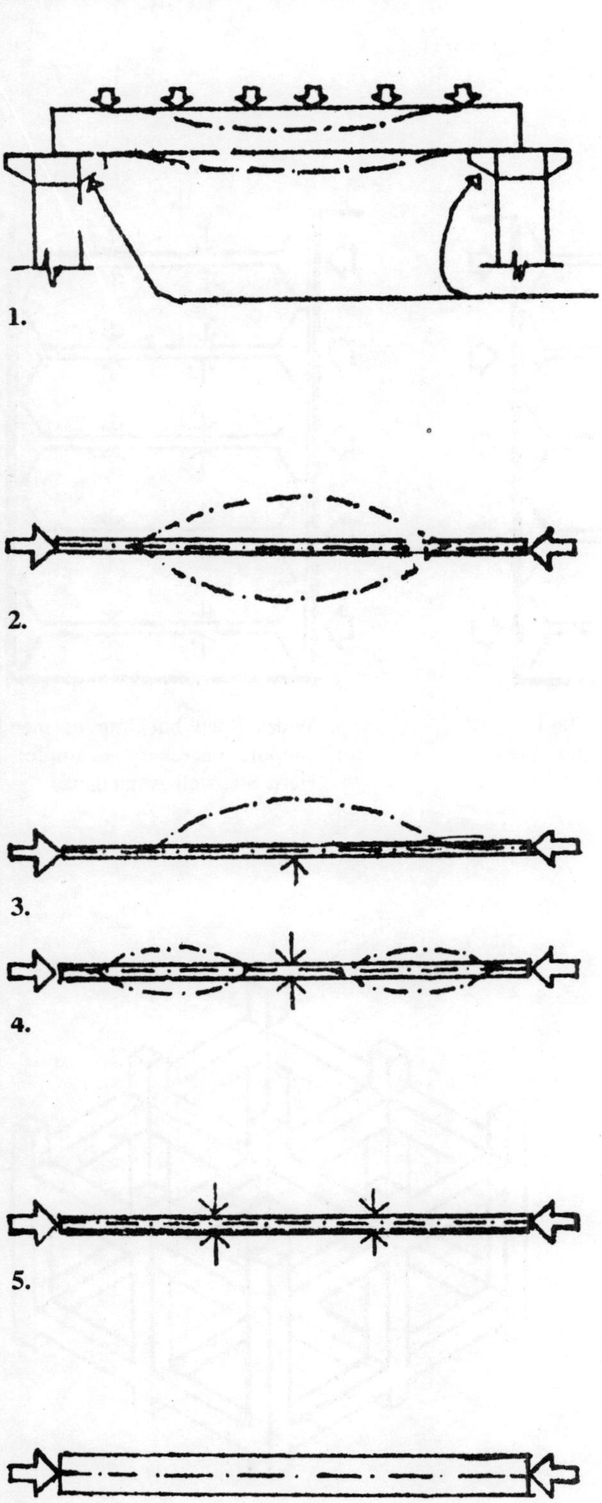

1. Point of maximum shear at support = Total load/2.

   Brackets help to take care of shearing forces, and to reduce bending moments and deflection.

2. Members under compressive forces tend to buckle if they are relatively thin and long.

3. & 4. This may be remedied by supporting it in more then one direction.

5. If necessary supports may be put at more then one point.

6. Alternatively the section may be increased. This however may not be suitable for reasons of heavy self loads etc.

Fig. 3

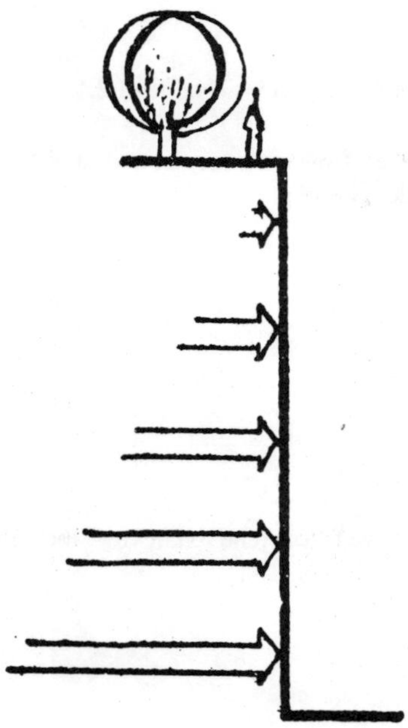

1. Thrust from side wall increases with depth in stepwell.

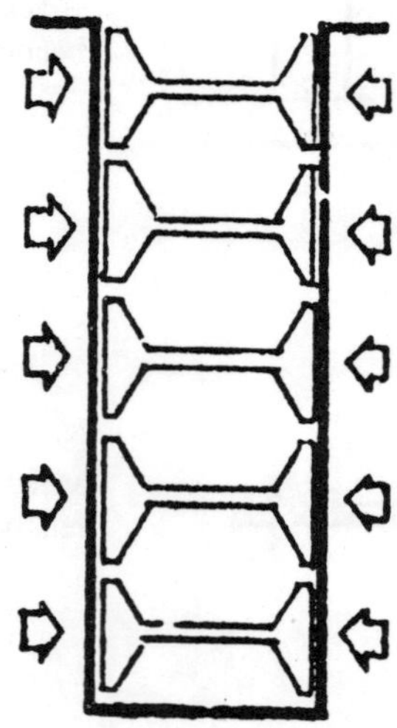

2. Small span, No buckling, example: Stepwell-Roho.

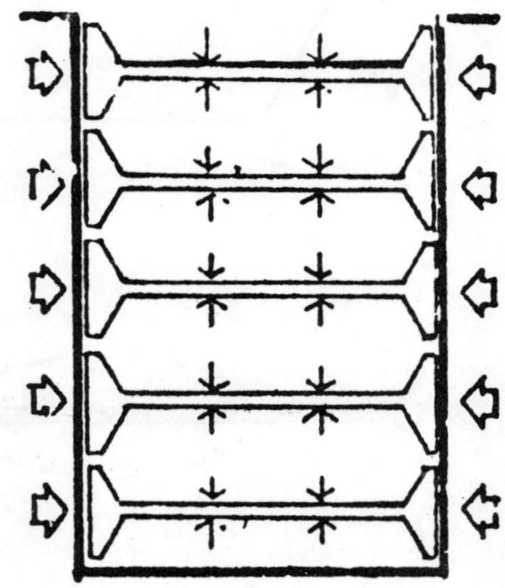

3. Wides Span buckling of member, support necessary example: Bai Harir Stepwell-Ahmedabad.

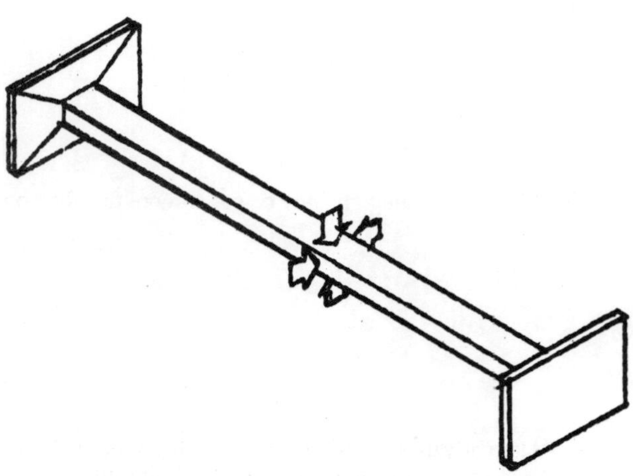

4. Support is necessary from all sides to prevent buckling.

5. Top side and bottom side. Support is through columns. Other side support is through beams.

Fig. 4

BAI HARIR STEPWELL

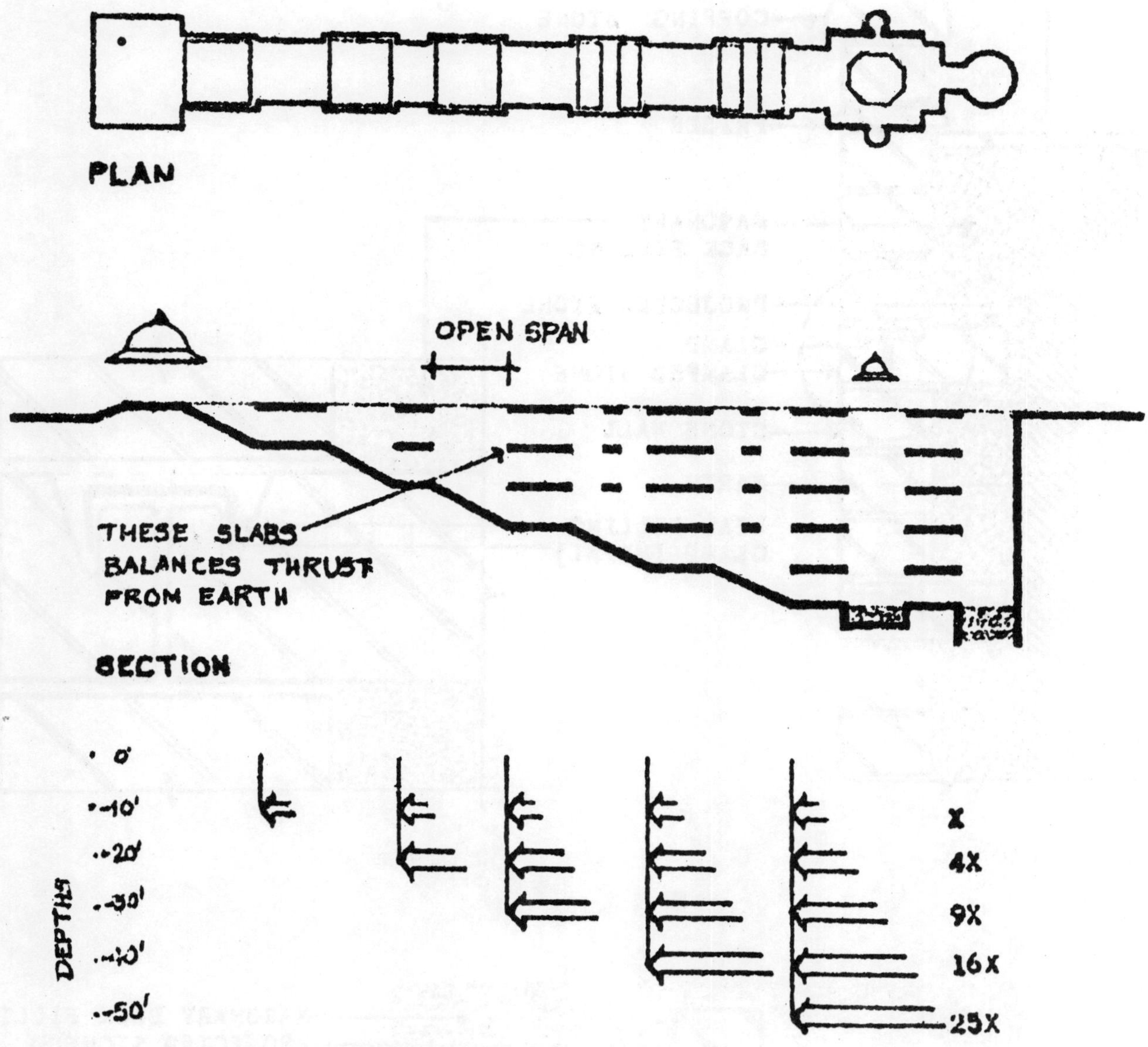

Graph Showing earth pressure on side walls at different depths

Fig. 5

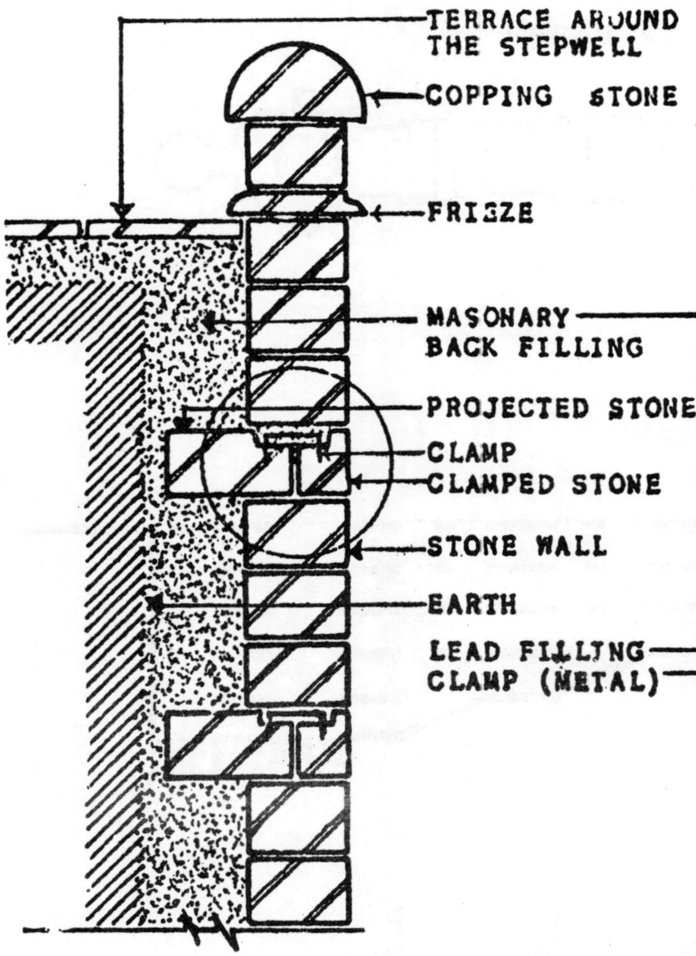

1. Section at 'BB'

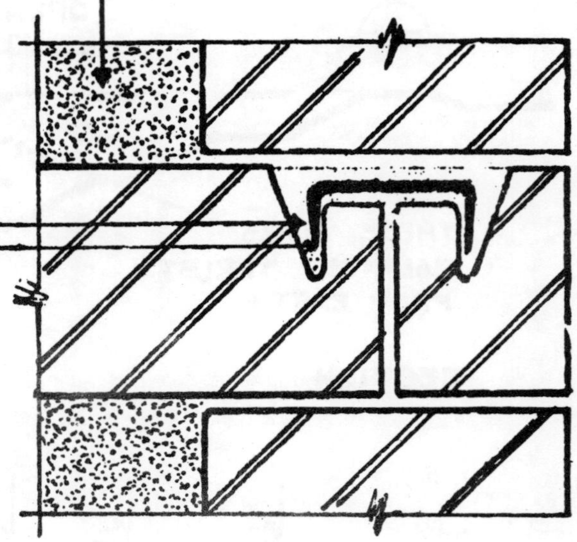

2. Detail at 'A'

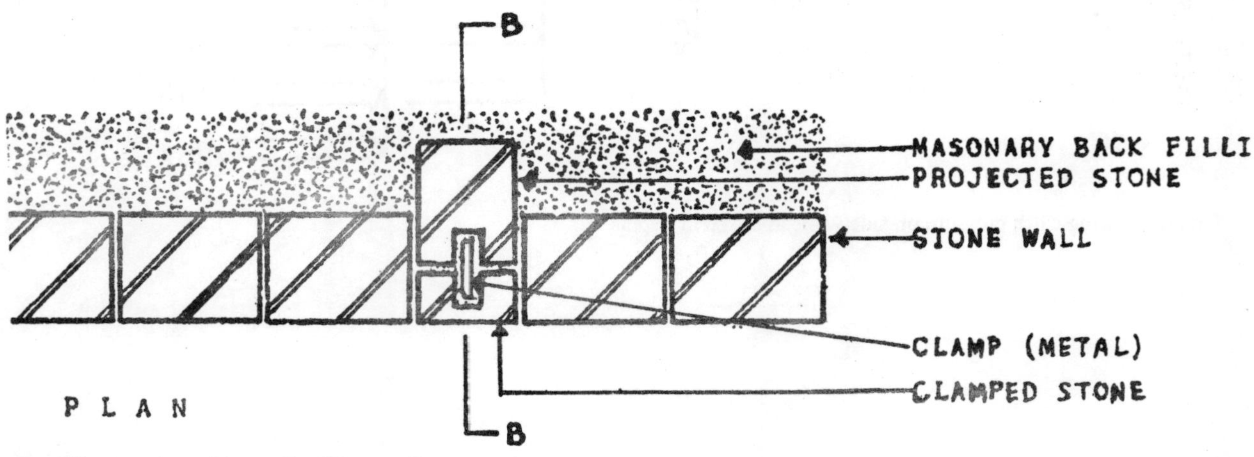

3. Details showing side wall of stepwell

Fig. 6

Columns, joints in Stepwell floors

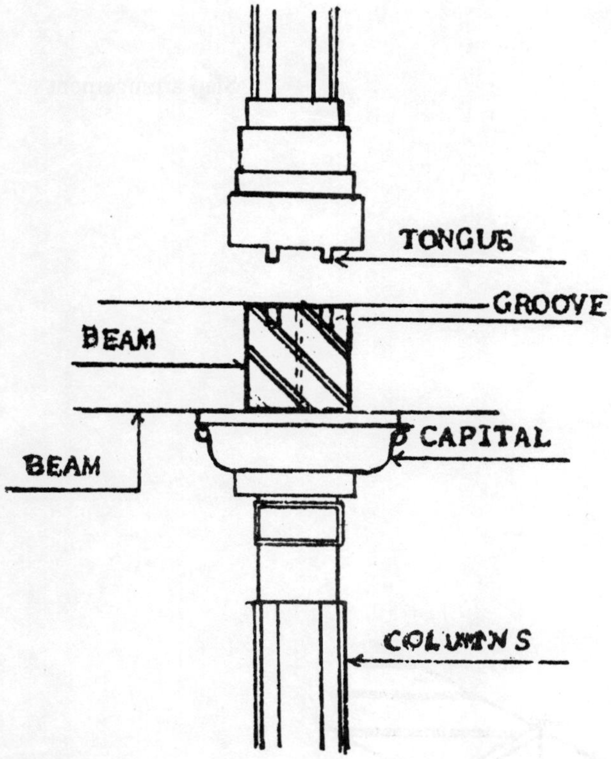

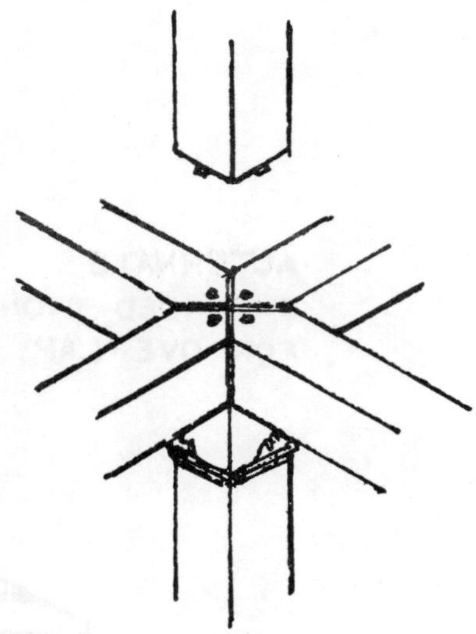

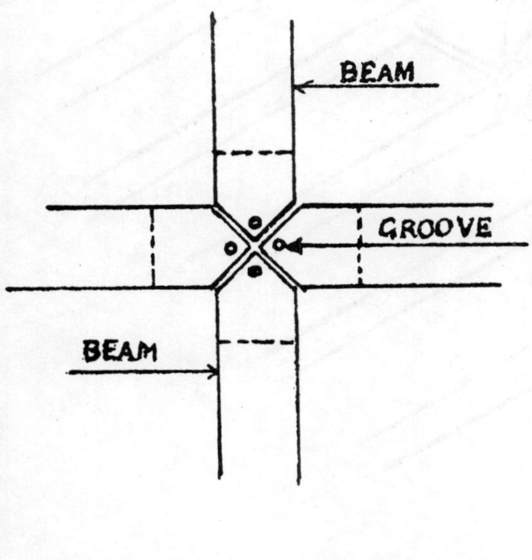

Fig. 7

Step arrangement

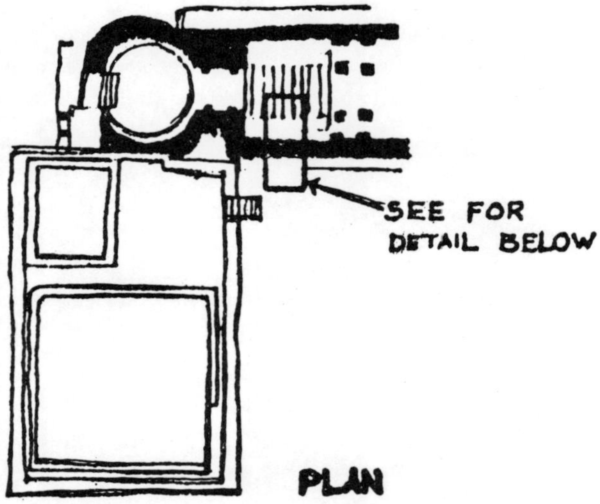

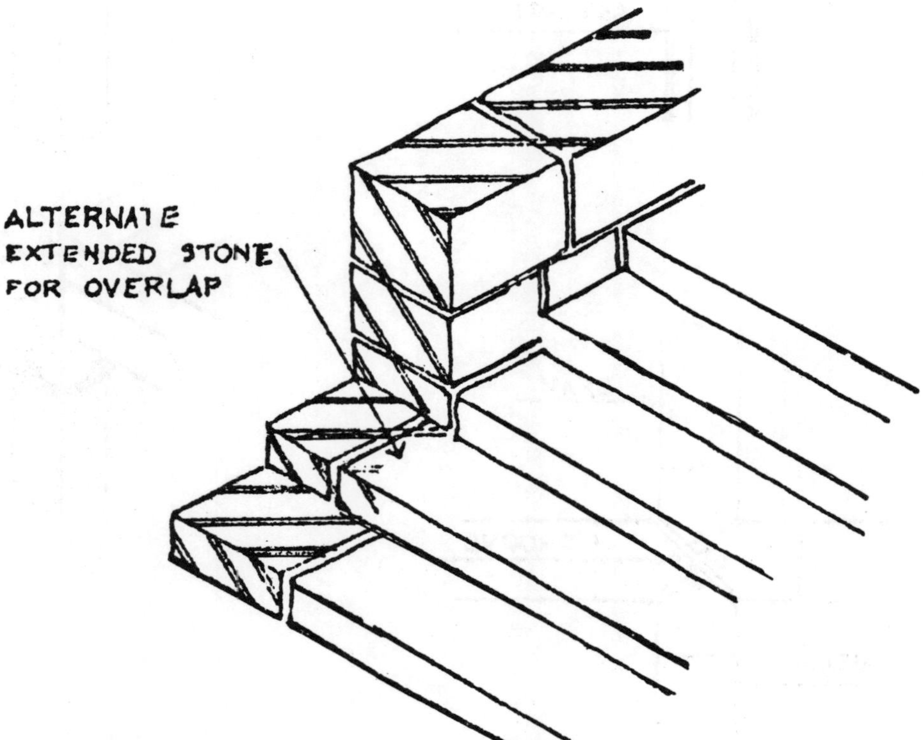

Fig. 8

other impervious facing is required.

Evaporation is least in a step-well because the surface of water exposed to the sun is less and it is situated at such a depth where the rays of the sun cannot penetrate directly.

Step-wells are basically outdated because of the mechanical means of water drawing. However, the idea of a resting place near the step-well could be exploited in villages and on highways. We can with cheap plastic and polymers convert many depressions into such water-areas and may be used for summer agriculture and entertainment. As for its symbolic value of uniting several architectonic elements we still need to rediscover the values. These new values must be original and meet the Indian environment.

REFERENCE

R. H. Karol. *Soil and Soil Engineering,* p. 11.

Usual concept of friction; the resisting force is a function of the normal pressure between sliding surfaces. Frictional resistance is one of the factors contributing to the shear strength of a soil, and it is measured by the friction angle, or angle of internal friction.

Sands and gravels generally have friction angles of 25^0. to 35^0. in the loose state, and 5^0 to 10^0 high in the dense state. Coarser materials generally show a tendency to higher friction angles. Silts will have values of 15° to 25° or 30°, while clays will have values ranging from 0° to 15° or 20°.

NOTES AND NEWS

Megaliths In Nagaland

Geographical Background

Nagaland, a small state in the north-eastern corner of India, was constituted in December 1963 out of a hill district of former undivided Assam. The state, lying between $23^0 54'$-$26^0 24'$ E and $92^0 26'$ and $94^0 39'$ N is composed of a compact landmass formed by rugged hill ranges of the Patkai Hill on the north-east and the Dorail range on the south-west forming a watershed of two great rivers of Asia - the Brahmaputra on the north and Chindwin-Irrawady system of Myanmar (Burma) on the south-east as well as deep gorges formed by the rivers - Doyang and Diphu, which flow into the Brahmaputra and the Tizu river which joins the Chindwin. The hill ranges are mainly of Eocene. Oligocene and Miocene sedimentary rocks, especially sandstones and clacarious splintary shale. The topography is highlighted with hill ranges and narrow valleys and deep gorges–all covered by dense tropical rain forest.

Ethnographic Account

The population of Nagaland is almost entirely tribal. Under the blanket term'Naga' there exists in Nagaland tribes like Angami, Ao, Chakesang, Chang, Chirr, Khiamunggan, Konyak, Lotha, Makware, Phom, Rengma, Sangtam, Tikher, and Zeliang. These ethnic groups have still preserved their cultural identity and linquistic characteristics; every ethnic group having its own dialect. In the field of socio-economic life and subsistence pattern, these ethnic groups follow their traditional system. Thus, some groups like Ao, Sangtam and Konyak etc. are primarily shifting cultivators; while some others like Angami, Chakesang and Zeliang etc. have developed very elaborate method of irrigated and terraced cultivation and reap bumper crops.

Megalithic Monument of Nagaland

In the Nagaland megalithism is a living tradition and among the Nagas it is closely related with the great social event called 'feasts-of-merit'. A person desiring to erect a monolith or menhir is required to offer a series of feasts-of-merit in order to attain the status to quarry a stone pillar or monolith for erecting the same in memory of his dead ancestors or in the name of living husband and wife or even to commemorate some social events.

The present author made a survey of the districts of Kohima and Phek, where such megalithic remains are found in plenty.

Megaliths in Kohima District (Map 1)

The Angami Nagas occupy the Kohima district which forms south-western part of Nagaland, and may be called the homeland of the Angamis. In addition, other Naga groups found here are the Rengma and the Zeliang.

In this part of Nagaland, megalithic tradition seems to be very rich and plays significant part in the everyday life of the people. Megalithic monuments of various types are found in large numbers and also in the forests and the vicinity of the present-day villages. In fact almost every Angami village may be considered as a megalithic site. There are 43 villages inhabited by the Angami Nagas, of which for the study, the following villages, where megalithic remains are abundant were selected for study these are : Jotsoma, Khonoma, Mezoma, Kohima village and Viswema sites.

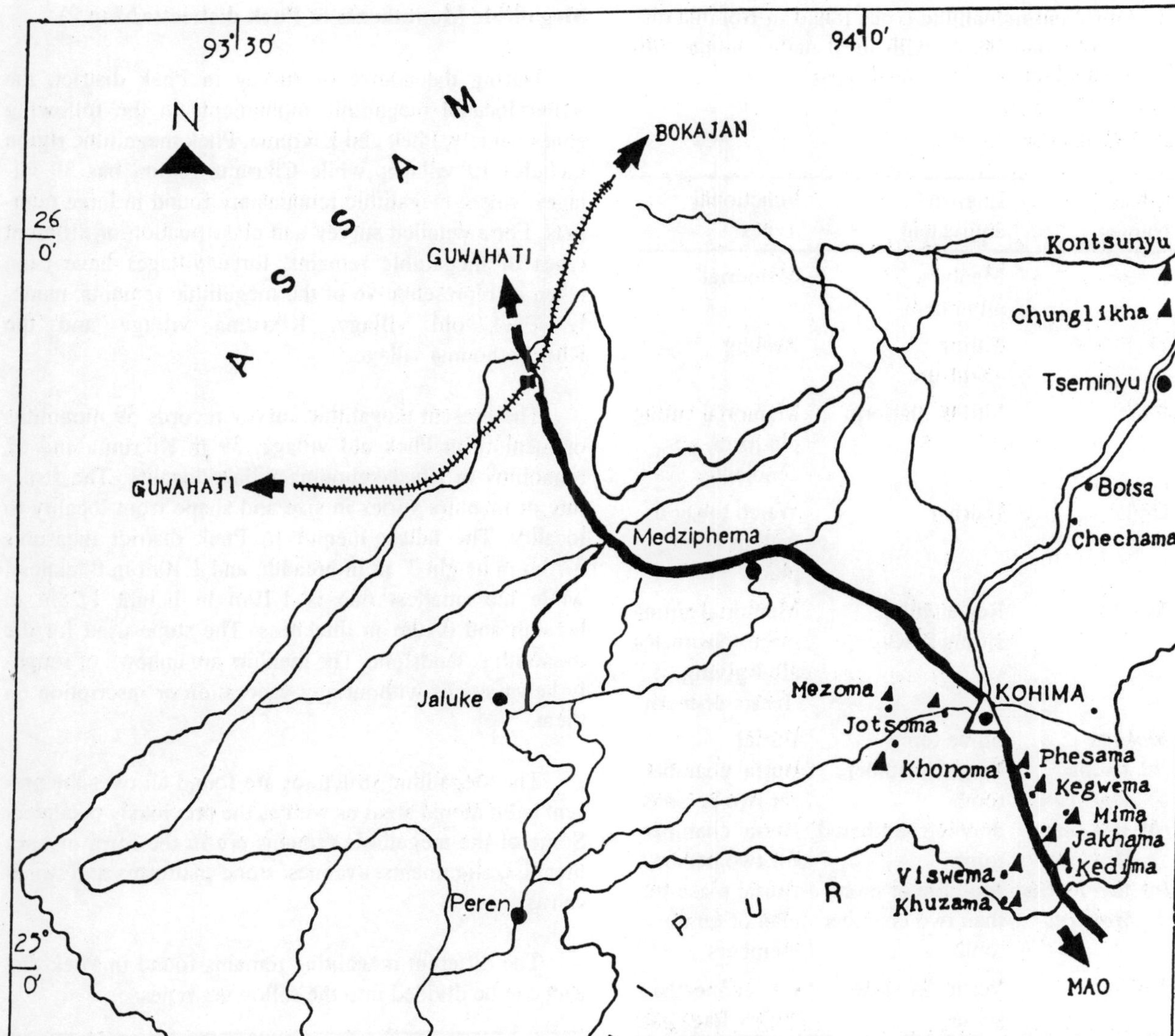

Map:1 Megalithic survey map of Angami Inhabited Area in Kohima District

The different megalithic types found in Kohima district sites are listed below with local names along with English equivalent and functional types.

(Angami dialect)

Sl. No.	Local Names	English equivalent	Functional types
1	*Tsiese*	Menhirs, alignment	Memorial
2.	*Thehouba*	Sitting enclosure	Resting
3.	*Badze*	Sitting platform	Memorial sitting platform, a cenotaph
4.	*Dahu*	Cairn	Watch tower as well as sitting place
5.	*Kwehou*	Rectangular, sitting place	Memorial sitting place constructed after giving 'feasts-of-merit'
6.	*Mokhru*	Stone tomb	Burial
	(a) Miapu Mokhru	Single chamber tomb	Burial chamber for two persons
	(b) Mia kenie Mokhru	double chambered tomb	Burial chamber for two person
	(c) Mia Kekra Mokhru	Multiple or more than two chamber tomb	Burial place for clan or family members
7.	*Kharu*	Vertically raised stone	It is connected with village gate

Megalithic remains found in Kohima district consist of menhirs, alignment, avenue and miscellaneous types such as stone platform, stone-walls, stone-chamber tombs and stone gate. The present survey in five localities shows 52 monoliths in Jotsoma site, 75 in Khonoma, 256 in Mezoma (highest number found among the Angami villages) and 117 in Viswema megalithic site. The rock used for the construction of such structures is sandstone. The stones are roughly hewn or are undressed. The tallest menhir found in Khonoma village measures about 5.28m. in height 0.78 m in breadth and 0.48 m in thickness and the smallest monolith found is 0.28m in height, 0.33m in breadth and 0.10m in thickness.

Megalithic Monuments in Phek district: (Map 2)

During the course of survey in Phek district, the writer located megalithic monuments in the following zones namely, Phek and Kikruma. Phek megalithic rigion includes 19 villages while Cikruma region has 39 villages, where megalithic remains are found in large numbers. For a detailed survey and classification of different types of megalithic remains, three villages have been taken as representative of the megalithic remains, namely, Phek old village, Kikruma village and the Khezakenouma village.

The present megalithic survey records 59 monoliths or menhirs in Phek old village, 39 in Kikruma and 62 monoliths in Khezakenouma village/locality. The structure of menhirs varies in size and shape from locality to locality. The tallest menhir in Phek district measures 3.70m in height 3 m in breadth, and 1.10m in thickness, while the smallest one is 1.10m in height 1.28m in breadth and 0.10m in thickness. The stone used for the monolith is sandstone. The menhirs are unhewn or roughly hewn stones without any decoration or inscription on them.

The megalithic structures are found all over the present habitational areas as well as the previously occupied. Some of the megalithic remains are in the form of ones menhirs, alignments, avenues, stone-platforms and stone-cairns.

The different megalithic remains found in Phek district can be divided into the following types:

Sl. No.	Local Names	English equivalent	Functional types
1	*Zhothotsu*	Menhirs, alignment avenues	Commemorative stones raised by a rich man who has given a series of feasts of merit
2.	*Khoho*	Raised platform	Meeting place for khel members
3.	*Sahini*	Rectangular stone	Heap of stone boulders raised after the death of a richman

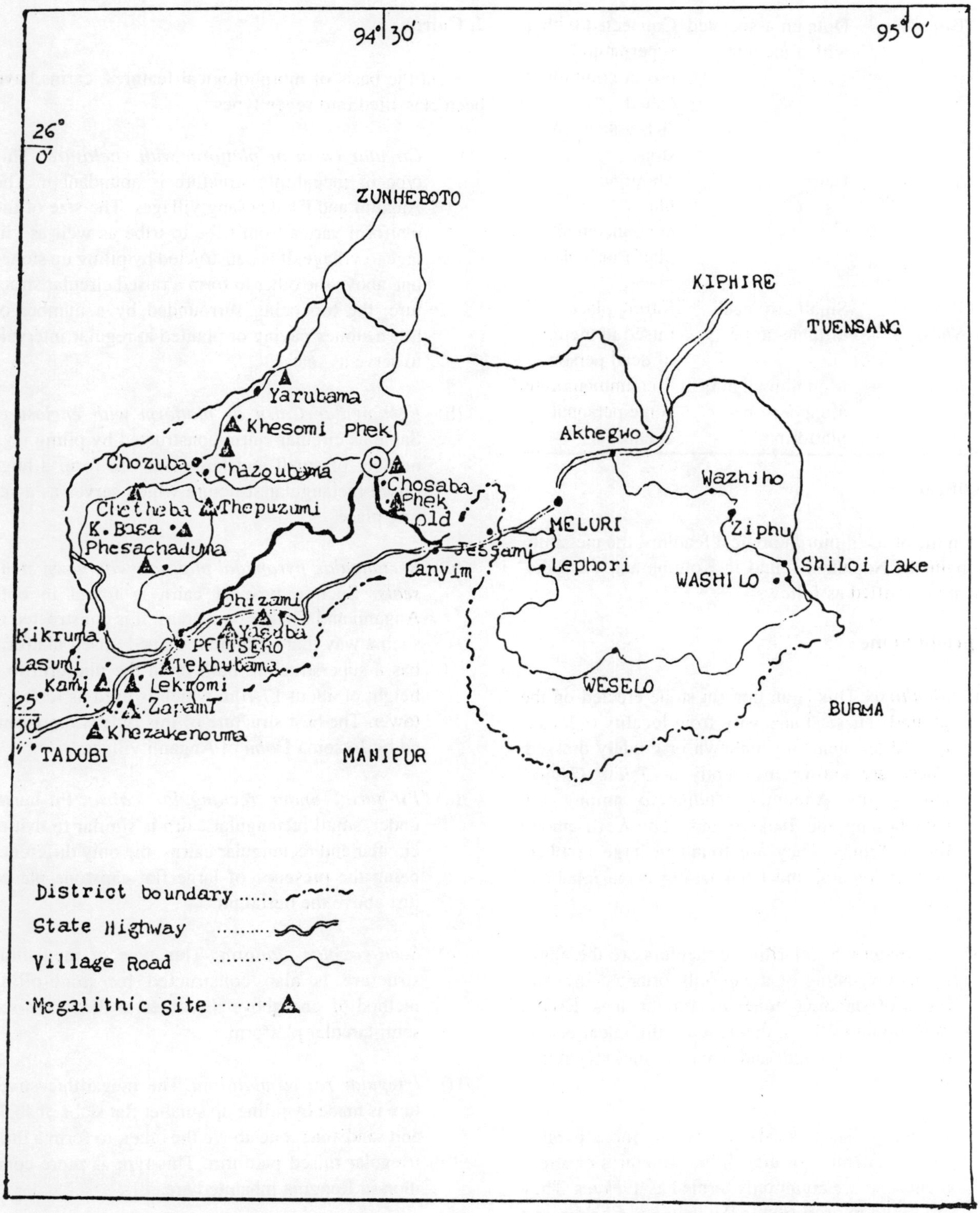

Map:2 Megalithic survey map of Chakhesang Inhabited Area in Phek District.

4.	*Tsotagwu*	Dolmen associated with a menhir	Connected with a supernatural power commonly called 'Khezakenouma stone'
5.	*Naseba*	Cairn	Shouting place/ announcement platform/lookout place
6.	*Verosa/ Nhose*	Small cromlech or table-stone	Sitting place raised in memory of dead person
7.	*Kosa moro*	Monolith alignment along a stone-platform	To commemorate some personal event

Classification

On the basis of morphological features, the megalithic remains of Nagaland found in Kohima and Phek districts are classified as follows:

1. Upright Stone

(a) *Menhirs* - This is an upright stone erected on the ground. These stones vary from locality to locality, and are generally unhewn or crudely dressed. These are known differently as *Tsiese (Tsowe)* among the Angamis; *Zhothotso* among the Chakhesang and Tsokulo and *Abon Keya* among the Rengmas. They are found in large numbers among Angami and Chakhesang Naga inhabited areas.

(b) *Alignment* - Similar to the menhirs are the alignments consisting of a carefully oriented row and series of standing stones in straight lines. Except in Rengma villages, this type of alignment occurs in all the Angami and Chakhesang megalithic sites.

(c) *Avenues* : They consist of two or more parallel rows of menhirs or megalithic structures or alignments and are commonly termed as avenues. They are found in profusion in Angami and Chakhesang areas but not seen in Rengma megalithic fields

2. Cairns

On the basis of morphological features, carins have been classified into seven types :

(a) *Circular cairn or platform with enclosure:* This type of megalithic structure is abundant in The Angami and Chakhesang villages. The size of the platform varies from tribe to tribe as well as village to village. It is constructed by piling up stones one above the other to form a raised circular structure, the top being surrounded by a number of hewn stones paving or planted at regular intervals to serve as seats.

(b) *Rectangular Cairn or platform with enclosure:* Same as circular cairn, constructed by piling up a number of small and large slabs to form a huge raised rectangular structure which serves as a sitting place.

(c) *Rectangular, pyramidal platform with hewn stone seats:* Such a type of cairn is found in both Angami and Chakhesang areas. It is constructed in such a way that pyramidal shaped raised platform has a superstructure built upon the platform to a height of about 17.10m which is used as look-out tower. The best structure of this type is represented by Jotsoma *Dahu* of Angami village.

(d) *Pit-burial under rectangular cairn:* Pit-burial under, small rectangular cairn is similar to that of circular and rectangular cairns, the only difference being the presence of large flat capstone placed just above the burial pit.

(e) *Semi-circular platform:* This type of megalithic structure is also constructed by stone-piling method of one above the other to form a raised semi-circular platform.

(f) *Irregular raised platform:* The megalithic structure is made by piling up smaller flat slabs of shale and sandstone, one above the other, to form a little irregular raised platform. This type is more common in Rengma inhabited areas.

(g) *Miniature irregular Cairn:* Stones are randomly

piled one above the other to form an irregular raised platform or cairn which serve as shouting or announcement cairn. This type is a common megalithic structure in all the Naga villages of Kohima and Phek districts.

3. Dolmen along with Menhir

This type of megalithic structure consists of a flatstone, resting on three or four smaller vertical or piled up stones. Just adjacent to it, a huge monolith or menhir is also erected. This type is found in the Angami and Chakhesang megalithic fields.

4. Dolmen without menhir

This structure consists of a flat stone, resting on some slabs, sometime on a few vertical pillars or piled up stones. Dolmen without menhir is also a common megalith found among Angami, Chakhesang and Rengma inhabited areas.

5. Stone Seats

The 'stone seat' consists of a number of dressed or undressed stone slabs placed at regular intervals either in the form of circular, semi-circular, rectangular fashion. In some structures, a separate central stone is erected for use of the leader of the village or the chief. Stone seat structures are found in Angami, Chakhesang and Rengma inhabited areas.

6. Burial Chamber Tombs

Traditional tomb was constructed in such a way that stones were arranged one above the other to form a crude structure or platform called *Mokhru.* In some example a huge flat stone is placed covering the entire raised platform.

For erecting a burial chamber tombs in modern day, cement, mortar and dressed sandstone blocks are used. Three different types of traditional burial have been identified.

(a) *Miapu Mokhru* - Single burial chamber (for one dead body)

(b) *Miakenie Mokhru* - Double burial chamber (for husband wife)

(c) *Miakekra Mokhur* - More than two burial chambers (for family members or clan members)

7. Miscellaneous Types

(a) *Terhotsiere* - It is an upright natural stone or monolith found in the vicinity of the village and is associated with some traditional tribal beliefs.

(b) Kepuchi - This structure is composed of two stones of irregular shaped place horizontally on the ground. It is unhewn natural stone found inside the present habitational area. It is a worshipping stone.

(c) *Dba* - It is a small monolith erected adjacent to the tombstone. It is connected with burial.

(d) *Mavezhodzo* - This structure consists of a natural undressed block of stone used by the head-hunters upon which records of captured heads by a particular head-hunter are inscribed.

(e) *Thonookhruchtse* - It consists of small stones erected in the form of an alignment and found associated with *Kosa Moro* megalithic structure.

(f) *Thiripi* - Thiripi consists of small monoliths and sometimes wooden structures as replicas of stone. These are erected in an alignment along with the *Kosa Moro* monument. This structure is found both inside and outside of the village.

(g) *Avo* - Structurally, these are miniature monoliths erected in a cluster as an abode of a deity. These are found inside the village.

(h) *Tsa* - This megalithic structure is a stone fortification constructed by using regular-sized stones and boulders. It is found along with *Dahu* megalithic structures.

(i) *Village Gate* - This structure was constructed by piling up smaller stones in such a way to form a rectangular entrance gate to the Naga villages.

Discussion and Conclusion

Megalithic tradition in Nagaland has not died because of the continuing tribal social customs and obligations and beliefs. As it is related to perpetuating the memory of a person or ancestors, the tradition will not get extinct. It is also observed among the Nagas who have been converted to Christianity because they also construct, even when alive, burial chambers, chamber tombs *'Mokhru'*, both for husband and wife side by side for their burial inside the compound of their house or near it. The concept behind such a practice appears to have survived in Naga custom of erection of monolith or construction of *Mokhru* in the lifetime of a person.

Therefore, Nagaland, a small state bordering Myanmar (Burma) and connected thence to Thailand and other South-eastern Asian countries and China, which form a common ecological zone, has preserved prehistoric cultural tradition, among which the tradition of erecting megalithic monuments is very conspicuous. Authors like C.B. Clark P.R.T. Gurdon, J.H. Hutton, J.P.Mills and Haimendorf and several others, who have studied and written about the megalithic monuments of Nagaland, are of the opinion that megalithic culture of the north-east India found among the Khasis and Nagas is of prehistoric origin. The megalithic culture discovered and exacavated in other parts of India, including south India, dated by ^{14}C method, is found to occur from c. 1000 B.C. to 200 B.C., but in Nagaland, these are yet dated scientifically. The most important point about the Naga megaliths is that it is an old tradition which still persists and megalith-building is a living culture.

BIBLIOGRAPHY

Aiyappan, A 1945. The Megalithic Culture of Southern India. Indian Science Congress Association XXXII Presidential Address. Anthropology and Archaeology section.

Allchin, F.R. 1956. "The Stone Alignment of Southern Hyderabad". *Man* LVI 150.

Banerjee N.R. 1956. "The Megalithic problems of Chengleputt in the light of recent exploration". *Ancient India,* pp. 21-34.

Ball, V. 1872. "Stone Monuments in the District Singbhum, Chotanagpur". *Indian Antiquary,* pp. 291-92

Cacile Mawlong 1990. "Classification of Khasi Megalithis - A Critique" Preseedings of North East Indian History Association, Eleventh Session, Imphal pp.9-16.

Clarke, C.B. 1874. "The Stone Monuments of Khasi Hill" *Jr. Royal Anthropological Institute.* Vol. III.

Childe, V.G. 1948. "Megaliths", *Ancient India,* No. 4, New Delhi. pp. 5-13.

Daniel, G.F. 1963. *The Megalithic Builders of Western Europe.* Pelican Books.

Fergusson, James, 1872. *Rude Stone Monuments in all Countries, their Ages and Uses,* London.

Ghosh, B.B. 1982. *History of Nagaland,* New Delhi

Gurdon, P.R.T. 1914. *The Khasis,* London, pp. 144-155

Haimendorf, C.von .F. 1939 *The Naked Nagas,* London.

Haimendorf. C. Von F. "The Megalithic Culture of Assam" in Schnitger. F.N. (ed) 1964. *Jorgotton Kingdom of Sumatra* pp. 215-19

Hutton, J.H. 1922 "The meaning and method of erection of monoliths of the Naga tribes," *Journal of Royal Anthropological Institute* pp. 52 : 242-49.

_________ 1937, *The Sema Nagas,* London.

_________ 1921. *The Angami Nagas,* London.

_________ 1922. Carved Monolith at Dimapur and an Angami Naga Ceremony," *Jr. Royal Anthropological Institute,* London LII, 55-70.

_________ 1926. "The use of Stone in Naga Hills, *"Jr. Royal Anthropological Institute.* LVI: 7-83.

_________ "The Mixed Culture of the Naga Tribes" *Jr. of the Anthropological Institute,* Vol. 95: Part I

Kramer, C. 1976. *Ethnoarchaeology : Implication of ethhnography for Archaeology,* New Delhi.

Lanusosang,1987. *"A study of Social Geography* Nagaland.

Lubbock, J. 1865. *Pre-Historic Times - As illustrated by Ancient Remains,* London.

Mills, J.P. 1926. *The Lotha Nagas,* London (Reprinted, Kohima 1980).

Mills, J.P. 1937. *The Rengma Nagas,* London.

Pakem, B. 1992. Megalithic Problems of Meghalaya: A case study of the megalithic of Jaintia Hills. *Journal of North East India Council for Social Science Research.* 16:1.

Peets, T.E. 1912. *Rough Stone Monuments and Their Builders,* London .

Wheeler, Sir Mortimer, 1960. *Early India and Pakistan.* London, pp. 150-169.

Lecturer, Dept. of Anthropology
Kohima Science College, Jotsom
Nagaland. 797001

WATIJUNGSHI JAMIR

The Living Megalithic Culture of Manipur

Introduction

Nagas of the North East India—Nagaland, and Manipur and the Khasis and Jaintias of Meghalaya still erect megaliths in memory of their dead. This paper is confined to the living megalithism of one of the states of the NE India viz. Manipur.

The Megalithic Tradition in Manipur

The megalithic monuments found in large numbers among the Nagas of Manipur comprising, eleven ethnic groups, such as the Kabui, the Kareng, Liangmais, the Mao, the Marams, the Maring, the Paumais, the Thangal, the Tangkhul and the Chakhesangs, each distinguished by their distinct dialects, cultural traditions, dress and ornaments, were noticed first by T.C. Hudson. There was a long period of inactivity till 1978, when Dr. O.K. Singh attempted to describe the megalithic types found among the Mao Nagas of Manipur. The investigation into the Megalithic culture of Manipur was taken up seriously by a Manipur Anthropologist, Dr. P.Binodini Devi, who carried an extensive survey of the megalithic sites and the monuments found among all the eleven Naga tribes of Manipur during 1988-91. This work undoubtedly forms the basis for all further work in the region. She came across the most exciting part of her study i.e. the living customs, traditions and rituals associated with the erection of megaliths, mainly menhirs, which when excavated, give us some grave goods from which we may reconstruct the material culture and chronological sequence of the prehistoric culture. But when we ventured to live among the present-day megalithic builders of Manipur, we were also able to gather a fund of information.

The rites and rituals associated with the erection of a menhir among the Nagas of Manipur, are in memory of their dead for the merit of living husband or wife, involving huge expenditure over feast-of-merit entertaining the villagers and the relatives, beginning from the initial feast and then progressing through six or seven higher ones. The ascending order terminates in the last feast in order to qualify the performer to transport a monolith from the quarry site to the hill top, where it is to be erected. Only a rich person of the village having a very rich harvest could ever aspire to erect a megalithic monument in memory of the dead ancestors or in the names of living husband or wife. At each feast-of-merit a large number of animals beginning from the most prized meat animals found in N.E. India, called *mithun* (*Bos frontalis*), a semi-feral bison, which are reared in the jungles and with which the owner of the herd gets familiarised by visiting them from time to time and feeding them with salt. When necessary for sacrife in a megalithic ritual, the animal is caught by a number of villages by enticing it with salt and bringing to the owner. Other animals sacrificed include buffalo, cow and pig, as many as necessary so as to feed the villagers sumptuously and also distributing a piece of meat, about a kilo, to each family of the village. In addition, the performer is required to brew about 3 to 4 thousand litres of rice-beer and preserve it in huge drums or vats for which a large quantity of rice is necessary. Besides, about 10 to 15 quintals of rice are necessary to be cooked for feeding.

During the days of feast, one normal feast in a year and a bigger feast after every 2 or 3 years, the performer of the ritual thus spends nearly half of his life time giving feasts only and spends all his earnings and agricultural products to feed the villagers. The performer also called donor, is to observe many social restrictions called *genna* in Naga dialect, involving confinement to the house, not talking to any one except the village priest, observing food restrictions, taking giner and rice-beer, as well as sleeping restrictions, particularly avoiding sleeping with his wife. All these expensive rites, rituals, are performed generally by the wealthy persons of a Naga village in order to qualify himself to erect a rough stone monolith in front of the house of the donor in memory of his dead ancestor or for himself and his wife when still alive. This social status is displayed on the roof of his dwelling house in the front gable of which a decorated house-horn or eaves, anciently made of timber now of G.I. Sheet, painted with red, black and white colours making circle disigns at regular intervals. Similarly, the megalithic builder is entitled to decorate the front veranda wall of his dwelling with wood carvings of Naga warriors, heads with elegant horns of the *'mithun' (Bos frontalis)* as well as other attractive designs and sun symbols, all decorated with bright red, yellow and black colours. In addition to this, the Naga villager, who had performed such elaborate rituals to drag up a rough stone monolith to be erected in front of his house, is rewarded by the society by honouring him with a special status distinguished by a special shawl, and ornaments of special precious beads. Thus dressed, he occupies a special seat in all village gatherings and village council meetings.

There appears to be very deep rooted social tradition in perpetuating and performing prehistoric megalithic tradition, giving us an opportunity to observe and understand fully the rites, rituals and religious beliefs of prehistoric times which have died out long ago in many parts of the world leaving for us only the material remains in the form of burial chambers or cists, dolmen, menhirs, cairns, etc. with their associated remains in the form of grave goods. Further, the social mechanism evolved by the traditional Naga society appears to have served a very useful purpose of social security and peace by maintaining economic equillibrium involving sharing of wealth accumulated by a family, in offering series of feasts with the sole aim of erecting a monolith and acquiring social status, so that in such primitive primary agricultural society, the evils of economic inequality i.e., the rich and poor is socially controlled.

The megalithic types found among the Nagas of Manipur consist of menhirs, alignments, avenues, dolmens, cairns with or without a stone–circle, capstone over the burial pit, stone-circles and stone seats raised in the memory of dead ancestors and some miscellaneous types, such as megaliths associated with head hunting, small menhirs erected in alignment called lover's stones by a person or his sons in recognition of the love affairs, a person may have had during his life time.

BIBLIOGRAPHY

Devi, P. Binodini 1994. "A study on the Megalithic culture of Manipur". Ph. D. Thesis, Gauhati University (Unpublished)

Haimendorf, C. Von Furer. 1964. "The Megalithic Culture of Assam" in Sohnitgar F. M. *(ed), Forgotten Kingdom of Sumatra* Leiden, Appendix I pp. 215-222

Hodson, T.C. 1911. *The Naga Tribes of Manipur.* Macmillan, London.

________ 1921. *The Angami Nagas,* Macmillan, London "The meaning and method of erection of monolith by Naga Tribes". *Jr. Royal Anth. Inst.* London, LVIII (2) : 399-408.

________ "Assam Megaliths", *Antiquity,* Cambridge III(2) : 399-408.

Rao, S.N. 1991. "Megalithic Practices among Khasis and Nagas of North–Eastern India, in J.P. Singh and Gautam Sengupta, (ed) *Archaeology of North–East India.* History Dept. North–Eastern Hill University, Shillong.

Singh, O.K. 1978. "A Live Megalithic Culture of Manipur," in V.N. Misra and Bellwood, (ed) *Recent Advances in Indo-Pacific Prehistory* Oxford Publishing Co. New Delhi, pp. 191-186.

Wati, Jungshi, 1997 : Megalithic Tradition in Nagaland : An Ethno-archaeological Study Ph. D. Thesis, Guahati University

T.C. Sharma

Nagaland University,
Kohima

Recent Trends in South Indian Megalithic Studies

Introduction

Earlier speculations about the megalithic culture was that it was the outcome of socio-economic problems in Western Europe arising out of the Industrial Revolution. Increasing thrust on diffusion and migration was evidenced in the works of German ethnologists such as Friedrich Rartzel, Franz Boas, and the Viennese school of Anthropology developed by Roman Catholic priests, Fritz Graefner and Wilhem Schmidt who advocated a non-Indian origin of megaliths.

Thus the diffusionists viewed human ability for innovation as limited; hence the thesis that basic discoveries had taken place in a unipolar region and then spread in various places.

While examining the role of ideology in the construction of megaliths in Europe, Kristiansen sees them as representing a ritualized extension of production through the communal lineage structure. Surplus production for lineage chieftains is transformed into ritual feasting and ancestor worship. This is mainly due to the perception of Marxist archaeologists that society is defined as the forces and relations of production. However, the Marxist approach of rejecting social reality has been opposed by Lull and Picazo who have correlated tombs and their contents to social cost and relative social value, thereby discarding the functionalist idea of an economic time of labour, separate from a social time of labour. Although this theory is based on historical materialism, it brings out the contradictions within the Marxist School.

Thoughts of fertility and sexuality predominate funeral practices according to certain anthropologists, and Bachofen who feels that "The funeral rite glorifies nature as a whole, with its two fold life and death giving principle." That is why the symbols of life are so frequent in the tomb. A graveyard has been depicted as a symbolic representation of the social order by Firth. The studies by Morin as well as Thomas cover a wider span, including the sociological, symbolic and psychoanalytical aspects of tombs, but they are a critique of Western approach towards death. In Germany, Herbert Jankuhn's interdisciplinary approaches and diachronic studies have fuelled an intensive debate on the social aspect of tombs, but it has completely shelved the contemporary Anglo-American debate on the question.

For Agostino, the study of tombs of a necropolis involves the reassembling of a system of structured signs which represent the society of the living in its social and functional hierarchy. Neustupny argues that tombs symbolise 'social stratification' as there are differences in the cultural material as well as in the arrangement of tombs.

Anthropological studies

From about the second half of the nineteenth century human skeletal remains from the megalithic burials have been subjected to critical analyses and several theses have been propounded. Prominent among them are Zuckerman who studied the skull from Adichchanallur and found Veddoid elements. S.S. Sarkar, H.K. Bose, Gupta and Dutta, Kenneth A.R. Kennedy and a host of others have contributed to the study of skeletal remains. The literature is enormous and it is not possible to recount every aspect of the human remains in this short note.

Skeletal evidence from burial from the megalithic and post-megalithic periods have gained importance because of the recent development in the sciences of taphonomy and forensic anthropology.

Palaeobotanical evidence

Palaeoethnobotanical studies have yielded evidences of cultivated plants. Paiyampalli in Tamil Nadu

Veerapuram in Andhra Pradesh, Hallur and Koppa in Karnataka, Adichanallur in Tamil Nadu. Gajjalkonda in Andhra Pradesh, Parambantalli and Chokkanad in Kerala ar have yielded evidence for cultivated grains. Rice, barley, wheat, kodo millet, common pea, lentil, horse gram, common bean, black gram, belric myrabolan and cucurbitaceous seed have been recognised from these sites.

Archaeozoological evidence

Archaeozoological vestiges from megalithic remains and associated early historical sites have shed light on the domesticated animals like cattle, buffalo, sheep, goat, pig, horse and the ass. The economy of megalithic period as observed from faunal remains was a combination of stock breeding, farming, hunting and occasional fishing. But main occupation was cattle pastoralism as evident from the large number of cattle bones found from the sites. This assumption that the megalithic-folk were practicing agro-pastoral economy needs reconsideration on the basis of emerging archaeological evidences.

The vexed problem of the pattern of subsistence of the megalithic people—whether they were nomadic pastrolists, depending heavily on cattle wealth and a little agricultural production or cultivctors. of sort in the dry semi arid zone is yet to be solved. However, the artifacts recovered from megaliths sites are related to the environmental diversity of south India which vary from region to region.

Hence an inter–disciplinary and a collective study and analysis is essential to understand the social dynamics and subsistence pattern of the megalithic culture of south India, as also the cultural interactions with other regions.

BIBLIOGRAPHY

Bachofen, J.J. 1967. *Myth, Religion and Mother Right,* p. 39, (trans. E. Mannheim). London : Routledge and Kegan Paul.

Bose, H.K. 1959. Preliminary Reports on the Faunal Remains, *Ancient India,* Vol. 15, pp. 40-42

Chatterjee, B.K. and P. Gupta. 1963. *Report on the Adichanallur Skulls.* Anthropological Survey of India.

Childe, V. Gordon 1948. "Megaliths", *Ancient India* No. 4, pp. 5-13.

Deo, S.B. 1973. *Problem of South Indian Megaliths,* Dharwar : Karnataka University.

Gupta, P. and P.C. Dutta. 1962. Human Remains Excavated from Megaliths at Yeleswaram, *Man in India* (42), pp. 19-34.

Gupta, P., A. Basu and P.C. Dutta. 1970. *Ancient Human Remains : a Study of Nagarjunakonda Skeletons.* Calcutta : Anthropological Survey of India.

Hunt, E.H. 1924. Hyderbad Cairns and their Significance, *Journal of the Royal Anthropological Institute* (54), pp. 140-156.

Hutchinson, Joseph 1976. *India : Local and Introduced Crops,* Phil. Trans. R. Soc. Land. B 275, pp. 129-141.

Iyer, L.A. Krishna 1929-30. Prehistoric Archaeology of Kerala *Quarterly Journal of Mythic Society.* Vol. (20), pp. 115-126. Bangalore :

Kajale, M.D. 1980. Palaeobotanical and Pollen Analytical Investigations. *Indian Antiquary* 1977-78, pp. 91-92.

Kajale, M.D. 1984. New Light on Agricultural Plant Economy during First Millennium BC : Palaeobotanical study of Plant Remains from excavations at Veerapuam, district Kurnool, Andhra Pradesh, pp. 1-17, appendix B n T.V.G. Sastri, Kasturi Bai and J. Vara Prasada Rao. *Veerapuram, A Type site for Cultural Study in the Krishna Valley.* Hyderabad : Birla Archaeological and Cultural Research Institute.

Kennedy, K.A.R. 1975. *The Physical Anthropology of the Megalith Builders of South India and Srilanka,* Canberra: Australian National University Press. pp. 75-76,

Kennedy, K.A.R. 1994. Identification of Sacrificial and Massacre Victims in Archaeological Sites : The Skeletal Evidence. *Man and Environment* XIX (1-2), pp. 247-251.

Kristiansen, K. 1984. "Ideology and Material Culture—An Archaeological Perspective, in Marxist Perspectives in Archaeology (M. Spriggs Ed.)." Cambridge, Cambridge University Press.

Mishra, P.K. 1969. Nomadism in India, *Journal of the Indian*

Anthropological Association (4), pp. 79-80.

Morin, E. 1970. *L. Homme Al mort.* Paris : Edition du Seuil.

Nath, B. 1963. Animal Remains from Brahmagiri (Mysore State, India), *Records of the Zoological Survey of India.* 61, pp. 65-68.

Neustupny, E. 1991. Recent Theoretical Achievements in Preistoric Archaeology in Czechoslovakia, in Hodder (Ed.), *Archaeological Theory in Europe* London : pp. 253.

Prasad, R.R. 1994. *Pastoral Nomadism in Arid Zones of India-Socio-Demographic and Ecological Aspects,* New Delhi : Discovery Publishing House.pp. 10-101.

Sarkar, S.S. 1960. 'Human Skeletal Remains from Brahmagiri', *Bulletin of the Department of Anthropology,* Calcutta (9), pp. 5-26.

Taylor, P. Meadows. 1851. 'Ancient remains at the village of Jiwurgi near Farozabad on the Bhima', *Journal of the Royal Asiatic Society* Bombay Branch 3., pp. 179-93.

Thomas, P.K. 1984. Faunal Assemblage of Veerapuram in (T.V.G. Sastri et al. Ed.), *Veerapuram : a Type Site for Cultural Study in the Krishna Valley,* pp. i-xi. Hyderabad : Bhavani Printers.

________ 1992. Faunal background of the Iron Age culture of Maharashtra. *Man and Environment,* Vol. XVII (2), Indian Society for Preistoric and Quaternary Studies Pune. pp. 75-79.

________ 1994. Holocene faunal studies in India in *Man and Environment,* Vol. XIX No. (1-2), pp. 179-203.

Vishnu—Mittre, 1972. Palaeobotany and the Environment of Early Man in India in S.B. Deo (Ed.), *Archaeologycial Congres Seminar Papers.* Nagpur : Nagpur University). pp. 206-212.

Zuckerman, S. 1930. *'The Adichanallur Skulls',* Bulletin of the Madras Government Museum (2), pp. 1-24.

Department of Archaeology,
Deccan College,
Pune

B.S. HARISHANKAR

Archaeological Investigation in Central Orissa

Introduction

Archaeological research on the early historical sites in Orissa is mostly based on the documented evidence like inscriptions or a few isolated material objects. Quite often, conclusions are drawn on the basis of a few coins and objects of artistic value that were unsystematically recovered in the past. However, in addition to ceramics and coins, bones and grains recovered from archaeological sites can also provide vital information about the cultural *milieu* of the past.

Lack of systematic and extensive survey has been the major drawback in understanding the early historical Central Orissa, particularly regarding the sites mentioned in literature. Absence of proper recording of the several components of the material culture such as ceramics, small finds, bones and grains add to confusion.

Archaeological research in Central Orissa is limited except for a small-scale excavation at Manamunda-Asurgarh[1]. However, extensive explorations carried out during 1995-97[2] have brought to light a number of early historical sites. These sites have yielded besides usual archaeological artifacts and faunal remains, large quantity of iron slag and iron ore. This note discusses recent archaeological investigations made during 1995-96 and 1996-97 field season at three early historical sites in the central part of Orissa namely. Manamunda, Deuli and Marjakud in Boudh district, by the first author. Here an attempt is made to study the faunal remains of the sites explored in the region and an effort is also made to analyse the material culture and other related information to understand ancient trade activity in the region with other parts of Orissa.

The Area of Study

District Boudh (Fig. 1) is located in Central Orissa and is bordered by the Districts Angul (north), Nayagarh (east), Sonepur (west) and Khondmal (south). The vegetal cover in this district is mostly of dry deciduous type. There are large forest tracts forming part of the northernmost extremity of the Eastern Ghats. The annual rainfall in Boudh district is 1500 mm.

The Sites

Marjakud (20^0 47'–20^{0}50' N and 84^0 20'–84^0 21' E)

The early historical site of Marjakud is located on an island in river Mahanadi and the village is under the administrative control of the Notified Area Council of Boudh. The mound is locally called as Guriamunda and is about 400 m away from the village towards south covering an area of 200 x 150 sq. m. The habitation deposit is 1.50 m. It is partly disturbed due to the fluvial activity of the river on the western side.

The mound was subjected to a random sampling and plotting. From the surface a large quantity of potsherds, iron slags have been recovered. To understand the nature of habitation, a trial pit was laid measuring 1 x 1 m on the periphery of the mound and dug up to a depth of 0.5 m. This trench yielded a few fragments of potsherds and charred bones.

The ceramic assemblage of the site is similar to that of other excavated and explored early historical sites in coastal part of Orissa[3]. Especially, the black slipped ware of different shapes, has a striking similarity with that of the Northern Black Polished Ware (Plate IB) in the Ganga Valley[4]. About 80% are sherds of Black and Red ware (Plate II A) of different shapes like bowls, dishes, globular pots, etc. Most of the potsherds bear decoration on the interior with incised linear patterns and horizontal bands (Pl II B).)Prior to the early historical people here it is evident that the site was occupied by the Black and Red ware users. Other finds include semi-precious stone beads (Plate IIIA) and terracotta lids, and handles (Plate III B).

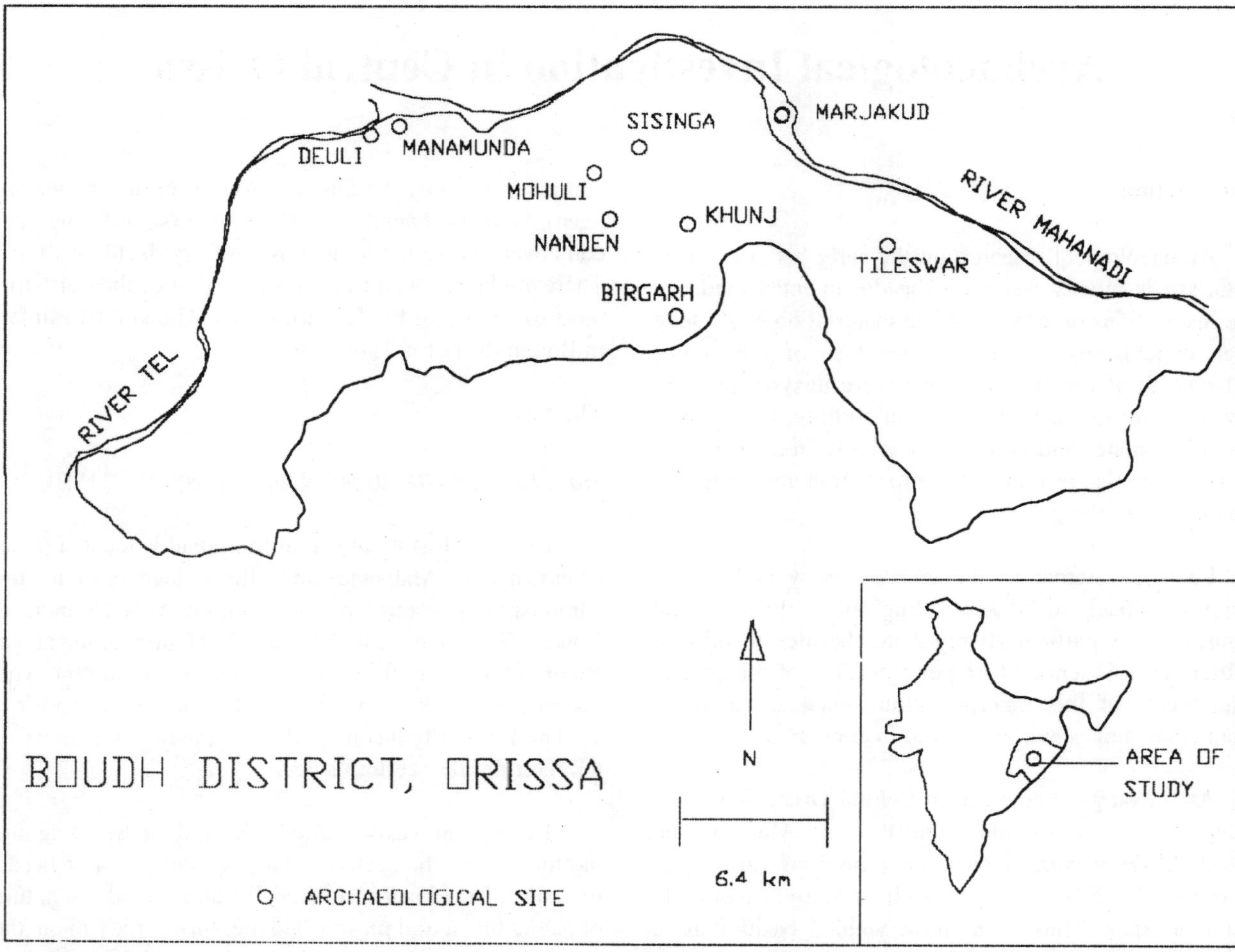

Fig. 1. Archaeological Sites in Boudh District, Orissa

During trial dig at Marjakud, only 16 bone fragments (55 gm) were recovered. All these fragments are completely charred and fragmentary. It was possible to identify 4 fragments. This collection has revealed presence of cattle or buffalo, sheep or goat and a mammal of the size of hare *(Lepus nigricollis).*

Manamunda (20⁰51′ N and 83⁰ 59′ E)

The site of Manamunda is located 50 km from Boudh town on its west. The complex is located on the confluence of river Mahanadi and river Tel and contains a number of mounds parallel to the river bank. The site was reported and partly excavated earlier[5]. From the section scrapings and the erosional part of the mound a large number of potsherds, iron objects and bone specimens have been recovered. A major part of the mound has been washed away by the river. Consequently it is difficult to ascertain the original size of the mound. The available habitation deposit is about 2 m thick.

The finding of knobbed ware at the site which is associated with the most of the early historical sites in the coastal part of Orissa clearly suggests the cultural contact of the people with other parts of Orissa through trade network[6]. A punch-marked coin with five symbols found in the excavations at this site[7] dates to 3rd century B.C. Apart from the above findings a large number of Black and Red ware, Black slipped ware, Red slipped ware dull red ware and skin rubbers, sling balls and ear-ornaments made of terracotta have been noticed. From the surface, a large number of iron slag fragments and ore nodules have been recovered, These findings point to an iron smelting activity of the people at the site. This has been substantiated by the presence of the considerable amount of iron implements. Presence of a few pieces of iron nails that are used exclusively in the boat construction work in this part of Orissa nowadays is noteworthy. This perhaps indicates Orissan trade activity in the early historical times.

At this site a total of 17 bone fragments were collected weighing 322 g. of which 13 were identifiable. (Pl. IV A & IV B) This collection revealed presence of cattle *(Bos indicus)*, buffalo *(Bubalus bubalis),* wild pig *(Sus scrofa)* and deer *(Cervus sp.)*. The fragments, one each of cattle, sheep/goat and deer had cut marks and marks of charring indicating that they have been butchered and consumed. A piece of antler (MND 12) perhaps was cut and charred in order to make a tool from it. Earlier in 1981, a few bones collected from Manamunda Mound III revealed that cattle bones (with charring and cut marks), sheep (*Ovis aries*) and wild pig (*Sus scrofa*) were present[8].

Deuli (20^0 49′ N and 83^0 54′ E)

The early historical site of Deuli is a part of the culture complex of Manamunda itself. It is located on the banks of the river Tel, a tributary of river Mahanadi. The habitational area measures about 200 x 200 m and the thickness of the deposit is 2 m. The mound is partly disturbed due to the river; the central part however, has remained intact. The artifacts at Deuli include ceramics, bones, iron objects, iron ore nodules and a large number of slag pieces. The ceramic assemblage of Deuli consists of Black and Red ware, red slipped ware, gray ware and black slipped wares. Specifically shapes in Black and Red ware consisted of bowls and dishes. Black slipped ware forms were dishes and lids while that of red slipped ware were pots, jars, shallow bowls and lids. The site also yielded a complete bowl of Black and Red ware with a graffiti mark on the exterior surface.

The bones collected from Manamunda as well as Marjakud have been dated to the time bracket of the early historic period in Orissa based on fluorine/phosphate technique (Table 1).

Table 1 Results of the fluorine/phosphate dating

Site	% F	% P	% P_2O_5	100F/P^2O_5
Manamunda	0.074	15.00	32.91	0.215
Marjakud	0.072	14.37	34.35	0.218

Concluding Remarks

The information gathered can be corroborated with that of known sites of coastal Orissa to highlight the early historical period of this region. The current exploration work carried out provided adequate data in terms of material culture along with faunal wealth of the early historical Central Orissa. The information gathered can lead to further investigations and bring out the archaeological richness of this less explored area in Orissa.

Acknowledgements

The authors wish to thank Prof. V.N. Misra for giving constant encouragement and Dr. R.K. Mohanty for his valuable suggestions and comments. Dr. A.A. Kshirsagar has kindly analysed the bone material on priority basis and, therefore, the authors are grateful to her.

REFERENCES

1. Mishra, C.R. and S. Pradhan 1990. *Excavation at Manamunda.* Sambalpur : Sambalpur University.

2. Tripathy, B. 1996. (in press). Archaeological Exploration in Boudh District, Orissa, *Bulleting of the Deccan College Post-graduate and Research Institute.*

3. Lal, B.B. 1949. Sisupalgarh 1948: An Early Historic Fort in the Eastern coast, *Ancient India* 5:62-105

4. Makhan Lal 1982. *Early Human Colonization Patterns in the Ganga–Yamuna Doab.* Ph.D. Dissertation, University of Poona.

5. Benarjee, R.D. 1929. Antiquities of the Boudh State, *Journal of the Bihar Orissa Research Society* XIV : 64-86; also Mishra and Pradhan, 1910 *op cit.*

6. Tripathy, B. (in Press). Archaeology of Boudh, Central Orissa, in K.K. Basa and P. Mohanty (Eds.). *Archaeology of Orissa* New Delhi, Pratibha Prakashan. 1998

7. Pradhan, S. 1995. A Note on a Punch-marked Coin found from Manamunda Excavation, *Journal of the Numismatic Society of India,* LIV (1-2) : 26-28.

8. Personal communication from Dr. P. K. Thomas

9. A.A. Kshirsagar Personal Communication.

Department of Archaeology
Deccan College, Pune 411 006

BALARAM TRIPATHY AND P.P. JOGLEKAR

Faunal Remains from Tharsa

The Site

Tharsa (21^0 13´ N; 79^0 23´ E) is 42 km north-east of Nagpur (District Nagpur, Maharashtra) on the left bank of river Sand (Fig. 1). The Department of Ancient History and Archaeology, University of Nagpur laid a single trench of 10 x 10 m on the ancient mound in 1985-86.

The excavations revealed four occupation layers belonging to Megalithic culture with Chalcolithic affini-

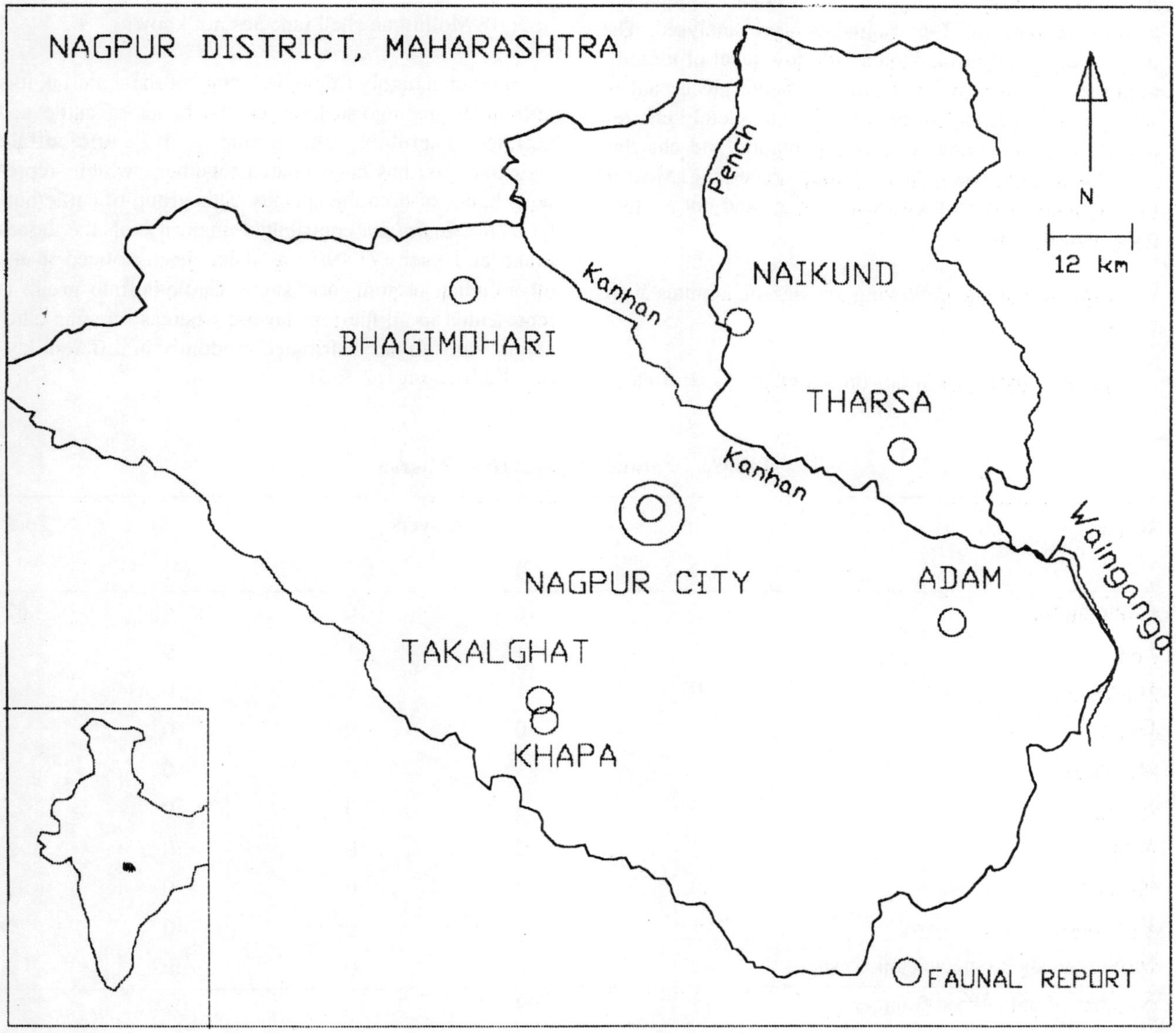

Fig. 1

ties[1]. Total cultural deposit was 85 cm thick which yielded pottery, terracotta hop-scatches, beads and animal bones. The pottery at Tharsa compares well with that from Adam II and Adam III, i.e. the Chalcolithic and Iron Ages respectively.

Faunal Material

Bones collected from Tharsa were handed over to the Archaeolozoology laboratory at Deccan College for analysis. A total of 196 fragments were analysed. The bones were highly fragmented with low level of identifiability i.e. about 30% (137 unidentifiable pieces out of 196). A large number of bones were completely charred as well as fragmented. This fragmentation and charring were due to activities related to food processing. Most of the fragments weighed between 5-15 g and not a single piece was measurable.

Remains of the following species of animals were noticed :

(1) *Bos indicus* (Cattle)/*Bubalus bubalis* (Buffalo)
(2) *Canis familiaris* (Dog)
(3) *Antilope cervicapra* (Black buck)
(4) *Axis axis* (Chital)
(5) *Axis porcinus* (Hog deer)
(6) *Cervus unicolor* (Sambar)
(7) *Sus scrofa* (Wild pig)
(8) *Rattus rattus* (house rat)
(9) Bird (species not known)
(10) Molluscan shell (species not known)

In such a highly fragmentry state of the material, it is difficult to distinguish between the bones of cattle and buffalo. Therefore, the group of cattle/buffalo *(Bos/Bubalus)* has been treated together, which represents bones of both the species. This group of cattle/buffalo *(Bos/Bubalus)* contributed majority of the bones found at Tharsa (71.19%) as it has been noticed in the other Indian protohistoric sites[2]. Cattle/buffalo group is represented in all the four layers; whereas remains other animals are found distributed randomly in different layers (Table 1, Figs. 2 & 3).

Table 1 : Faunal remains from Tharsa

Species	Layers				Total
	(1)	(2)	(3)	(4)	
Cattle/buffalo	12	16	10	4	42
Dog	0	1	1	0	2
Blackbuck	0	1	0	0	1
Chital	1	0	0	0	1
Hog Deer	0	1	0	0	1
Sambar	0	3	0	0	3
Wild Pig	1	2	0	0.	3
House Rat	0	2	0	0	2
Bird (speecies not known)	1	1	0	0	2
Molluscan shell (species unknown)	0	2	0	0	2
Number of indentified fragments	15	29	11	04	59
Total unidentified fragments	68	32	26	11	137
Total bone fragments	83	61	37	15	196

Bones of common rat *(Rattus rattus)* and of the domentic dog *(Canis familiaris)* are devoid of charring and cut marks. In this faunal assemblage dog bones could have been brought within the site by scavengers including the dogs. It is commonly observed that rats intrude into ancient habitation deposits. Therefore, these species have not contributed to the food of the people at Tharsa.

Table 2 Presence/absence of wild mammals at Megalithic/Chalcolithic sites in Nagpur District

	THR	BMR	NKD	ADM III	TKP
Gaur	–	–	+	+	–
Nilgai	–	–	–	+	–
Chowsingha	–	+	–	–	–
Blackbuck	+	–	–	+	–
Chital	+	–	+	+	–
Hog Deer	+	–	–	–	–
Sambar	+	+	+	+	+
Muntjak	–	+	–	–	–
Wild Pig	+	–	+	+	–
Hare	–	+	+	–	–

THR : Tharsa

BMR : Bhagimohari

NKD : Naikund

ADM : Adam

TKA : Takalghat Khapa

\+ : Present

– : Absent

Faunal assemblages from here can be compared with those at Naikund[3], Takalghat Khapa[4] Bhagimohari[5] and Adam[6]. The comparison of occurrence of wild mammalian species. (Table 2) reveals that the gaur and nilgai found at Adam III and Naikund are absent at other three sites. Blackbuck which is common both at Tharsa and Adam III is not present at Bhagimohari, Naikund and Takalghat–Khapa. Except Bhagimohari and Takalghat Khapa, wild pig bones have been found at rest of the sites. Even at present, wild pig and several species of deer are commonly seen in the Vidarbha region. Presence of deer, particularly sambar at all the sites is noteworthy. Except at Bhagimohari, chital has been seen at all the sites. Bones of hog deer and *muntjak* have been found at Tharsa and Bhagimohari, respectively. As has been suggested by Thomas[7] the faunal assemblages at all the sites indicate an environment similar to that found in this region today.

The faunal material examined from Tharsa is only from a trial trench and therefore, final conclusion on the presence or absence of species cannot be made at this stage. However, it is important to note that even such a small trial excavation at Tharsa has added to our information of the fauna at the megalithic sites in Vidarbha.

Concluding Remarks

The bones studied are from only one trench of 10x10 m and therefore, inadequate for any quantitative analysis. Therefore, it is not possible to comment on the food economy at Tharsa. However, presence of five wild animals in just 59 fragments is interesting. This shows that probably the people at Tharsa were not only engaged in raising cattle but also exploting a wide range of wild fauna as has been noticed at Adam[7]. The study has provided scope for future inter-site comparisons and clues for examination of faunal remains in the area in wider perspecive.

Acknowledgements

The authors wish to thank Dr. K. Ismail of the Nagpur University for entrusting the faunal material to them and Dr. P.S. Joshi, Deccan College for his help in preparing the map.

REFERENCES

1. *Indian Archaeology 1985-86 –A Review* and also personal communication by K. Ismail.

2. Thomas, P.K. 1988. Faunal Assemblage, in M.K. Dhavalikar, H.D. Sankalia and Z.D. Ansari (eds.) *Excavaion at Inamgaon* Vol. I part ii, pp. 822-961. Pune : Deccan College also Thomas, P.K. 1992. Faunal Background of the Iron Age Culture of Maharashtra, *Man and Environment,* XVII (2) : 75-80.

3. Badam, G.L. 1982. Faunal Remains from Naikund With Special Reference to Animal Domestication in S.B. Deo and A.P. Jamkhedkar (eds.), *Naikund Excavations 1978-80* pp. 70-91. Bombay : Government of Maharashtra

4. Thomas, P.K. 1993. Faunal Remains from the Megalithic Habitation Site of Bhagimohari, *Man and Environment* XVIII (2) : 105-118.

5. Thomas, P.K., P.P. Joglekar and Arati Deshpande-Mukherjee. Faunal Assemblage at Adam. : A Multi-cultural site in the Vidarbha Region of Maharashtra. Report submitted to the Archaeological Survey of India.

6. Thomas 1993 op cit

7. Thomas et al. in press

P.P. JOGLEKAR AND P.K. THOMAS

Department of Archaeology
Deccan College,
Pune 411 006

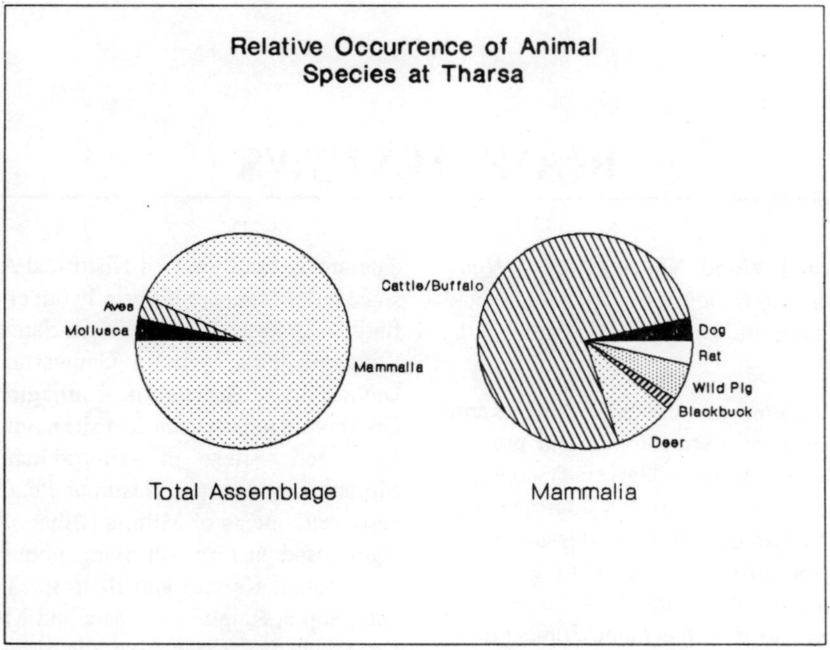
Relative Occurrence of Animal
Species at Tharsa
Aves
Mollusca
Mammalia
Total Assemblage
Cattle/Buffalo
Dog
Rat
Wild Pig
Blackbuck
Deer
Mammalia

Fig 2

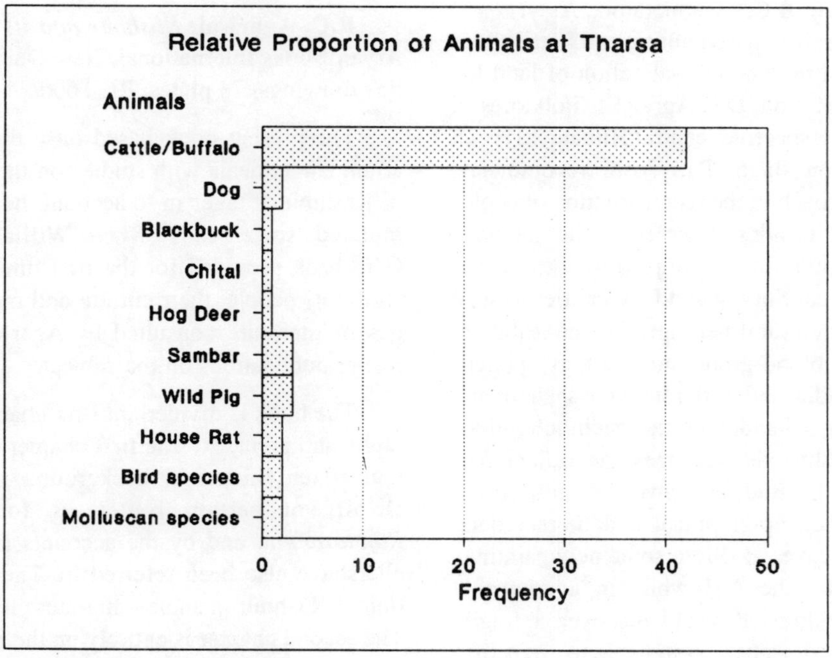
Relative Proportion of Animals at Tharsa
Animals
Cattle/Buffalo
Dog
Blackbuck
Chital
Hog Deer
Sambar
Wild Pig
House Rat
Bird species
Molluscan species
0
10
20
30
40
50
Frequency

Fig 3

BOOK REVIEWS

B.M. Khanduri and **Vinod Nautiyal** (eds.) *Him-Kanti (Prof. K.P. Nautiyal Felicitation Volume)*, Book India Publishing Co. Rampura, Delhi 110035, pp. 1-301, figures 29, Price Rs. 1800/-.

This Felicitation volume in honour of Prof. Kanti Prasad Nautiyal, an eminent archaeologist and present Vice-Chancellor of H.N.B. Garhwal University contains critical and fresh research papers by his admirers and senior Indologists. The large number of articles are on the central Himalayan region providing interesting glimpses of the rich but little known cultural tradition, history and archaeology of the area justifies the name *Hima-Kanti.* Papers on prehistoric archaeology covers a vast area from the Ganga plains, Himalaya terrain to Gujarat and Goa. S.P. Gupta in his thought provoking paper speaks about eco-friendly and eco-unfriendly parameters and avers that during third millennium B.C. Mesopotamia, Assyria and Egypt witnessed prosperity in agriculture and horticulture whereas in the second millennium salination of land led to large scale desertification. D.P. Agrawl's 'Folklores in the interdisciplinary perspective (central Himalayas) is an interesting contribution. Jagat Pati Joshi recommends multidisciplinary approach in the reconstruction of ecology, and environment besides other scientific methods including the pedological studies adopted by the excavator of the Archaeological Survey and Universities as well as for preservation of cultural heritage. The contributors have also discussed blood-group archaeology, pottery making in ancient India and different views about the identification of King Chandra of the Mehrauli pillar-inscription. M.N. Deshpande describes the salient features of paintings in the Buddhist caves of India in the context of their lay-out, epigraphical and literary data. Recently in Buddhist caves at Ellora some new paintings have been exposed by the ASI while in a *vihara* at Thanala (Konkan) he himself could discover a fragile painting illustrating Bodhisattva, assignable to *circa* fifth century. Another note by Krishna Deva which may be useful to students and layman alike incorporates the upto date and overall view of Historical Archaeology in India since independence. He briefly but critically discusses the finds from key-sites like Sunet, Sanghol, Harsha-ka-Tila. Sringaverapura, Mathura, Ganwaria, Rangmahal, Akota, Devnimori, Sisupalgarh, Ratnagiri, Nagarjunakonda, Dharnikota (a port-*cum*-fort site), Salihundam, Pauni, and excavated sites in Uttarakhanda viz. Thapali, Moradhawaj, Panipat, Kashipur etc. Other articles discuss early settlements of Mithila (Bihar); Dhatris, Kinnaras in legend and history, surviving pottery making tradition, hero-stones, Katyuri and Bharasivas, feudalism, temples and people, Rajput, Sultanate and Mughal relations with Uttarakhanda. Absence of diacritical marks is a great lapse. The book will be useful to scholars, general readers and the libraries.

P.K. Trivedi.

R.C. Agarwal, *Kashmir and its monumental glory*, Aryan Books International, New Delhi, 1998, pp.208, 73 line drawings, 73 plates, Rs. 1600/-.

The present book based on a thematochronological arrangement deals with studies on the monumental glory of Kashmir. It takes in to account the vast material accumulated since 1841 when William Moorcroft and G.Treback provided for the first time an account of the Kashmiri people, their culture and monuments. The corpus of literature consulted by Agarwal includes all the earlier publications on the subject.

The book is divided into six chapters with a bibliography and an index. The first chapter deals with the ecological and historical background of Kashmir Valley. Details of certain routes as found in Kalhana's *Rajatarangini* and by the accounts left by foreign travellershave also been referred to. The geographical position of Kashmir in ancient literature has been worked out. The second chapter is entirely on the neolithic-megalithic culture in the valley. The excavations carried out at Buzahom during 1960 and 1968 provided new data which brought into focus cultural contacts outside the frontiers of Kashmir in China and Pakistan across the Chinese Republic. The presence of menhirs in Kashmir connects them with similar ones in Himalayan ranges. The third chapter is on the early historical remains as noticed at Burzahom Gufkral and Semthan. In this region Kushanas succeeded the Indo-Greeks. The apsidal *stupa* at Harwan has become a landmark of early artistic activity (3rd-4th century AD) in this Himalayan region. Chapter four deals with the development of temple architecture and all the important ones starting from Narang to Kakpura which are now lying in rupinous condition. Chapter five is on Islamic architectural heritage in Kashmir beginning from the mosque of Shah Hamdan and ending with Akhun Mulla Shah mosque built by Dara Shukoh. The last chapter dealing with conclusion is very short.

The author has presented a masterly analysis while describing the development of temple architecture in the valley especially the domical ceilings which are remarkable features of temples of Kashmir. Fundamentally these are different from the domes of the Islamic buildings in the region.

It will be seen from the contents of collected data that the work so far as it goes, is quite analytical and thought provoking. It has excellent potential material-wise to inspire future researchers.

K.N. Dikshit

Pramod Kumar Mishra, *Archaeology of Mayurbhanj,* D.K. Printwold (P) Ltd. New Delhi pp, 1997 XIII+40, 49 Plates, figures, Appendix, bibliography and Index Price Rs. 480.

Mayurbhanj, is derived from two medieval ruling dynasties of Orissa, the Mayuras and the Bhanjas, the latter subordinates of the Bhauma-Karas of Orissa; and they adopted the Bhauma era for their epigraphs.

The Mayuras of Bonai Mandala disappeared from the historical scene of Orissa much earlier. The Bhanjas, of the Khijjinga Mandala, however, continued to survived till the middle of the 20th century, though as a princely state. They initially ruled from Khijjingakotta, modern Kiching. Khijjingakotta, was overrun by Firozshah Tugluk in 1361 and the Bhanjas shifted their capital in 1400 to Haripur or Hariharapur, named after the then Bhanja ruler Harihara Bhanja Deo. Hereafter the kingdom came to be known as Mauyrbhanj. The peacock the original eblem was replaced with the Bull as the state insignia. The Britishers conquered the state in 1801 and henceforward it became princely state subordinate to the British rule.

Consequent upon the merger of this princely state in 1949 with the state of Orissa, Mayurbhanj became a district covering an area of over six thousand square kilometres.

Mayurbhanj has a hoary past commencing right from the Palaeolithic times - the sites are located on the banks of Burhabalanga and its tributaries Sone and Ganghar. The area was explored by N.K. Bose, Dharani Sen, Mohapatra and others and their accounts have been published. Kuliana is the type site. Besides the Palaeolithic sites we perceive activities of the Neolithic people - Baidipur and Kuchai - the latter was excavated by the late B.K. Thapar and the results noticed in the *Indian Archaeology a Review* which brought to light the peculiar characteristics of Orissan Neolithic.

The present book by Prof. Mishra is an attempt to recapture the past archaeological glory of a bygone princely state. In the process, we see in the book more of art and architecture represented by temples and sculptures at Haripur and Kiching; the other aspects of the culture of the district are confined to brief statement of facts.

The book is in four chapters with a post script. The first recounts the history of the Bhanjas till 1947 besides a brief account of persons who researched in this area. The second deals with the structural remains of Haripur and their maintenance and research. Temple and sculptural vestiges of Kiching are embodied in the next chapter. In these two chapters, the efforts of the archaeologists involved in the upkeep of monuments and the budget involved are highlighted.

The post script updates the research done in this district in the post-independence times.

Illustrations in the book pertain to temples and sculptures: photographs or line drawings of the vestiges of Stone Age Mayurbhanj have been completely omitted, otherwise, the book is very informative.

K.S. Ramachandran

Amarendra Nath, *Further Excavations at Pauni* 1994, Archaeological survey of India, New Delhi, 1998, pp. 124, 35 line drawings, 48 plates, price Rs. 275.

The excavations at Pauni undertaken in 1994 are the accounts of field work under taken by the author in the Wardha - Wainganga valley while he was posted in Excavations Branch (I), Nagpur. The site was earlier jointly excavated by S.B. Deo and J.P. Joshi who brought out the remains of one of the largest brick *stupas* in Vidharbha. The present excavation, while confirming the earlier chronology has widened the time-span of human occupation at the site.

The report is divided into eleven chapters. The first chapter deals with the scope of work and summary of results of the excavations, whereas second chapter is devoted to the cuttings in habitational and rampart areas. The third devoted to chronology based on numismatic data. The fourth is about structures of various periods. The fifth chapter is on pottery and has been dealt in detail. Chapters six, seven and eight deal with minor antiquities including coins and seals. Chapters nine and ten are devoted to plant and animal remains respectively. The last chapter is conclusion. A bibliography is also appended.

The report is an important contribution on the growth of early historical urban centres of the eastern Vidarbha and their relationship with other urban centres situated on the trans-peninsular trade routes. The cyclopean wall was constructed immediately over the existing rampart.

The report is a welcome addition and throws refreshing light on many knotty historical problems of the region.

K.N. Dikshit

Rekha Jain, *Ancient Indian Coinage,* D.K. Printworld(P) Ltd., New Delhi, XIII+24, 50 illustrations, map, Bibliography and Index, Price : Rs. 350/-.

Coins in general, as Casey would aver "are perceived as dating evidence, as art objects and as a unique species of evidence that is left to numismatists and confined to Museum strong room at the earliest possible moment". This perception is changing rapidly and coins and currency - both forming money–are being viewed in a broader economic parameters as evidences for reconstructing and assessing the wealth of a state authority issuing them and also the quantum and extent of trade relations; they being the means of exchange.

This aspect is emphasised in the definition of a coin by Casey. "The essential defining characteristic of a coin is not its shape, or metal but it should expressly or implicitly show the authority by which it was issued and which in the last analysis guarantees its utility as a means of exchange".

In Rekha Jain's *Ancient Coinage* this view is reflected. Her study spans a wide area both in space and time right from the coins of the *Janapadas* down to the medieval times—. 6th century B.C. to century A.D. It shows that metallic currency predominated ancient India. From a study of the various issues of the several dynasties Ms Jain enunciates some salient features: a sort of standardisation of coins was initiated during the regime of the Nandas; the Mauryans introduced different denominations in their coinage; gold coins emerged during the Mauryan rule; coins were also made legal tender. Her analysis shows that money economy started to decline during the Gupta period and its revival was only during the early medieval times, primarily due to a spurt and revival of trade activities i.e. in the 9th century and afterwards. The author deals also with barter and other medium of exchange– cowrie shells, metal-ratio and source of metals, the technique of manufacture of coin, besides their nomenclature such as *Karshapana, suvarna, rusika, purana* etc. Denominations, standard weights and other cognate information regarding the coins are also mentioned.

The book is divided into several chapters - the first two being of a general nature detailing what money is about and the methodology of research. The subsequent chapters tell us about coins and related matters of specific period viz. *Janapada, Maurya,* etc. ending with a chapter on the coins of early medieval times.

The tome is a comprehensive study of the subject spanning over a time span of eighteen hundred years and gives a graphic description of how coins and currency developed over the period. The author perceives coins - to her money - as a medium of exchange and its role in trade and prosperity.

A good bibliography, an index besides several illustrations add value to the book.

The author needs to be congratulated on a good job done.

K.S. Ramachandran

Report of the XXXI Annual Conference of Indian Archaeological Society held at Srinagar (Garhwal) from the 16th Through the 18th October, 1997

The annual session of three Societies namely Indian Archaeological Society, Indian Society for Prehistoric and Quaternary Studies and Indian History and Culture Society for the Year 1997 was held in collaboration with Department of Ancient Indian History, Culture and Archaeology, H.N.B. University, Srinagar(Garhwal) in Srinagar, Garhwal and was inaugurated by Prof. K.P. Nautiyal Vice-Chancellor of the University on the 16th October, 1998.

After the inaugural function, Dr. K.M. Srivastava delivered the Presidential Address of the Indian Archaeological Society; Prof. Allchin delivered the Presidential address of the Indian Society for Prehistoric and Quaternary Studies and Prof. Rasesh Jamindar of the Indian History and Culture Society. The closing function was held on 18th October and the Valedictory Address was given by the Pro-Vice Chancellor of the Srinagar University.

The number of papers presented at the seminar were fairly large. In order to save time and give opportunity to every one parallel sessions were organised on all the three days of the seminar. A number of scholars presented their papers on the 'Himalayan Archaeology', a seminar organised on this occasion by the Indian Archaeological Society. It included a variety of subsidiary and cognate subjects ranging from the prehistory and palaeo-environment of the Himalayan region to early historic cultures.

Those who presented papers in all the three societies exceeded a hundred.

Programme

Thursday, 16 October: Afternoon Session

Professor H.D. Sankalia Memorial Lecture by Prof. Raymond Allchin: Interface of History and Archaeology

PRESENTATION OF PAPER FOR H.D.SANKALIA YOUNG ARCHAEOLOGIST AWARD.

Dilip Rajgor	Rediscovering the Janapada Punch-marked Coins of Early Historic India
Arati Deshpande-Mukharjee:	Shell fishing and Shell Craft Activities - During the Harappan Period with Special Reference to Gujarat.

PRESENTATION OF PAPERS AT COMBINED SESSION

P. Ajithprasad	Palaeolithic Settlements in Jogpura.
J.N. Pal	Recent Exploration of Palaeolithic Culture near Kerwa Dam, Bhopal, Madhya Pradesh.
Ravi Korisettar	Geoarchaeology of the Lakhmapur Palaeolithic Site.
Ramawtar Sharma	Prehistoric Exploration of Gwalior District.

Friday, 17 October: Forenoon Session

K.S. Shukla	Achievements of Indian Archaeology since Independence
J.N. Pande	Prof. G.R. Sharma: Fifty Years of Archaeology, Allahabad University
D.N. Tripathi	Proto-Indo-European Archaeology and Vedic Literature
S.K. Bhatt	Contribution of Madhya Pradesh in

	the field of Indian Archaeology during the last fifty years.
B.Tripathy and P.P. Jogelekar	Archaeological Investigations in the Middle Mahanadi Valley, Central Orissa
Purshotam Singh	Recent Exploration in Eastern U. P.
Atusha M. Bharucha	The Archaeology of Western Kshatrapas
S.K. Bhatt	Archaeological findings in from Delchi, Madhya Pradesh
B.M. Khanduri	Sanana: Ancient Burial Complex in Kumaon
Tripathy, B.	Early Historic Trade in Central and Western Orissa: An Ethnic archaeological Perspective
W.S. Siddiqi	Two Newly Discovered Medieval Sculptures from District Bareilly
S.B. Singh	The Sculptural Art in the Uttarakhand

Friday, 17 October: Afternoon Session

S. Kharakwal	The Archaeology of Uttarakhand
Ashok Kumar Singh	Ceramic Industries of Imlidih Khud, district Gorakhpur a study
Atusha M. Bharucha	Pottery Patterns of Gujarat and their Implications on the Settlements
P.P. Dandawate	Little Known Ardhanari Images of Brahmanical Dieties
S.K. Rai	Maurya kalina Naukarasahi Banama Samanya Jana (Hindi).
Lalit Pandey and J.S.Kharakwal	Fifty Years of Archaeology in Rajasthan: A Review
Ashwani Asthana	Origin of Saraswati River – A recent Research Development
A.K. Singh	Yakshi Medallion from Bharhut
D.N.Goswami	Saktism and Sakti Worship in Ancient Assam
S.K Jha and S.Jha	A Rare Vishnu image from Dumra (Madhuvani)— Looking for an Ethnographic Explanation

Saturday, 18 October: Forenoon Session

Kumkum Mathur	Mughal Chitrakaron Ka Pahari Rajyon Men Agaman Thatha Paharishaili Par Prabhava (in Hindi)
S.K.Bhatt	Discovery of *Nishka* the Earliest Indian Money.
D. P. Dubey	Art Remains of the Gahadavala Period.
Tulika Banerjee	Antiquities of Kushan Period found from Basti.
Kumar Anand	Archaeology remains on Kaimur Hills of Bihar.
Arakhita Pradhan	Exploration at Bhejidihi and it's neighbourhood in Karandi Valley, Orissa.
K.P. Padhy	Buddhist Vestiges of Orissa— A reference to Vajrayana chool of art of ?
Sumita Chakravarty and N.C.Ghosh	Archaeology Background of Rishikesh, District Dehradun
D.P. Sharma and Madhuri Sharma	Newly discovered Copper Hoard from U.P.
D. Bhengra	Archaeology of Chhota Nagpur Division: Fresh evidence

Saturday,18 October: Afternoon Session

A. Sundara	Some Rare Early Sculptures from North Karnataka: Their Significance
R.C. Bhatt and B.P. Badoni	Some interesting Kubera Icons from Garhwal
Mahesh C.Srivastava	Vindhyn Rock Art with reference to Dhausara Rock-shelter
B.M. Khanduri	Supanna: An Early Historical site in Garhwal, Himalaya
J.Manuel	Re-enumeration of the Exposition on Anthropomorphic Figures of Copper Hoard as Rigvedic Indra
Pradeep Saklani	Living Tradition of Kharak Chan in Garhwal, Himalaya: A New Light

	in Early Pastoralism and its Morphogensis.
D.P. Tiwari	Excavation at Romasarpurwa.
Ashwani Asthana	Water management and conservation planning at Dholavira – A Harappan city.
Rajendra Yadav	Madhya Kalin Mandir Sthapathya Ki Annupum Krit Chatturbhuj mandir, Darchha. (in Hindi)

The Conference passed the following three resolutions

Resolved that Indian Archaeology should be included as an independent subject in the Competitive Examinations conducted by this Union and State Public service Commissions.

The conference appreciates the initiative taken by the Government of India in developing the infrastructural facilities for places along the Buddhist circuit. However, the three Societies strongly feel that the states of Uttar Pradesh and Bihar directly concerned with the development of these facilities should he advised by the Government of India to get ancient Buddhist sites and Routes properly explored and identified with the help of the institutions and departments connected with archaeological studies. This will ensure the implementation of the Project on sound and scientific lines.

Apart from ιhe danger posed to archaeological heritage because of different development projects, uncontrolled tourist traffic and unbridled tourism policy is causing harm to our archaeological and cultural heritage. The Indian Archaeological Society, therefore, resolves that the various state Tourism departments as well as the Central Tourism department adopt a more serious attitude about the objections, if any, raised by the archaeological survey of India or State Departments of Archaeology.

B-17, Qutub Institutional Area
New Delhi-110016

K.N. Dikshit
General Secretary
Indian Archaeological Society

INDIAN ARCHAEOLOGICAL SOCIETY
BALANCE SHEET AS ON 31ST MARCH, 1998

LIABILITIES		AMOUNT	ASSETS	AMOUNT
Capital Fund			**Fixed Assets**	
Op. Balance	14,74213.89		(As per schedule "A" attached)	51,17,496.52
Add: L. M. Fees	24380.00			
Income over Expenditure	93455.40	15,92,049.29		
Corpus Fund		15,00,000.00		
Building Fund				
Op. Balance	723951.00			
Add. Receipts during the year	4005000.00	47,28,951.00	**Current Assets & Investments**	
			Fixed Deposit	20,70,000.00
Dr. A.K. Narain (Award) Fund		50,000.00	Vardhman Construction Co.	60,298.00
Vardhman Construction Co.		1,00,000.00	S.B.I. - 45062	35,778.17
			S.B.I. - 45082	7,29,787.21
Dr. S.P. Gupta Loan A/c		7,000.00		
Rajan Sharma & Co.		7,000.00	Indian Bank - 460017	10,000.00
VAP Enterprises		15,815.57		
Aquarelle		43,285.60	Cash in Hand	20,741.56
		80,44,101.46		80,44,101.46

Sd/
GENERAL SECRETARY

Sd/
TREASURE

Sd/
For Rajan Sharma & Co.,
Chartered Accountant

In terms of our Audit Report of even date attached.

Place: New Delhi
Dated: 24.10.1998

INDIAN ARCHAEOLOGICAL SOCIETY

INCOME AND EXPENDITURE ACCOUNT FOR THE YEAR ENDING 31ST MARCH, 1998

EXPENDITURE	AMOUNT	INCOME	AMOUNT
To Honorarium	75,560.00	By Grant	48,750.00
To Ground Rent	23,000.00	By Donations	47,305.00
To House Tax	13,500.00	By Annual Membership Fees	410.00
To Publication Exp.	59,100.00	By Institutional	
To Tour and Travel	385.00	Membership Fees	5,000.00
To Medical Exp.	160.00	By Sale of Publication	31,103.00
To Telephone Exp.	9,137.00	By Bank Interest	3,18,648.27
To Conveyance	39,475.00	By Service Charges	900.00
To Printing & Stat.	8,276.00		
To Conference Exp.	52,162.00		
To Office Expenses	4,561.00		
To Repairs & Maint.	25,380.00		
To Staff Welfare	7,156.50		
To Postage & Stamps	7,892.00		
To Accounting Charges	10,000.00		
To Audit Fees	7,000.00		
To Bank Charges	675.37		
To Miscellaneous Exp.	756.00		
To Professional Chg.	750.00		
To Electricity Exp.	3151.00		
To Depreciation	10,584.00		
To Excess of Income			
over Expenditure	93,455.40		
TOTAL	4,52,116.27	TOTAL	4,52,116.27

Sd/
GENERAL SECRETARY

Sd/
TREASURER

Sd/
For Rajan Sharma & Co.
Chartered Accountant

(Rajan Kumar Sharma)
Prop.

Place: New Delhi
Dated : 12.09.98

INDIAN ARCHAEOLOGICAL SOCIETY

BOARD OF MANAGEMENT

OFFICE BEARERS OF THE INDIAN ARCHAEOLOGICAL SOCIETY

Amarendra Nath : Rakhigarhi General view of the excavated trenches (RGR 2) showing structural remains of the Mature Harappan phase.

Amarendra Nath : Rakhigarhi North-south extended Harappan burial (RGR-1) showing courses of mud-brick on one side of the pit line.

Amarendra Nath : Rakhigarhi Mud Brick lined Animal sacrificial pit from the Mature Harappan phase.

Amarendra Nath : Rakhigarhi Three circular fire-altars of the Mature Harappan phase.

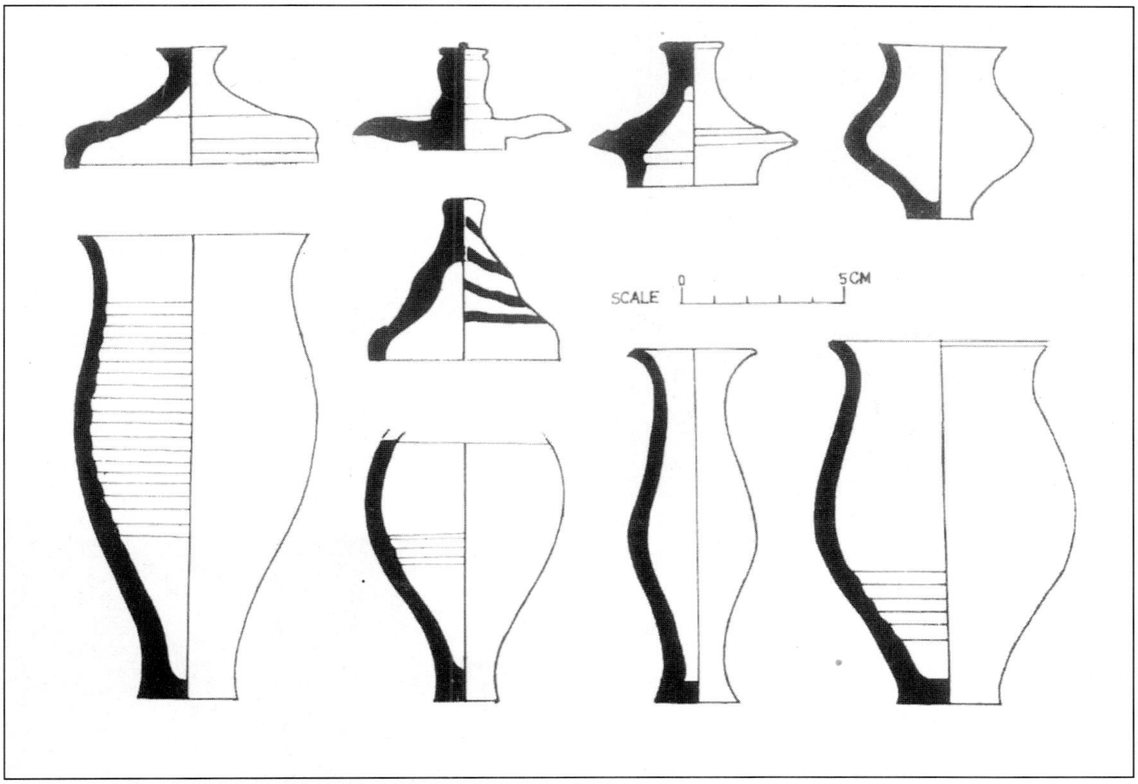

Amarendra Nath : Rakhigarhi Painted pottery from the Mature Harappan phase.

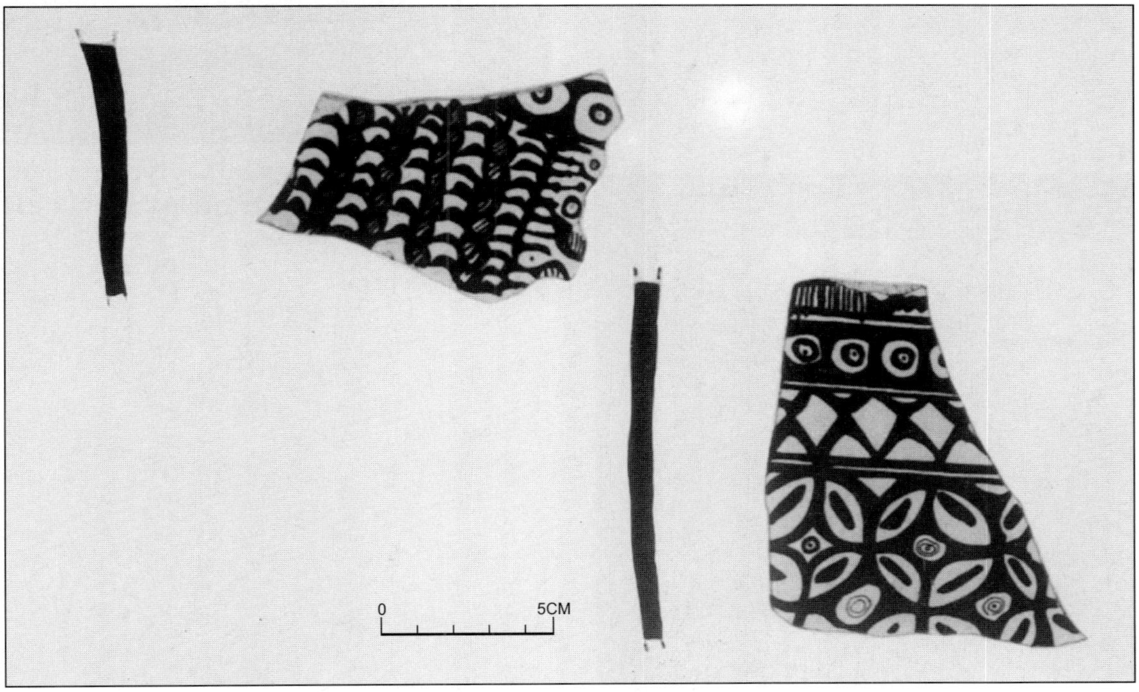

Amarendra Nath : Rakhigarhi Goblet, lid etc. from the Mature phase.

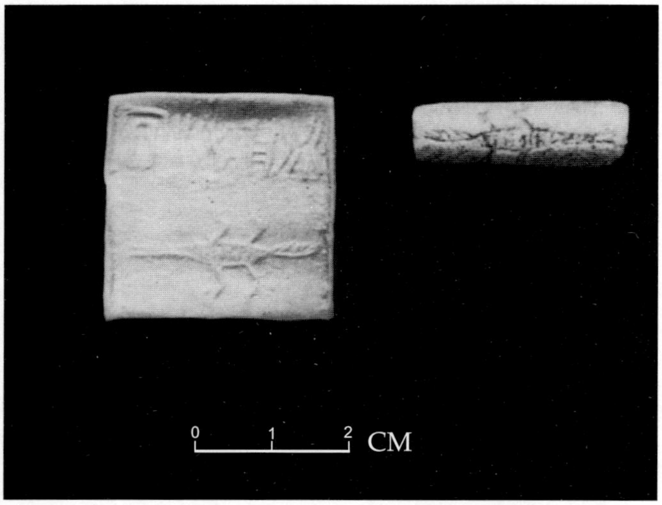

Amarendra Nath : Rakhigarhi Faience cylindrical seal from the upper Mature Harappan phase.

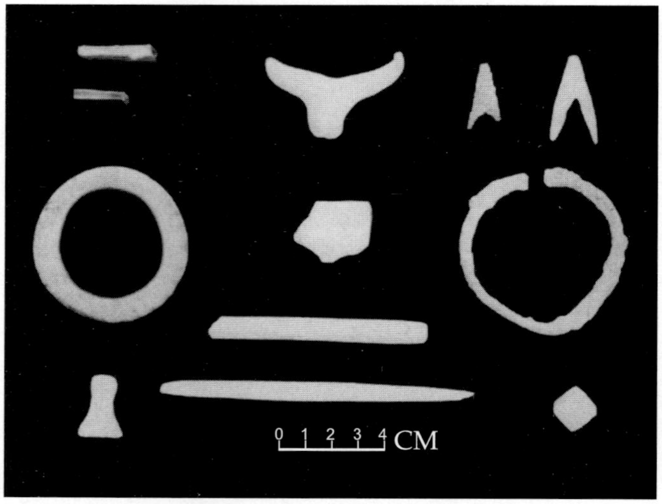

Amarendra Nath : Rakhigarhi Types of antiquities reported from the Mature Harappan phase.

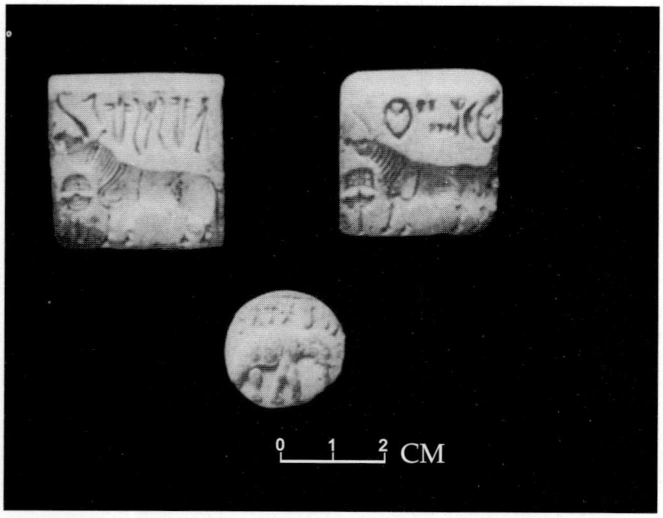

Amarendra Nath : Rakhigarhi, Seals and amulet from the Mature Harappan phase.

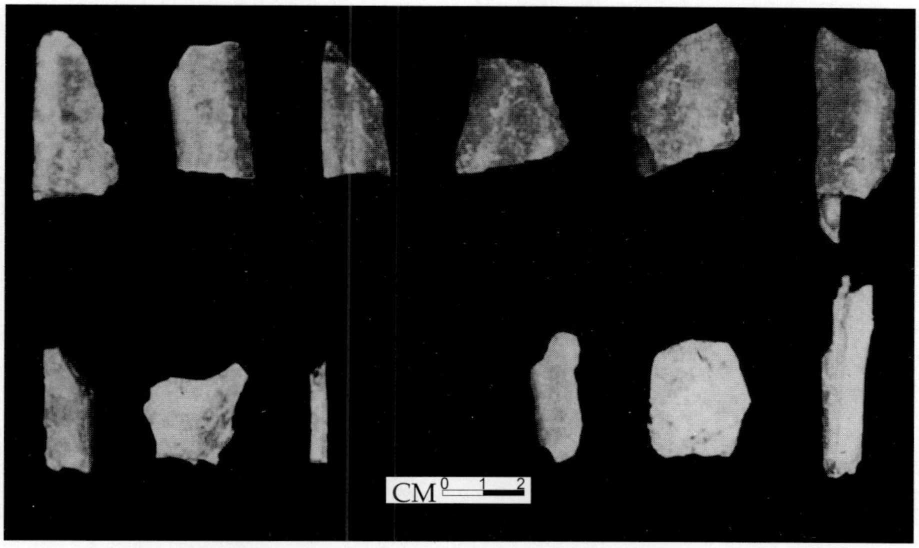

1 a. Tripathy and Joglekar : Charred bones from Marjakud.

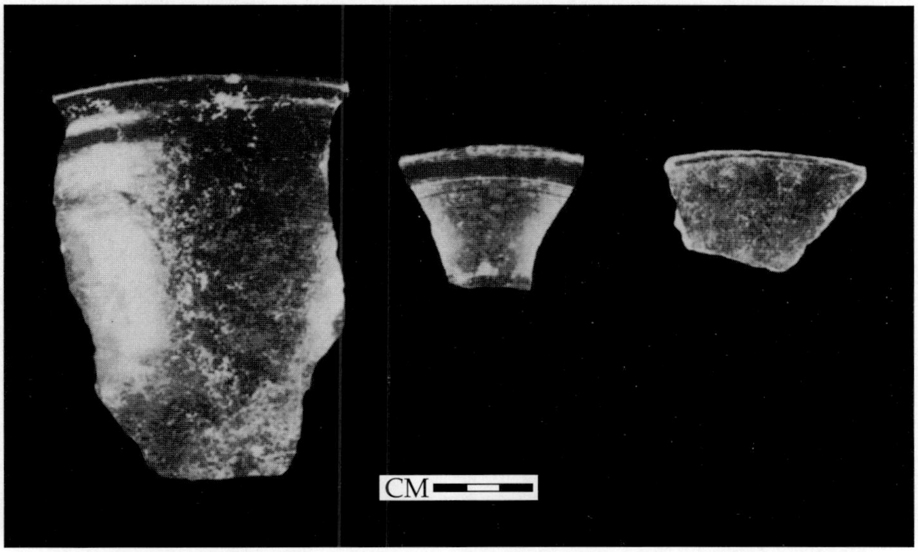

1 b. Tripathy and Joglekar : Black polished ware from Marjakud.

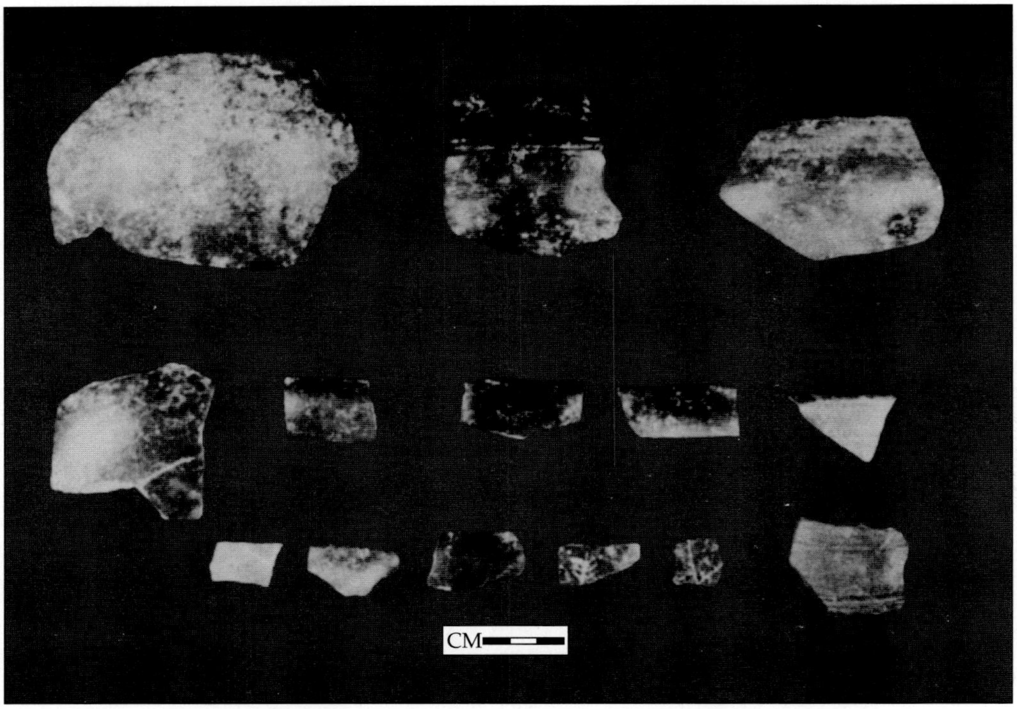

2 a. Tripathy and Joglekar : Black and Red ware from Marjakud.

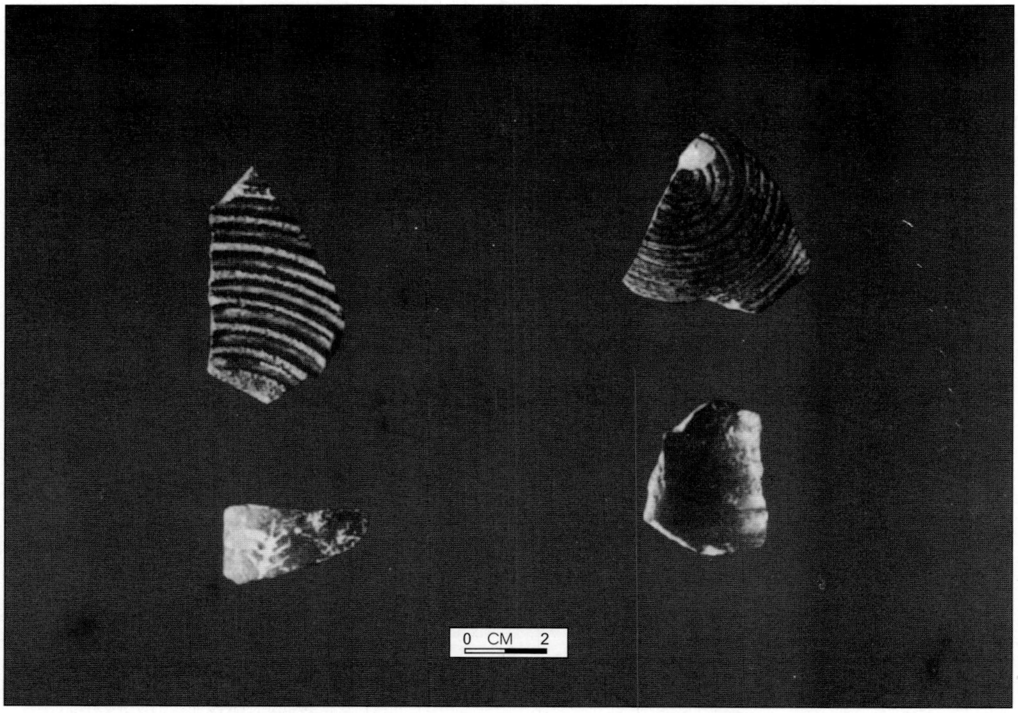

2 b. Tripathy and Joglekar : Decorated and graffiti bearing sherds : Marjakud.

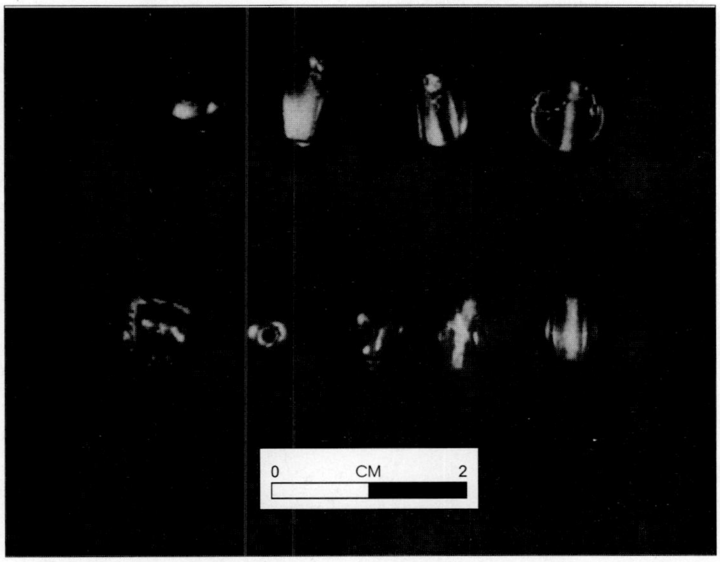

3 a. Tripathy and Joglekar : Semi-precious stone beads from Marjakud.

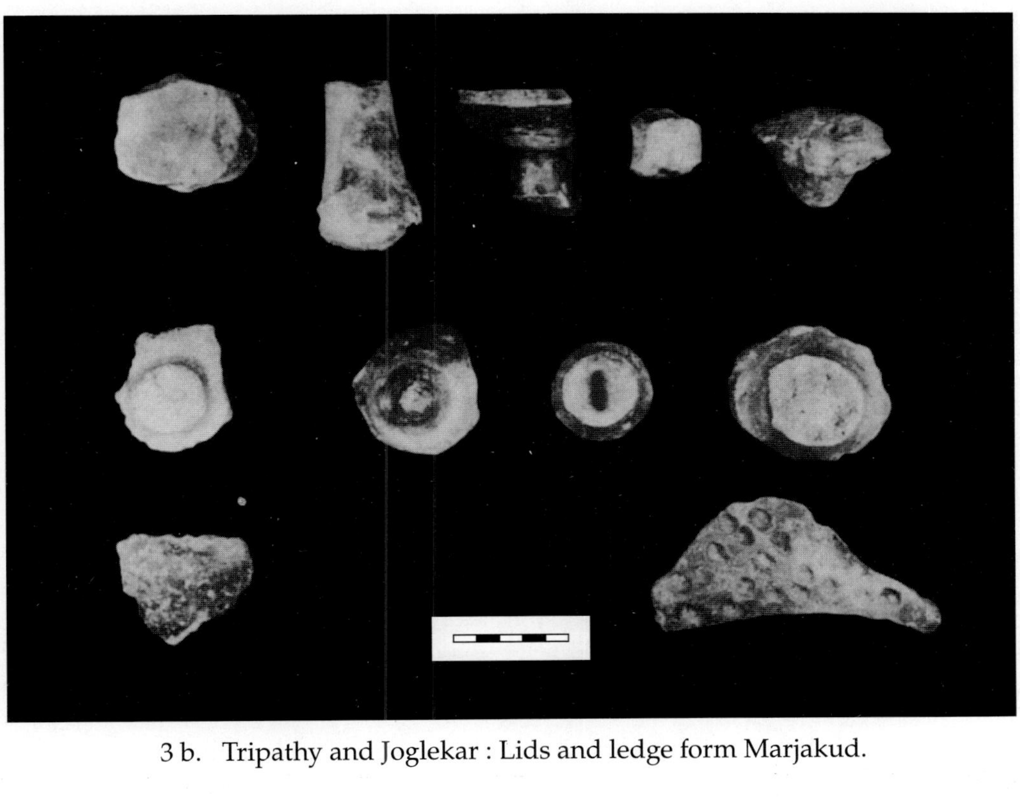

3 b. Tripathy and Joglekar : Lids and ledge form Marjakud.

4 a. Tripathy and Joglekar : Bones form Manamunda.

4 b. Tripathy and Joglekar : Turtle carapace fragments from Deuli.